VOTES WITHOU᠁
WOMEN IN AMERICAN ELECTO᠁

M000084663

Votes without Leverage reexamines a long-standing puzzle in women's electoral politics, namely why the increasing importance of women's votes throughout the 1920s did not imply increasing success for the lobbying efforts of women's organizations during the same period. Applying recent theoretical developments in the political economy of institutions and electoral behavior, Professor Harvey argues that female disfranchisement prior to 1920 created incentives for leaders of women's organizations to invest in the pursuit of suffrage as a first step to achieving other policy benefits for women. When the battle over the right to vote was finally won, those leaders then required time to adapt their organizations to pursue a broader legislative agenda through conventional electoral politics. During this time, however, the major party organizations were able to initiate their own electoral mobilization of women, giving the parties significant advantages in imperfectly competitive markets for women's electoral mobilization. Without women's votes, those organizations ceased to be able to win policy concessions from vote-minded legislators, a state of affairs that would not significantly change until the accelerated decline of the parties as mobilization organizations in the 1960s.

Anna L. Harvey is Assistant Professor of Politics at New York University.

Series list continues on page after index.

VOTES WITHOUT LEVERAGE

WOMEN IN AMERICAN
ELECTORAL POLITICS, 1920–1970

ANNA L. HARVEY

CAMBRIDGE
UNIVERSITY PRESS

PUBLISHED BY THE PRESS SYNDICATE OF THE UNIVERSITY OF CAMBRIDGE
The Pitt Building, Tumpington Street, Cambridge CB2 1RP, United Kingdom

CAMBRIDGE UNIVERSITY PRESS
The Edinburgh Building, Cambridge CB2 2RU, UK   http://www.cup.cam.ac.uk
40 West 20th Street, New York, NY 10011-4211, USA   http://www.cup.org
10 Stamford Road, Oakleigh, Melbourne 3166, Australia

© Anna L. Harvey 1998

First published 1998

Printed in the United States of America

Typeset in Sabon 10/12, in Penta [RF]

Library of Congress Cataloging-in-Publication Data
Harvey, Anna L. (Anna Lil). 1966–
Votes without leverage : women in American electoral politics,
1920–1970 / Anna L. Harvey.
p. cm. – (Political economy of institutions and decisions)
Includes biographical references and index.
ISBN 0-521-59239-9 (hb) – ISBN 0-521-59743-9 (pb)
1. Women – Suffrage – United States – History – 20th century.
2. Elections – United States – History – 20th century. 3. Women in
politics – United States – History – 20th century. 4. United States –
Politics and government – 20th century. I. Title. II. Series.
JK1896.H45   1998
324.6'23'09730904 – dc21   97-41730
                                                        CIP

*A catalog record for this book is available from
the British Library*

ISBN 0 521 59239 9 hardback
ISBN 0 521 59743 9 paperback

Contents

Series Editors' Preface

The Cambridge series on the Political Economy of Institutions and Decisions is built around attempts to answer two central questions: how do institutions evolve in response to individual incentives, strategies, and choices, and how do institutions affect the performance of political and economic systems? The scope of the series is comparative and historical rather than international or specifically American, and the focus is positive rather than normative.

Anna Harvey provides a fresh, thought-provoking perspective on women in American electoral politics in the half century after their enfranchisement. She artfully combines rational choice approaches to participation with careful historical analysis of social movements. Her explanation of the turnout of cohesive groups begins with the assumption that many eligible voters vote because they receive cues during an election campaign from others whose opinions matter to them. These cues indicate to them that voting in a particular way is required in order to be an accepted group member. Because of their previous electoral exclusion, newly enfranchised groups are more likely to be mobilized by parties, not by independent group organizations. Skeptical about the party elites' responsiveness to voters' policy preferences when parties mobilize voters, Harvey argues that a benefit-seeking organization pursuing an electoral strategy in return for policy concessions is a necessary but not sufficient condition for its obtaining group-specific policy benefits. In the historical cases she studies, benefit-seeking group entrepreneurs possessed both informational and organizational advantages that enabled them to be the first entrants into new markets for group electoral mobilization.

The goals were women's goals, and politicians' attitudes were the attitudes of men toward women. Nevertheless, Harvey shows how the rational strategy that men would have chosen in the same position, and the disadvantage they would have faced, would have been the same. In this way she offers an innovative theoretical and empirical analysis that transcends yet is still suffused with gender.

Preface

Electoral markets are often characterized as economic markets used to be characterized: candidates offer policy positions for sale, and voters buy shares of a candidate's wares with their votes. Given any set of electoral laws and any distribution of voter preferences, election outcomes should be efficient: the victorious candidate wins because he promises to make more voters better off than do any of the losing candidates.

But scholars of economic institutions have cast doubt on whether economic markets can produce efficient outcomes under typical circumstances. Certain market institutions can encourage inefficient investment in information, organizations, and skills. And because in the real world searching out alternative information and creating new organizations is costly, leaders of economic organizations such as firms often have strong incentives to persist in inefficient practices. As a result, economic markets can produce inefficient outcomes for generations.

This study suggests that the same may be true of electoral markets as well. Efficiency in electoral markets is heavily dependent upon the existence of intermediary organizations that can coordinate individually insignificant votes into powerful voting blocs. Only then will voters exert any leverage over candidates. Like their counterparts in economic markets, leaders of such intermediary organizations are guided by electoral institutions to make investments in certain kinds of knowledge and organizations. Given an electoral institution that encourages some leaders to make investments in organizations that are inefficient from the standpoint of the larger electoral market, electoral markets can also produce inefficient outcomes for generations.

This study examines the effects of one such electoral institution, namely the laws prohibiting the participation of women in most electoral markets in the United States until 1920. But this study is not just about the effects of this institution on female voters. The unusual position of women in the U.S. electoral market after 1920 highlights the fragile conditions necessary for electoral markets to be efficient for any group.

It is an understatement to say that scholarly work is made more arduous in the absence of financial and intellectual support from others. The work for this project was made easier through financial support from the Woodrow Wilson National Fellowship Foundation, through its programs for the Andrew W. Mellon Fellows and the Princeton Society of Fellows, the Graduate School of Princeton University, the Woodrow Wilson School of Public and International Affairs at Princeton University, the Herbert Hoover Presidential Library, and New York University. I have also benefited from the intellectual support of colleagues at both Princeton and New York Universities, as well as at numerous universities and conferences where this work has been presented, and from the press and series editorial support at Cambridge University Press. In particular I would like to acknowledge the help of Darwin Neher, Jennifer Hochschild, Larry Bartels, John Londregan, John DiIulio, Alan Ryan, Russell Hardin, Kristi Andersen, Nancy Burns, Jim Alt, and Alex Holzman. I thank all those who have sought to make this study a better work.

Abbreviations

DNC	Democratic National Committee
DNEC	Democratic National Executive Committee
NAWSA	National American Woman Suffrage Association
NLWV	National League of Women Voters
NYT	*New York Times*
OWA	Office of Women's Activities
RNC	Republican National Committee
RNEC	Republican National Executive Committee
TWC	*The Woman Citizen*
TWV	*The Woman Voter*
WJCC	Women's Joint Congressional Committee
WSP	Woman Suffrage Party

1

The Legacy of Female Disfranchisement

Women in the United States have labored under the long shadow cast by a history of disfranchisement. Even after approximately seventy years of organized efforts simply to win the vote, efforts that finally paid off with the passage of constitutional female suffrage in 1920, American women were to endure fifty more years of the consequences of not having had that right in the first place. In what we can now identify as a predictable sequence of events, women's exclusion from the suffrage created conditions that were to lead to distinctive patterns of postsuffrage female electoral politics. Those unique electoral dynamics can in turn ultimately be held responsible for the oft noted decline in the political influence of women's organizations by the mid-1920s, a decline that would last until 1970. Only by this latter date would a significant feature of the institutional context of women's electoral politics have changed sufficiently to allow women's organizations once again to exercise influence over the course of public policy.

These are relatively startling findings, particularly after decades of scholarship in which the difficulties of women's organizations in the political arena were ascribed to the allegedly timid, self-effacing, and unambitious characteristics of women themselves.[1] For too long scholars assumed that because men and women possessed equal rights to vote after 1920, they possessed equal opportunities to influence political outcomes. Any differences in those outcomes by gender must therefore be attributable in some way to women themselves. But recent theoretical developments in the fields of political science and economics have focused scholarly attention on the lasting consequences of institutional arrangements, even after those arrangements have been altered. Because

[1]For a review of such scholarship, see Susan C. Bourque and Jean Grossholtz, "Politics an Unnatural Practice: Political Science Looks at Female Participation," *Politics and Society* 4, no. 2 (Winter 1974): 225–266.

institutional rules guide the investment by instrumentally rational political actors in particular kinds of knowledge and organizations, those rules can have enduring effects.[2] This new scholarship has enabled us to take a fresh look at the problems faced by women in American electoral politics.

More specifically, this book argues that the differential treatment of women by electoral laws prior to 1920 created incentives for reform-seeking women's leaders to invest in organizations to attain suffrage as a first step to achieving other policy benefits for women. When women were finally granted the vote, those leaders required time to adapt these organizations to pursue a broader legislative agenda through conventional electoral politics. During this time, however, the major party organizations were able to initiate the electoral mobilization of women, giving the parties significant advantages in imperfectly competitive markets for women's electoral loyalties. Those advantages would prove insurmountable to postsuffrage women's organizations, which would within a few years leave the markets for women's electoral mobilization. And without women's votes, those organizations ceased to be able to win policy concessions from vote-minded legislators. This state of affairs would not significantly change until the accelerated decline of the parties as mobilization organizations in the 1960s.

This chapter lays out the historical puzzle that this study seeks to solve, namely the odd nature of the rise and fall of the political leverage of women's organizations, and briefly surveys the existing literature that has addressed this puzzle. Later chapters will evaluate both the theoretical and the empirical merits of these explanations in greater detail. This chapter also discusses the way in which the argument made here may provide fresh insights into thinking about the role of gender in politics, and the extent to which those insights can be generalized to other groups and/or women in other countries. The chapter concludes by discussing the methodology and data employed to test the book's arguments against competing explanations in the subsequent empirical chapters.

THE HISTORICAL PUZZLE

The decade of the 1970s in the United States saw a dramatic increase in the success rate of women's organizations pursuing congressional support of legislation designed to remove barriers to the progress of women in economic, political, and social arenas. Although women's organiza-

---

[2]The theoretical claim is well made in a number of works, of which one of the most prominent is Douglass C. North, *Institutions, Institutional Change, and Economic Performance* (Cambridge: Cambridge University Press, 1990).

tions, including both older organizations such as the National Federation of Business and Professional Women's Clubs (NFBPWC) and newer organizations such as the National Organization for Women (NOW), had lobbied Congress before 1970, that year saw their first major lobbying success. House passage of the Equal Rights Amendment (ERA) in 1970 was followed by full congressional passage of the ERA and Title IX of the Educational Amendments Act (prohibiting sex discrimination in education) in 1972, the Equal Credit Opportunity Act and the Women's Educational Equity Act in 1974, the Pregnancy Discrimination Act and the (unprecedented) congressional extension of the ratification period for the ERA in 1978, and a host of measures prohibiting sex discrimination in federal programs. The legislative success of women's organizations has continued, albeit with some fits and starts, into the 1980s and 1990s with pension equity reform, child support enforcement legislation, child care subsidies, and parental leave legislation as important examples. As documented by numerous scholars, in all these cases women's organizations provided the primary lobbying support for the successful legislation.[3]

In addition to these congressional policy initiatives, women's organizations also won benefits for women within both political parties shortly after 1970. Under pressure from the National Women's Political Caucus (NWPC), the Democratic National Committee (DNC) as of 1972 required state parties to select women as national convention delegates roughly in proportion to their presence in the state's general population. If the number of women in a state delegation did not match this proportion, then the burden of proof would be on state party officials to prove that they had not discriminated in the delegate selection process.[4] The rule had immediate effects; in 1972, the percentage of Democratic National Convention delegates who were women rose to 40 percent

[3]On the pre-1970 lobbying activity of women's organizations, see Betty Friedan, *It Changed My Life: Writings on the Women's Movement* (New York: Random House, 1976), pp. 80–86, 101. On their post-1970 lobbying activity, see Helene Norma Silverberg, "Political Organization and the Origin of Political Identity: The Emergence and Containment of Gender in American Politics, 1960–1984" (Ph.D. dissertation, Cornell University, 1988), pp. 153–206. More generally see Anne N. Costain, "Women's Claims as a Special Interest," in Carol Mueller, ed., *The Politics of the Gender Gap* (Newbury Park, Calif.: Sage, 1988), pp. 150–172; Anne N. Costain, *Inviting Women's Rebellion* (Baltimore: Johns Hopkins University Press, 1992); W. Douglas Costain and Anne N. Costain, "The Political Strategies of Social Movements: A Comparison of the Women's and Environmental Movements," *Congress & the Presidency* 19 (Spring 1992): 1–27. These studies document what I call the "success rate" of women's organizations.

[4]Byron E. Shafer, *Quiet Revolution: The Struggle for the Democratic Party and the Shaping of Post-Reform Politics* (New York: Russell Sage Foundation, 1983), pp. 138–142, 169–172, 465–486.

from 13 percent in 1968. Explicit quota provisions for women in the Democratic Party were then further expanded in subsequent years. Republican Party elites acted similarly: a national committee on party reform authorized by the 1968 Republican National Convention recommended the expansion of affirmative action language in the selection of national convention delegates. The 1972 national convention, at which female delegates composed 30 percent of the delegates compared with 17 percent in 1968, approved this recommendation and created a committee to work with state parties to implement this reform.[5]

Although seldom remembered, this surge of legislative and party activity conferring benefits upon women as a group had a precedent, namely a similar albeit shorter-lived trend that occurred between 1920 and 1925. In fact, the entrance of women into the electorate in 1920 had been heralded as a momentous event in American electoral politics. The passage of the Nineteenth Amendment, guaranteeing to American women the constitutional right to vote, had appeared to many contemporaneous observers as only the first step in what would be an inevitable shifting of the political landscape to accommodate the demands of newly powerful women's organizations.

And for the first four to five years after suffrage, the anticipated political clout of women's organizations in national politics appeared to be realizing itself. As historians have amply documented, women's organizations led by the National League of Women Voters (NLWV) were the primary lobbyists for several successful congressional bills immediately after the passage of constitutional female suffrage.[6] The first and most visible of these congressional victories occurred in 1921 when a coalition of women's organizations led by the NLWV successfully lobbied Congress for the Sheppard-Towner Maternity and Infancy Protection Act.[7] Sheppard-Towner, which provided matching grants to states

---

[5]Winifred Wandersee, *On the Move: American Women in the 1970s* (Boston: Twayne Publishers, 1988), pp. 20, 25; Denise Baer, "The National Federation of Republican Women: Women's Auxiliary or Feminist Force?," paper delivered at the Annual Meeting of the American Political Science Association, Chicago, August 31– September 3, 1995, p. 3.

[6]For discussions of the legislative activities of women's organizations during the 1920s, see Clarke A. Chambers, *Seedtime of Reform: American Social Service and Social Action, 1918–1933* (Minneapolis: University of Minnesota Press, 1963); J. Stanley Lemons, *The Woman Citizen: Social Feminism in the 1920s* (Chicago: University of Chicago Press, 1975); Nancy F. Cott, *The Grounding of Modern Feminism* (New Haven: Yale University Press, 1987); Robyn Muncy, *Creating a Female Dominion in American Reform, 1890–1935* (New York: Oxford University Press, 1991); and Theda Skocpol, *Protecting Soldiers and Mothers: The Political Origins of Social Policy in the United States* (Cambridge, Mass.: Belknap Press of Harvard University Press, 1992).

[7]This coalition, the Women's Joint Congressional Committee (WJCC), had been

4

for pre- and postnatal care under the administration of the Children's Bureau in the Department of Labor, had been the legislative priority of the NLWV and was the first federal social policy measure ever enacted. The act's opposition, led by the influential American Medical Association, called the successful coalition of women's organizations "the most powerful lobby in Washington";[8] a supporter of the act in the Senate noted that "If the members could have voted on that measure secretly in their cloak rooms it would have been killed as emphatically as it was finally passed in the open under the pressure of the Joint Congressional Committee of Women."[9] In the eyes of many political elites, the passage of Sheppard-Towner signified that the "woman movement" had gained enormous leverage with the passage of female suffrage.

Subsequent national policy victories appeared to confirm this impression. Also in 1921 women's groups were successful in lobbying for the Packers and Stockyards Control Act, providing for federal regulation of the meat industry (after the passage of which an influential senator wrote the NLWV that the bill "could never have been passed without the work of the women"),[10] and obtained increased appropriations for the Women's and Children's Bureaus in the Department of Labor (regarded by women's organizations as "their particular stake in the government").[11] In 1922 the NLWV successfully lobbied for the Cable Act, providing for independent citizenship for married women, and for a bill establishing the U.S. Coal Commission to regulate the coal industry; appropriations for the Women's and Children's Bureaus were again increased. In 1923 the NLWV's successes included a "Filled Milk" bill, prohibiting interstate shipment of condensed or evaporated milk containing oil substitutes for butter fat, and the Sterling-Lehlbach Reclassification Act, which inter alia instituted the principle of equal pay for equal work irrespective of sex in the civil service. The Division of Home

formed at the instigation of the NLWV in November 1920 for the sole purpose of congressional lobbying on measures of interest to member women's organizations. Lemons, *The Woman Citizen*, pp. 55–56. Brief histories of the WJCC's first major success, the Sheppard-Towner Act, may be found in Lemons, *The Woman Citizen*, chap. 6, and Skocpol, *Protecting Soldiers and Mothers*, chap. 9. A full history of the act is available in Joseph Benedict Chepaitis, "The First Federal Social Welfare Measure: The Sheppard-Towner Maternity and Infancy Act, 1918–1932" (Ph.D. dissertation, Georgetown University, 1968).

[8]The congressional liaison for the American Medical Association, in *Journal of the American Medical Association* 77 (December 10, 1921), pp. 1913–1914, quoted in Lemons, *The Woman Citizen*, p. 166.

[9]Senator Kenyon, in Lemons, *The Woman Citizen*, p. 167.

[10]Papers of the National League of Women Voters, 1918–1974, microfilm edition (Frederick, Md.: University Publications of America, 1985), Pt. II, Reel 1, Frame 50.

[11]Belle Sherwin memo, January 28, 1929, Campaign and Transition Papers, Box 43, Herbert Hoover Papers, Herbert Hoover Presidential Library, West Branch, Iowa.

Economics in the Department of Agriculture was raised to bureau status under lobbying by the league and other women's organizations, and the Women's and Children's Bureaus again received increased appropriations. In 1924 the NLWV was "instrumental" in securing passage of the Curtis-Graham bill, providing for a separate institution for female federal prisoners,[12] and in winning congressional passage of the child labor amendment; yet again appropriations for the Children's and Women's Bureaus were increased.

In addition to these policy victories, women made steady advances in the immediate postsuffrage years in winning access to previously all-male party committees. In order to lure new female voters, both parties shortly before constitutional enfranchisement created women's divisions within their organizations, both nationally and in most states, staffed solely by women and, to all appearances, autonomous from the men's organizations. In fact, these women's divisions in both parties were ultimately controlled by male party elites through the latter's powers of personnel appointment and removal. Not content with this status, women in both party organizations sought access to the men's party committees; the NLWV included the demands of female party leaders on its lobbying agenda. And as will be documented in Chapter 5 for the national and New York State party organizations, both Republican and Democratic, between 1920 and 1924 partisan women made consistent if incremental progress in this endeavor.

After 1924, however, the success rate for women's organizations in both Congress and the party organizations diminished dramatically. In both 1925 and 1926 appropriations for the Women's and Children's Bureaus were reduced, and only one substantive bill supported by the NLWV passed, providing for compulsory school attendance for the District of Columbia. A bill to renew Sheppard-Towner's appropriations was held up in the Senate by a filibuster. In 1927 Sheppard-Towner was extended for two more years but with the provision that the law itself would expire in June 1929, an effective repeal of the bill.

In the subsequent two years no more bills passed if their support came primarily from women's organizations, despite continued lobbying activity, and the Women's and Children's Bureaus continued to receive the reduced appropriations of 1926. But the real blow to the legislative progress of women's organizations came under the Hoover administration. Leaders of the major women's organizations that had originally supported the Sheppard-Towner Act had hoped that they would be able to renew the act in 1929 as though it were simply being reappropriated. This same coalition of women's organizations, again led by the NLWV,

---

[12]"Women Progress under Suffrage," *NYT*, August 22, 1926, VIII p. 10.

mounted a campaign as early as 1927 to ensure that the existing state programs for maternal and infant health care under Sheppard-Towner would be permitted to continue operations.[13]

But Hoover's administration was firmly on the side of the male medical profession and the surgeon general's predominantly male Public Health Service, which (as it had in 1921) strenuously opposed the administration of a maternal health program by the predominantly female Children's Bureau. Women's organizations were unable to counter this opposition, and Sheppard-Towner was not renewed after its expiration in 1929.

And as will be documented in Chapter 5, the NLWV-supported efforts of female party leaders to win access to the men's party committees stalled abruptly at precisely the same point as did the legislative progress of women's organizations. After 1924 women in neither party organization, New York State or nationally, would make further gains in enhancing the organizational status of partisan women. In fact, in all four of these organizations, women would experience some form of organizational setback by the late 1920s or early 1930s.

There is quite clearly a change in the mid-1920s in the success rate of women's organizations in both the legislative and the party arenas. Moreover, this pattern appeared at the level of state policy making as well, as Theda Skocpol's work on mothers' pensions has demonstrated. Although women's organizations were quite successful during the 1910s and early 1920s in getting mothers' pension enabling legislation passed in several states, by the mid-1920s women's organizations found themselves ineffective in pushing for the programs' funding and expansion.[14] Similar patterns may be found in states' extension of jury service to women and the progress of the child labor amendment's ratification within the same time frame.[15]

Even more striking, the severely diminished efficacy of women's organizations after 1925 was to last for approximately forty-five years, until 1970. During this period women's organizations were by all accounts simply unsuccessful in influencing the course of policy. During

[13]Irvine L. Lenroot to Herbert Hoover, February 4, 1929, enclosing memo from Belle Sherwin, president of the NLWV, Campaign and Transition Papers, Box 43, Herbert Hoover Papers. The coalition in 1929 included the American Home Economics Association, the American Association of University Women, the National Women's Trade Union League, the Young Women's Christian Association, the National Council of Jewish Women, the National Consumer's League, the American Nurses Association, the American Federation of Teachers, the Service Star Legion, and the General Federation of Women's Clubs.

[14]Skocpol, *Protecting Soldiers and Mothers*, p. 479.

[15]On jury service see Lemons, *The Woman Citizen*, pp. 72–73; on the child labor amendment see ibid., pp. 216–225.

the New Deal years, for instance, money for maternal and infant health was restored and money for mothers' pensions, in the form of Aid to Dependent Children (ADC), was finally appropriated at the national level. But whereas women's organizations had lobbied for, and had originally won in the case of Sheppard-Towner, non-means-tested programs for women administered by female-led administrative agencies, these were not prominent features of New Deal social programs. The aid for maternal and infant health care under the Social Security Act of 1935 was earmarked for "needy" families only, critically undermining the program's appeal to all women, and, while administered by the Children's Bureau, that bureau was increasingly less able to favor the hiring of female personnel as it had previously done.[16] The administration of ADC, which the Children's Bureau had expected to receive, was given to the Social Security Board (SSB) instead as an income-maintenance program, again undermining the potentially universal appeal of mothers' pensions. Under the administration of the SSB, clear distinctions emerged between this program for needy mothers and children and programs for male "breadwinners" like Social Security and unemployment insurance.[17] The primary explanation given by those who have documented these distinctions in ADC is that the concerns of women's organizations about the program's implementation were easily subordinated to the concerns of more politically powerful groups such as labor unions.[18]

[16]Muncy, *Creating a Female Dominion*, pp. 154–155; Skocpol, *Protecting Soldiers and Mothers*, pp. 535–536.

[17]See Winifred Bell, *Aid to Dependent Children* (New York: Columbia University Press, 1965); Russell L. Hanson, "Federal Statebuilding during the New Deal: The Transition from Mothers' Aid to Aid to Dependent Children," in Edward S. Greenberg and Thomas F. Mayer, eds., *Changes in the State* (Newbury Park, Calif.: Sage, 1990), pp. 93–114; Barbara J. Nelson, "The Origins of the Two-Channel Welfare State: Workmen's Compensation and Mothers' Aid," in Linda Gordon, ed., *Women, the State, and Welfare* (Madison: University of Wisconsin Press, 1990), pp. 123–151; Christopher Howard, "Sowing the Seeds of 'Welfare': The Transformation of Mothers' Pensions, 1900–1940," *Journal of Policy History* 4, no. 2 (1992): 188–227; Skocpol, *Protecting Soldiers and Mothers*, pp. 534–539; Suzanne Bridget Mettler, "Divided Citizens: State Building, Federalism, and Gender in the New Deal" (Ph.D. dissertation, Cornell University, 1994).

[18]See, e.g., Mettler, "Divided Citizens." Other setbacks for women during the New Deal included Section 213 of the 1932 National Economy Act, which penalized the federally employed wives of federal employees (repealed in 1937), the approximately 25 percent of the National Recovery Act codes which allowed lesser wages for women, the 1934 decision of the Attorney General that sex discrimination in the civil service was legal, the refusal of the War Manpower Commission to appoint women between 1941 and 1945, and its concomitant refusal to consider the problems of job training, flextime, and day care for women wartime workers. Susan Ware, *Beyond Suffrage: Women in the New Deal* (Cambridge, Mass.: Harvard University Press, 1981), pp. 79, 90; Judith Sealander, "Moving Painfully and Uncertainly: Policy Formation and 'Women's Issues,' 1940–1980," in Donald T. Critchlow and Ellis W.

The Legacy of Female Disfranchisement

In the period between the New Deal years and 1970 only two congressional acts that appeared to be designed to provide benefits to women as a group were passed: the Equal Pay Act in 1963 and Title VII of the Civil Rights Act of 1964, prohibiting sex discrimination in the workplace.[19] However, these two bills are usually distinguished from the wave of legislation that followed in the 1970s because of the odd circumstances surrounding their passage. The Equal Pay Act was in fact originally a demand of male labor union leaders, who feared the displacement of male wage workers by lesser-paid women. Likewise, Title VII of the Civil Rights Act was originally an amendment to the act proposed by southern conservatives in an effort to kill the bill.[20] After 1925, we simply do not see a sustained recognition of women as a significant group in policy making until 1970. Moreover, as will be discussed in Chapter 6, women in the national parties fared no better during the New Deal years or later. Not until the party reforms of the early 1970s would women make any more significant advances in the party organizations.

EXPLAINING THE PUZZLE

What accounts for the long hiatus between these periods of congressional and party efforts to accede to the lobbying demands of women's organizations? More broadly, what accounts for the variation in such efforts? Existing accounts, which fall into two distinct classes of explanation, treat only the legislative activity benefiting women, and treat the two time periods separately at that. The first such class of explanation emphasizes the nonelectoral factors that may have influenced the provision of policy benefits for women, of which two have received the most attention in the literature: policy networks and ideological climates. With respect to the first argument, one group of scholars contends that legislators began enacting policies to benefit women both before and immediately after suffrage because of the development of a women's policy network linking the leaders of women's organizations, female academics, and female bureaucrats in the Children's and Women's Bureaus

Hawley, eds., *Federal Social Policy: The Historical Dimension* (University Park: Pennsylvania State University Press, 1988), pp. 79–96.

[19]On the interim period, see Eugenia Kaledin, *Mothers and More: American Women in the 1950s* (Boston: Twayne Publishers, 1984); Cynthia Harrison, *On Account of Sex: The Politics of Women's Issues, 1945–1968* (Berkeley: University of California Press, 1988); Patricia Zelman, *Women, Work, and National Policy: The Kennedy–Johnson Years* (Ann Arbor, Mich.: UMI Research Press, 1982).

[20]Jo Freeman, *The Politics of Women's Liberation: A Case Study of an Emerging Social Movement and Its Relation to the Policy Process* (New York: David McKay, 1975), pp. 171–178.

of the Department of Labor; an analogous argument has been made for the late 1960s.[21] If policy concessions for women dried up between the mid-1920s and 1970, then there must have been corresponding changes in the strength of these policy networks.[22] Another group of scholars argues that the policy victories won by women's organizations during these periods were due rather to the favorable ideological climates of the late Progressive period and the turbulent 1960s; the general ideological climate in the interim must simply have been hostile to reform legislation of any kind, including that sought by women's organizations.[23]

The second class of explanations for the variation in policies benefiting women relies upon a simple version of strategic electoral politics: women received policy benefits from legislators when legislators believed that women voted as a bloc. Legislators must have believed that women would vote as a bloc immediately after female enfranchisement, but not have believed in women's electoral distinctiveness between 1925 and 1970.[24]

How do these explanations fare when we extend them to both periods and to the case of women in the party organizations? The short answer is, not particularly well. (The long answer is the substance of this book.) As later empirical chapters will detail, neither class of arguments, the nonelectoral nor the simple electoral, can account for important facts that remain anomalous and unexplained under these stories.

Moreover, and perhaps not coincidentally, these arguments are also

---

[21]Two leading advocates of the policy network approach for the 1920s are Robyn Muncy in *Creating a Female Dominion* and Theda Skocpol in *Protecting Soldiers and Mothers*, although Skocpol distinguishes her argument by emphasizing the role that women's organizations also played in mobilizing their members to educate public opinion. Both scholars also rely somewhat on a "climate" explanation for the ebb and flow in the success rate of the policy network. On the late 1960s, see Freeman, *The Politics of Women's Liberation*, chap. 7; Freeman's is also in part a "climate" explanation.

[22]Thus, e.g., Skocpol suggests that the women's organizations composing the first policy network grew weaker over the course of the 1920s; *Protecting Soldiers and Mothers*, p. 519.

[23]For the 1920s, see William H. Chafe, *The American Woman: Her Changing Social, Economic, and Political Roles, 1920–1970* (London: Oxford University Press, 1972), p. 29; Chambers, *Seedtime of Reform*; Muncy, *Creating a Female Dominion*, pp. 129–135; Skocpol, *Protecting Soldiers and Mothers*, p. 521. For the 1960s and 1970s, see Freeman, *The Politics of Women's Liberation*, p. 229.

[24]For the 1920s, see Chafe, *The American Woman*, pp. 29–30; Lemons, *The Woman Citizen*, pp. 157, 174; Michael McGerr, "Political Style and Women's Power, 1830–1930," *Journal of American History* 77, no. 3 (December 1990): 882; Muncy, *Creating a Female Dominion*, p. 126; Eleanor Flexner, *Century of Struggle: The Woman's Rights Movement in the United States* (Cambridge, Mass.: Harvard University Press, 1975), p. 338; Skocpol, *Protecting Soldiers and Mothers*, p. 521. On the 1970s, see Silverberg, "Political Organization"; Silverberg argues a more nuanced version of the strategic electoral politics story.

unconvincing on purely theoretical grounds. As the next chapter will discuss in greater detail, the nonelectoral stories seem implausible because of their inattention to the constraints imposed on legislators by the rules that compose an electoral system. Given that legislators must compete for survival in an electoral "game" well defined by existing political institutions, it seems unlikely that electoral or strategic concerns would not outweigh expert opinions or legislators' ideological predilections.

But simple electoral stories about legislators' responsiveness to voter preferences are just that: too simple. These theories typically fail to consider the constraints that electoral rules impose on voters as well as on legislative and party elites. If voters in large electorates are instrumentally rational enough to want to see their policy preferences implemented by legislators, then they are calculating enough to figure out that they should not in fact vote if all they care about are policy outcomes: a single vote has too little impact on the eventual outcome of any election to justify even small opportunity costs of acquiring electoral information and voting (otherwise known as the collective action problem in voting). And if voters can be expected to reason thusly, then legislators will have negligible incentives to provide policy concessions to voters who cannot be motivated to vote by such concessions.

In this book I present an alternative approach to explaining the variation in the provision of legislative and party benefits for women as a group, one that seeks to combine the strengths of the foregoing explanations while avoiding their weaknesses, both theoretical and empirical. This approach builds upon the recognition of the importance of electoral institutions in structuring the choices of electoral elites, but extends this role played by institutions to *both* electoral elites and voters. The central prediction made by this approach is that voters' leverage over policy requires the intermediary action of policy-seeking interest group activity in electoral politics. Only when voters are coordinated to overcome the collective action problem in voting by such policy-seeking organizations will voters see their collective votes leveraged into policy influence.

In fact, this appears to have been the case for women between 1920 and 1970. Between 1920 and 1925, legislators and party elites both believed that women constituted a distinct and significant electoral group, *and* were being publicly threatened by women's organizations with electoral retaliation if their lobbying demands were not met. Between 1925 and 1968, even though electoral elites clearly believed for much of this time that women were still a distinct and significant electoral group, women's organizations were not threatening these elites with electoral mobilization. After 1968, however, the threat of electoral retaliation by women's organizations resurfaced.

11

This extended strategic story thus works very well for explaining the waves of policy concessions for women as a group, better in fact than any of the existing explanations. But this explanation itself raises another question, namely, What determined the decisions of women's organizations either to pursue or not to pursue an electoral strategy? Given that there was little to no likelihood of policy concessions in the absence of such a strategy, why would women's organizations not seek to coordinate women's votes if women were in fact susceptible to such coordination?

For the case of women in the 1920s, scholars have again offered two kinds of answers to this question. The first relies on ideology as an explanation for the actions of former suffrage elites in the postsuffrage years: those elites were constrained either by an ideology of gender "sameness" or by an ideological tradition of nonpartisanship, either of which would have precluded the mobilization of women as a group in partisan electoral contests.[25] The second answer to this question infers from the absence of such mobilization the conclusion that former suffrage elites did not believe that women constituted a distinctive electoral group.[26] For the case of women in the late 1960s, surprisingly little attention has been given to the specifically electoral dimension to this question. Students of the development of this second women's movement have perhaps concluded that women did not pursue an electoral policy until 1984, with the first endorsement of a presidential ticket by NOW.[27]

As this book will document, both of these classes of answers for the 1920s, and the inference about the irrelevance of electoral politics to the women's movement of the 1970s, are empirically problematic. In addition to their empirical shortcomings, these explanations for the absence of an electoral strategy on the part of women's organizations between 1925 and 1970 pose theoretical problems as well. As already noted, and as will be discussed in greater detail in Chapter 2, ideology is a rather unpersuasive explanatory variable in the context of political competition well defined by the rules of an electoral game. Interest group leaders may have goals other than the pursuit of policy benefits for their group,

[25]For the "gender sameness" argument, see Sara Alpern and Dale Baum, "Female Ballots: The Impact of the Nineteenth Amendment," *Journal of Interdisciplinary History* 16, no. 1 (Summer 1985): 63; and Cott, *The Grounding of Modern Feminism*, p. 112. For the "gender difference" argument, see Paula C. Baker, *The Moral Frameworks of Public Life, 1870–1930* (New York: Oxford University Press, 1991), p. 148; Muncy, *Creating a Female Dominion*, p. 127; and Kristi Andersen, *No Longer Petitioners: Women in Partisan and Electoral Politics after Suffrage* (Chicago: University of Chicago Press, 1996), pp. 22–23, 30–31.

[26]See, e.g., Naomi Black, *Social Feminism* (Ithaca, N.Y.: Cornell University Press, 1989), pp. 249–250; Cott, *The Grounding of Modern Feminism*, p. 112.

[27]See, e.g., Silverberg, "Political Organization," pp. 205, 309.

but if they miss opportunities to pursue such policies effectively, they can be sure that others will rise to challenge their leadership by taking advantage of those opportunities. NLWV leaders who refused to pursue the electoral mobilization of women, in the face of the apparent viability of such mobilization, over time should have been replaced by others who could more successfully secure benefits for the group by threatening electoral retaliation on uncooperative legislators.

This problem appears to be addressed by simple strategic explanations that infer from the absence of such mobilization the conclusion that the group in question would not respond to mobilization appeals as a group. If groups *would* respond to such appeals, then logically interest group leaders should be making them. However, this is a faulty inference. The inference assumes a model of perfect electoral competition in which, if an electoral group exists, policy-seeking group leaders have every opportunity to leverage the group's votes into policy concessions. But just as many (if not most) economic markets do not reflect the conditions of perfect competition, so too may political "markets" be only imperfectly competitive.

In particular, it turns out that the most likely way for organizations to solve the collective action problem for voters leads to competitive advantages for the first organization to begin coordinating a group to vote. Moreover, while under the conditions of "normal" electoral politics in the United States we could expect policy-seeking organizations to be the first to initiate a new electoral group's electoral mobilization, under the conditions of the transition from female disfranchisement to female enfranchisement it was predictably the office-seeking party organizations that were the first to initiate women's electoral mobilization. The institution of elections creates the incentives for policy-seeking organizations to pursue legislative benefits through electoral politics. Without that institution (during the presuffrage years) many women's policy-seeking organizations came to focus on the exclusive pursuit of suffrage as a proximate goal to attaining policy benefits. Consequently the most successful of these organizations were not prepared to pursue a broader legislative agenda upon female enfranchisement, or to compete with the office-seeking party organizations for women's electoral mobilization.

When these two parts of the puzzle of women's organizations and policy outcomes are integrated into a chronological story, the implications are striking. For the story from start to finish is that exclusionary suffrage laws can have significant downstream effects on the efforts of previously excluded groups to take advantage of the opportunities presented by suffrage. The institutional context of female disfranchisement in the United States created initial conditions that had predictably neg-

13

ative consequences for the efforts of the former woman suffrage organization to compete with the major party organizations in the mobilization of women's votes after the passage of constitutional female suffrage in 1920. By the mid-1920s, the former suffrage organization had apparently been driven from the market in women's electoral mobilization. And without women's votes, the former suffrage organization could not effectively lobby vote-minded legislators for policies its leaders believed represented women's policy preferences. Due to the consequences of their prior exclusion from participation in electoral politics, as women grew more important electorally to the governing national party over the course of the 1920s, their leverage over national policy actually declined.

GENDER, IDEOLOGY, AND INSTITUTIONS

Recent years have seen the development of an interest in the study of gender as a significant analytical category in history and political science. Scholars have begun to ask the question whether explanatory theories based only on the experiences of men can be extended to explain political outcomes involving women. For example, many scholars have sought to understand the way in which gender as an ideology has shaped the beliefs and actions of female political actors, leading to the development of a shared and distinctive women's political culture. Specifically with respect to the relation of women to social policy, some scholars have argued that women both have had an understanding of the proper role of the state which differs from that of men *and* have used means different from those typically used by men to realize their different policy goals.[28] Therefore, perhaps we need different theories of public policy development to explain policy outcomes reflecting primarily the involvement of women as political actors.

A second scholarly effort involving the study of gender has rather sought to understand the way in which gender as an ideology has shaped the beliefs and actions of male public policy elites. That is, perhaps male policy makers have been motivated as much by their desire to reproduce

---

[28]See, e.g., Paula Baker, "The Domestication of Politics: Women and American Political Society, 1780–1920," in Linda Gordon, ed., *Women, the State, and Welfare* (Madison: University of Wisconsin Press, 1990), pp. 55–91; Theda Skocpol and Gretchen Ritter, "Gender and the Origins of Modern Social Policies in Britain and the United States," in Theda Skocpol, ed., *Social Policy in the United States: Future Possibilities in Historical Perspective* (Princeton: Princeton University Press, 1995), pp. 72–135; Ann Shola Orloff, "Gender in Early U.S. Social Policy," *Journal of Policy History* 3, no. 1 (1991): 249–281; Skocpol, *Protecting Soldiers and Mothers*; Gwendolyn Mink, *The Wages of Motherhood: Inequality in the Welfare State, 1917–1942* (Ithaca, N.Y.: Cornell University Press, 1995).

14

societal gender roles in public policy as they have been by concerns to alleviate problems such as poverty.[29] Again, perhaps existing theories about how public policies are developed do not apply when women are the subject of policy initiatives.

Empirically, these studies have greatly contributed to our awareness of often quite distinct male and female political cultures, and of the frequent incidence of gender bias in the development of public policies. Yet the causal account underlying much of this work is somewhat less satisfactory. First, these gender ideologies are assumed to provide incentives for action by both male and female political actors which consistently outweigh the incentives for action provided by the institutional rules of the game of electoral politics. For instance, female political actors maintain a distinct female tradition of political action even when their interests might be better served by pursuing different strategies. Male political actors continue to downplay the importance of the policy preferences of women even when their own reelection interests might be better served by closer attention to those preferences. Although gender ideologies might provide such strong incentives, it seems as though we would want that assertion demonstrated rather than assumed.

Second, our skepticism as to the plausibility of this causal account is perhaps enhanced when there is an alternative causal story for the existence of distinct female political strategies, and distinct policy outcomes for women, which does not conflict with the institutionally provided incentives inherent in the game of electoral politics. Perhaps different political practices develop, and different patterns of policy outcomes occur, because strategic political actors are responding to different institutional opportunities and constraints. For instance, if electoral laws treated men and women differently at any given point in time, then we would expect to see women as political actors making strategic choices that differed from those of their male counterparts. These choices would differ not because gender ideologies provided incentives that overrode institutionally provided incentives, but rather precisely because institutional rules provided different opportunities for political action to men and women. If the treatment of the sexes by electoral laws were reversed, then logically we would expect male political actors to have made essentially the same strategic choices made by female political actors under the previous scenario.

Similarly, it is also possible that the reluctance of male political elites

---

[29]See, e.g., Virgina Sapiro, "The Gender Basis of American Social Policy," in Gordon, *Women, the State, and Welfare*, pp. 36–54; Barbara J. Nelson, "The Origins of the Two-Channel Welfare State: Workmen's Compensation and Mothers' Aid," in ibid., pp. 123–151.

to grant policy concessions to women has been due not to any ideological gender bias, which overrode these elites' incentives to win women's votes, but rather to a more general strategic concern by office-seeking legislators to conserve their promises to voting groups. In a world of budget constraints, policy concessions to any given group will imply fewer resources available to reward other electoral groups. Reelection-minded legislators will therefore be reluctant to grant concessions to any group unless the electoral rewards or costs are relatively clear. If women have often received fewer and/or less valuable policy benefits than men, then the relevant question to ask would not be, In what way are men biased against women? but rather, Why have women apparently wielded so negligible an electoral threat to vote-minded legislators throughout much of the twentieth century?

In short, this study suggests a new way of thinking about the potential relevance of gender to political outcomes, one characterized more by an attention to the role of institutions rather than to the role of ideology. When institutional rules apply with equal force to both men and women, then we would not expect to see any relevant differences in male and/or female political behavior or outcomes that would necessitate bringing in gender as a category of analysis. But when institutional rules treat men and women differently, or more broadly impact upon men and women differently, then we would expect to see male and female political actors respond to the specific incentives presented to them by those rules. Those responses may require us to predict different outcomes for male and female political actors.

That is, it may not be the case that we need more than one theory to explain political outcomes. Both male and female actors should respond to the incentive structure of existing institutions in predictable ways. But we should be careful not to generalize our predictions based on the political experiences of men without *first* ensuring that women were not facing different institutional rules governing the behavior or outcome in question.[30]

---

[30]In *Protecting Soldiers and Mothers* and "Gender and the Origins of Modern Social Policies in Britain and the United States" (with Gretchen Ritter), Theda Skocpol seeks to address the interaction between political institutions and women's organizations in the following way: she argues that women's organizations were influential in the making of American welfare policy, as opposed to elsewhere, because those organizations enjoyed a good "fit" with the structure of the American state ("Gender and the Origins," p. 128). But since other nonfemale organizations have also enjoyed such a good "fit," according to Skocpol (see, e.g., *Social Policy*, p. 29), it is unclear either why the same institutions would not induce similar organizational forms among all interest groups or why electoral exclusion, e.g., would not produce women's organizations that were distinct from other interest group organizations.

The Legacy of Female Disfranchisement

This study thus at least tentatively argues for a single explanatory approach to studying political outcomes. Logically, we should therefore be able to use this study's theoretical framework to explain cross-national outcomes in postsuffrage female politics. However, the same framework may yield different predictions in countries possessing different institutional rules. For instance, electoral laws that make it easier for parties to form will affect the competition between parties and interest groups for voters' loyalties. Legislative rules distributing the leverage of individual legislators over policy will in turn affect the scale on which interest groups will have to organize in order to be able to influence policy. Constitutional rules concerning the authority of subnational governments will likewise influence interest group organizational incentives. All, or none, of these rules may alter the predictions of this book.

Similarly, the focus of this book on institutions rather than group characteristics implies that the arguments made here may apply to the postsuffrage politics of other previously disfranchised groups within the United States. The clearest analogues to the case of women in 1920 are those of black men in the Reconstruction South of 1867, and southern black men and women in 1965.[31] Again, however, in order for this book's predictions to hold, precisely the same institutional conditions would have had to govern electoral politics at these times. But we already know that this is not likely to have been the case. For example, electoral laws that affect the organizational strength of the parties have changed over time, and these changes would clearly affect our predictions concerning political outcomes. The same *framework* can be used to investigate analogous cases, but the predictions for those cases may be different depending upon the institutional context in each case.

TESTING COMPETING HYPOTHESES

Ultimately, our explanation for the puzzling policy outcomes of the 1920s and beyond rests on a chain of causally linked events that may be traced back to the effects of disfranchisement on the information available to and strategies chosen by suffrage and party elites. For each of the steps in this sequence, however, competing hypotheses also purport to explain the events in question. What are our standards for rejecting alternative hypotheses?

For the social scientist, testing these hypotheses is difficult because of

---

[31]This possibility is explored in my "Votes without Leverage: The Political Consequences of Black and Female Disfranchisement," paper presented at the Annual Meeting of the American Political Science Association, Washington, D.C., September 2–5, 1993.

the historical nature of the phenomena in question. The ideal technique for drawing conclusions on the basis of the available evidence, or making scientific inferences, would involve replicating the events in question in a carefully controlled laboratory setting in order to isolate the independent and dependent variables of interest. Obviously this is not an option for making inferences about the events of the 1920s, as it is not for much of social science. Nor is the social science analogue to controlled laboratory experiments, comparative case analysis (with either large or small numbers of observations), particularly apt in this case. We would like to be able to see whether the presence of prior disfranchisement negatively affects the later efforts of groups to leverage votes into policy, holding all other relevant variables constant. This latter requirement first forces us to remain within the United States to look for comparative cases, as we have good reason to believe that the different political institutions in other countries (including electoral laws and other constitutional rules) would affect the strategic interaction of electoral actors. Given that the institutional context of electoral politics has changed over time in the United States, we would also want to look to electoral groups mobilizing at approximately the same time as newly enfranchised women for relevant comparative cases. Our universe of potential cases for comparison is thus greatly restricted already to only one positive instance and three or four negative instances of the independent variable. Yet we can proceed with these comparisons (as in Chapter 2), mapping the sequence of electoral mobilization experienced by contemporary groups and demonstrating the uniqueness of the case of female electoral mobilization. Our argument, of course, is that the prior institutional history of women accounts for the distinctive features of their case.

Yet many will still argue that women are distinct in ways that do not relate to the effects of their treatment by institutional rules. This is a more general problem in doing comparative case analysis with a small number of cases, namely that our ability to control for other potential independent variables (such as gender ideology) is quite limited. Obviously we would want to examine the history of other enfranchised groups in the United States to see whether their patterns of postsuffrage electoral politics meet the theory's predictions (thus controlling for any effects of gender ideology). And we could do this, but the institutional context of postsuffrage electoral politics for enfranchised black men in the South of 1867, or southern black men and women in 1964, is different enough from that of women in the 1920s to render such comparisons suspect. Unfortunately, it seems we have a case of one with which to establish an inductive argument. The fact that this may be a more general problem in the social sciences, which few are willing to admit, does not ease our explanatory burden.

Indeed, our situation is most akin to that facing a homicide detective who wants to solve a murder case. The victim obviously cannot be murdered again and again in a series of controlled experiments in order to establish the murderer's identity, nor would it be particularly helpful to compare the murder to a statistical universe of similar cases. Yet it is not the case that the detective is left without any method with which to establish the identity of the murderer. Rather, the detective will compile a list of possible suspects, posit the likely chronological sequence of events linking each potential criminal to the crime, and investigate each step of those causal sequences to see if the evidence exculpates that individual or allows him to remain a suspect. If at the end of this process the detective is lucky enough to have only one suspect left, then she has the most likely suspect of those on the original list. And the more distinctive and complex the causal sequence linking that suspect to the crime, the more likely it is the case that it was in fact that particular individual who committed the homicide, and not a previously unknown suspect.

This methodology has been given several names, among which are "modus operandi analysis,"[32] "process tracing,"[33] "the method of subobjectives,"[34] or simply increasing the observable implications of a theory.[35] The basic procedure remains the same, however. The primary causal hypothesis for a given phenomenon must imply several subsidiary causal hypotheses in a chain of causation over time, each of which subsidiary hypotheses must allow for empirical verification. The more complex the causal chain, the better, as the multiplication of subsidiary hypotheses gives the investigator more opportunities to eliminate the primary hypothesis and thus strengthens her confidence in its causality if in fact all the implied subsidiary hypotheses are supported by the evidence. If competing hypotheses are being tested, the same should be done for each of these. The best explanation for the event in question will be the primary hypothesis whose "characteristic causal chain"[36] is the most fully realized, even if other causal chains are partially realized.

In other words, even though we have only one "case," namely that

[32]Michael Scriven, "Maximizing the Power of Causal Investigations: The Modus Operandi Method," *Evaluation Studies Review Annual* 1 (1976): 101–118.

[33]Alexander L. George and Timothy J. McKeown, "Case Studies and Theories of Organizational Decision Making," *Advances in Information Processing in Organizations*, 2 (1986): 21–58.

[34]Lawrence B. Mohr, *Impact Analysis for Program Evaluation* (Chicago: Dorsey Press, 1988), chap. 11.

[35]Gary King, Robert O. Keohane, and Sidney Verba, *Designing Social Inquiry: Scientific Inference in Qualitative Research* (Princeton: Princeton University Press, 1994).

[36]Scriven, "Maximizing the Power of Causal Investigations," p. 105.

of women in the United States, we actually have several testable hypotheses that flow from our primary causal hypothesis. And since our ultimate hypothesis concerning the importance of female disfranchisement is deductively linked to several subsidiary outcomes, we can test alternative explanations for each outcome. The more outcomes that can be explained by our primary causal hypothesis and its subsidiaries, and not by alternative explanations, the more likely it is that our primary hypothesis is in fact causal.[37] And as will become clear throughout this study, the available evidence does not support any of the previously discussed competing hypotheses in fully realized causal chains.

CHAPTER OUTLINE

Chapter 2 develops in much greater detail the theoretical foundations of our explanation for the puzzling variation in the treatment of women as beneficiaries of public policy. This chapter seeks to show that on purely theoretical grounds, our explanation is perhaps more convincing than its competitors. Because of the often limited nature of data in the social sciences, it makes our case stronger if we can in fact argue it on theoretical grounds.

However, theory is not particularly helpful if in the end it does not help to explain any more facts than existing stories. The subsequent chapters thus present previously unexplored data from 1917 to 1970 that support the revised strategic story presented in Chapter 2 while casting doubts on competing hypotheses. These data concern the strategic behavior of office-seeking party and benefit-seeking women's elites, the likely effects of these strategies on the partisan registration behavior of enfranchised women between 1920 and 1936, and the resultant outcomes within the parties as organizations between 1920 and 1970, outcomes that replicate the public policy outcomes for women discussed earlier. Although our primary outcomes of interest exist at the level of national politics and policy making, a state-level case study of New York State was also done to obtain more observations with which to test our predictions. New York is also significant to this book's story because it was the only state in which the NLWV and the parties competed head to head for women's electoral loyalties after constitutional enfranchisement.

Specifically, this study draws upon the following documentary sources

---

[37]The fact that our arguments are based on deductive logic makes the task of testing these arguments easier than if they were not so based. Deductive logic allows for the development of implied hypotheses, whereas nondeductive arguments typically do not.

for the period of the 1920s: the papers of Warren G. Harding, Calvin Coolidge, and Herbert Hoover; any article in the *New York Times* between 1917 and 1932 that included a reference either to women in the political parties, national or New York State, or to the National or New York State Leagues of Women Voters; the transcripts of every convention of the NLWV from 1919 through 1930, the minutes of every meeting of the NLWV's board, executive committee, or executive council during that same period, and the newsletters of the New York State Woman Suffrage Party, the New York State League of Women Voters, the National American Woman Suffrage Association, and the National League of Women Voters from 1909 through 1920. In addition, as a surrogate for analyzing women's voting behavior in the 1920s, I collected and analyzed women's partisan registration data from Boston, Philadelphia, Pittsburgh, and rural Pennsylvania counties between 1920 and 1936. For the later period, I drew upon the papers of John F. Kennedy and the official records of the Democratic National Committee and Democratic National Executive Committee between 1952 and 1964. For both periods I consulted secondary sources where appropriate.

Chapters 3 and 4 consider explanations for the decision of the NLWV in the mid-1920s to cease mobilizing women in electoral contests as a means to leverage policy concessions from office-seeking elites. In a chronological sequence, these chapters present evidence that undermines explanations for this decision based on ideology or on the assumption that women were not a mobilizable group. Rather, the evidence, both documentary and in the form of registration data, supports the deductively argued predictions made in Chapter 2.

Chapter 5 considers explanations for the decisions of office-seeking elites to cease providing policy benefits to women in the mid-1920s. Again, the evidence is not consistent with explanations for these decisions based on policy networks, ideology, or the assumption that women did not constitute a significant and distinct electoral group. Rather, the evidence supports the argument that it was the now publicly known decision by the NLWV to end its policy of electoral mobilization that best explains the decisions of office-seeking elites. This chapter examines as additional dependent variables the grants of representation made to women in both party organizations, both at the national level and in New York State, between 1917 and 1932. The evidence in all of these cases is consistent with the arguments made in Chapter 2.

Finally, Chapter 6 brings the argument up to the present by examining the period of 1952 to 1970 (secondary sources tell us that there was not much change in the variables in which we are interested in the interim period). This chapter examines explanations both for the decision of women's organizations in 1968 to resume an electoral strategy, and for the reappearance of women as specific beneficiaries of public policy in 1970. Again, it appears that explanations for these phenomena based on policy networks, ideology, or simple assumptions about women's voting behavior do not do a particularly good job at explaining the events in question. Rather, as argued in Chapter 2, some feature of the institutional context of electoral politics would have had to have changed significantly in order to lead to a change in women's politics. We know from other work that the institutional context of electoral politics was indeed undergoing significant changes during the 1960s; this chapter suggests the relevance of those changes to women's politics. The chapter concludes by discussing the way in which this study suggests the relevance of institutions and history to democratic theory.

2

The Logic of Policy Change:
Voters, Organizations, and Institutions

As discussed in the preceding chapter, the problems with the existing explanations for the puzzling fate of policy benefits for women between 1920 and 1970 are both theoretical and empirical. In this chapter I tackle the theoretical issues raised by these explanations; later chapters will examine the empirical issues.

In brief, the argument I make in this chapter is the following:

1. Eligible voters vote not on the basis of their policy preferences, but rather because voting in a particular way is required as a condition of acceptance by family members, friends, co-workers, or others in some larger group such as a party or interest group.
2. Both party and interest group organizations seek to capitalize on such group-based incentives during electoral campaigns, or to mobilize voters. Given the divergent motivations of party and interest group elites, however, we should expect party elites to be mobilizing voters solely in order to attain office, and interest group elites to be mobilizing voters in order to obtain policy benefits from those office-seeking elites.
3. Given the foregoing, it is a *necessary though not sufficient* condition of group-specific policy benefits that an interest group organization is pursuing a strategy of electoral mobilization in return for policy concessions from office-seeking elites.
4. Markets for group electoral mobilization are predictably characterized by imperfect competition, under which the first electoral entrepreneur to initiate a group's mobilization can have significant competitive advantages over later entrants to the group's market in mobilization.
5. Interest group elites typically appear to possess both informational and organizational advantages that enable them to be the first entrants to new markets in group electoral mobilization. These benefit

seekers then have competitive advantages over purely office-seeking elites in coordinating groups' electoral mobilization.

6. *Because of their previous electoral exclusion,* enfranchised groups are likely to be mobilized by parties, not by interest group organizations. And because parties are controlled by purely office-seeking elites who are reluctant to make policy concessions, the group's electoral mobilization will not induce party bosses or candidates to move toward endorsing the group's previously unrepresented policy preferences. By the logic of electoral mobilization outlined here, disfranchisement has significant downstream consequences for later attempts by enfranchised groups to attain electoral representation.

In order to generate these hypotheses, it is necessary to consider two distinct theoretical questions. The first question we must answer concerns the sources of policy change in the United States: what motivates legislators to provide policy benefits to groups? The second question concerns the electoral strategies of interest groups: what accounts for the decision of interest group elites to engage (or not) in the electoral mobilization of a group whose primary strength lies in votes rather than money?

This chapter addresses these questions in separate sections, taking up first the question of the sources of policy change and subsequently the question of the competition between interest group and party elites to mobilize voters. The final section considers the effect of a unique institutional context on this competition in the case of potential female voters, telling a story that links female disfranchisement to the diminishing political influence of women's organizations in the 1920s.

Convincing as these purely theoretical arguments may be to some, they are not particularly useful unless they actually help us to explain outcomes better than the alternatives. Ensuing chapters thus take up the testing of these arguments and the weighing of competing empirical claims for the puzzling events of the 1920s. As those chapters will demonstrate, it happily appears that strengthening our arguments on purely theoretical grounds helps us to explain more of the empirical phenomena in which we are interested.

EXPLAINING POLICY OUTCOMES: THEORETICAL APPROACHES

Existing explanations for the puzzling policy outcomes concerning women during the 1920s assume some sort of logic behind the generation of policy change in the United States more generally. Therefore, the first theoretical issue we must face is the quality of those more general arguments. Do they provide adequate accounts of the causal mechanism assumed to generate policy change, accounts that can be tested by the available evidence?

Although it is beyond the scope of this book to examine these arguments in detail, we can both broadly indicate the major classes of explanation for policy change in the United States that surface in the specific explanations for the events of the 1920s, and identify some potential problems with those explanations. This section thus briefly examines two such groups of explanations, namely arguments from nonelectoral mechanisms and those which instead focus on the electoral incentives of legislators. This section then articulates in much greater detail the basis for an alternative electoral story and its predictions for the course of policy change.

Nonelectoral Approaches: Policy Networks and Ideological Climates

One class of explanations for the variation in the extent to which women have been beneficiaries of public policies seeks the causes of policy change in nonelectoral factors such as the development of policy networks or the power of certain ideas to move legislators. Thus one group of scholars argues that we should look to the development of women's policy networks between 1920 and 1925 and after 1970 in order to explain the pattern in policy outcomes.[1] Another group argues that the policy victories won by women's organizations during these periods were due rather to the favorable ideological climates of the early 1920s and the 1970s.[2] More generally, such explanations rely on existing theories of policy change that focus on factors such as the expertise of policy specialists participating in "issue networks"[3] or "policy communities,"[4]

---

[1]For the 1920s, see Robyn Muncy, *Creating a Female Dominion in American Reform, 1890–1935* (New York: Oxford University Press, 1991), and Theda Skocpol, *Protecting Soldiers and Mothers: The Political Origins of Social Policy in the United States* (Cambridge, Mass.: Belknap Press of Harvard University Press, 1992); for the late 1960s, see Jo Freeman, *The Politics of Women's Liberation: A Case Study of an Emerging Social Movement and Its Relation to the Policy Process* (New York: David McKay, 1975), chap. 7.

[2]For the 1920s, see William H. Chafe, *The American Woman: Her Changing Social, Economic, and Political Roles, 1920–1970* (London: Oxford University Press, 1972), p. 29; Clarke A. Chambers, *Seedtime of Reform: American Social Service and Social Action, 1918–1933* (Minneapolis: University of Minnesota Press, 1963); Muncy, *Creating a Female Dominion*, pp. 129–135; Skocpol, *Protecting Soldiers and Mothers*, p. 521. For the 1960s and 1970s, see Freeman, *The Politics of Women's Liberation*, p. 229.

[3]Hugh Heclo, "Issue Networks and the Executive Establishment," in Anthony

or the power of ideas themselves (as in, "an idea whose time has come").[5] According to authors working in these traditions, electoral considerations are not the only or even the primary cause of policy change.

Arguments concerning issue or policy networks hypothesize that the roots of policy change must be sought in the entrepreneurial efforts of nameless, faceless policy specialists linked together in networks of technical expertise, networks that include congressional staff and agency bureaucrats. Motivated not by "interest" but rather by intellectual and/or emotional commitments, these policy experts seek to mobilize legislative action through persuasion rather than bargaining, selling legislators on the merits of alternative policy proposals rather than on their political appeal. The policies most likely to be legislated are therefore those with the most support from policy networks or communities.[6]

Although adopted policies often have the support of communities of policy experts, we might want to question the causal mechanism underlying this empirical relationship. No studies demonstrate that defeated policies do not just as often have the support of communities of policy experts. Policy advocates may be found for either side of any given issue; the real question is, What governs the response of electoral elites such as legislators to the various policy proposals by which they are continually besieged? Why do political elites respond to some policy networks and not others, or at some times and not at others?[7]

The most likely motivation of legislative elites in this regard is an electoral concern, given that those elites must compete for survival in an electoral "game" well defined by existing political institutions. No matter their ultimate goals, members of Congress must secure their reelection as a requisite proximate goal before they have the luxury of pursuing other aims. Note that the argument is not that legislators do

King, ed., *The New American Political System* (Washington, D.C.: American Enterprise Institute, 1978), pp. 87–124.

[4]John W. Kingdon, *Agendas, Alternatives, and Public Policies* (Boston: Little, Brown, 1984).

[5]Ibid., pp. 153–157; David R. Mayhew, *Divided We Govern: Party Control, Lawmaking, and Investigations, 1946–1990* (New Haven: Yale University Press, 1991), pp. 142–174; Arthur M. Schlesinger Jr., *The Cycles of American History* (Boston: Houghton Mifflin, 1986), pp. 31–34; Samuel P. Huntington, *American Politics: The Promise of Disharmony* (Cambridge, Mass.: Harvard University Press, 1981). The quoted phrase is from Theda Skocpol, "The Enactment of Mothers' Pensions: Civic Mobilization and Agenda Setting or Benefits of the Ballot?: Response," *American Political Science Review* 89, no. 3 (September 1995): 728.

[6]Heclo, "Issue Networks and the Executive Establishment," p. 102; Kingdon, *Agendas, Alternatives, and Public Policies*, pp. 131–134.

[7]Similar questions are raised and discussed by John Mark Hansen in *Gaining Access: Congress and the Farm Lobby, 1919–1981* (Chicago: University of Chicago Press, 1991).

not care about the merits of the policy proposals before them or value as an ultimate goal the enactment of better public policy, but rather that these concerns must take a back seat to the pursuit of reelection because of the structure of Congress itself. Those who framed the structure of this institution were in fact concerned that legislators would be responsive only to the needs of certain elite groups, and thus sought to ensure a "dependence upon the people" through regular elections. Although we can thus certainly recognize Richard Fenno's argument that members of Congress may have goals other than simply winning reelection, such as the making of good policy and the attainment of power and status within Congress,[8] we must as a matter of logic argue that given the constraints imposed upon legislators by the election cycle, the "electoral incentive" must arguably underlie legislators' decisions to take up particular policy proposals and to ignore others.[9]

Incidentally, the most prominent advocates of the policy network approach do not in fact sharply distinguish their arguments from those based on electoral politics. For instance, both Hugh Heclo and John Kingdon agree that the strategic calculations of political elites who must maneuver for electoral advantage play an important role in determining which policy communities become influential, and when this is likely to occur.[10] By most accounts, then, strategic concerns are likely to underlie the decisions of electoral elites to respond to some policy networks and not to others, or at some times and not at others.

Another explanatory argument for public policy development that is typically distinguished from arguments based on electoral strategy emphasizes the evolution of a grand idea that somehow captures the imagination of both the mass public and political elites, variously referred to as a "public mood," a public "passion" or "climate," or simply as a prevailing ideology. According to proponents of this argument, these moods or passions result in predictable periods of legislative activity: periods of strong public-minded moodiness during which many major pieces of reform legislation are passed alternate with a private-regarding moodiness on the part of the general public during which little congressional legislative activity occurs.

Although it may often seem as though legislators and the voting public are caught up in the same ideological "mood," we might again want

---

[8]Richard Fenno, *Congressmen in Committees* (Boston: Little, Brown, 1973).

[9]David R. Mayhew, *Congress: The Electoral Connection* (New Haven: Yale University Press, 1974), p. 16; John H. Aldrich, *Why Parties? The Origin and Transformation of Party Politics in America* (Chicago: University of Chicago Press, 1995), p. 14.

[10]Heclo, "Issue Networks and the Executive Establishment," p. 117; Kingdon, *Agendas, Alternatives, and Public Policies*, p. 20.

to speculate further as to the causal mechanism generating this empirical relationship. In the absence of any alternative story, the most likely candidate for such a mechanism is again an electoral account. Given the institutional context of the U.S. Congress, legislators simply have no choice but to be concerned about their electoral futures. We should therefore expect shrewd legislators to make some effort to correlate their ideological moods with those of their constituents. Following ideological whims that do not correspond to those of the public at large could spell electoral disaster for the legislators who dared such a course. And indeed, strategic electoral concerns do appear to lurk more or less visibly behind the discussions of mood and climate found in the works of those who study them.[11]

Given the constraints imposed on legislators by political institutions, plausible explanations for policy change seem to require a theoretical underpinning of strategic action. But that underpinning may not be as simple as, "Legislators respond to constituency preferences." What we still need is a good argument about the conditions under which electoral elites will be likely to respond to electoral pressures by enacting public policy. It is to this issue that we now turn.

"Simple" Electoral Approaches

The second class of explanations for the variation in policies benefiting women relies upon a simple version of strategic politics: women received policy benefits from legislators when legislators believed that women voted as a bloc. When legislators believed that women did not vote as a bloc, there were no longer any electoral incentives for legislators to grant women policy benefits in order to win their votes.[12]

More generally, we may include these explanations in a category of approaches to the study of policy outcomes that are based on the electoral constraints faced by lawmakers. Common to these approaches is the contention that legislators are forced by the rules of the electoral

[11]Mayhew, *Divided We Govern*, p. 172; Kingdon, *Agendas, Alternatives, and Public Policies*, p. 156.

[12]For the 1920s, see Chafe, *The American Woman*, pp. 29–30; J. Stanley Lemons, *The Woman Citizen: Social Feminism in the 1920s* (Chicago: University of Chicago Press, 1975), pp. 157, 174; Michael McGerr, "Political Style and Women's Power, 1830–1930," *Journal of American History* 77, no. 3 (December 1990): 882; Muncy, *Creating a Female Dominion*, p. 126; Eleanor Flexner, *Century of Struggle: The Woman's Rights Movement in the United States* (Cambridge, Mass.: Harvard University Press, 1975), p. 338; Skocpol, *Protecting Soldiers and Mothers*, p. 521. On the 1970s, see Helene Norma Silverberg, "Political Organization and the Origin of Political Identity: The Emergence and Containment of Gender in American Politics, 1960–1984" (Ph.D. dissertation, Cornell University, 1988).

market to develop policies primarily in response to the policy preferences held by voters. In other words, legislators and other office-seeking electoral elites produce policy (or policy promises) to maximize votes.[13]

The nuances of these arguments, theoretical and empirical, are unimportant for our purposes, as my contention is that they tend to share a common logical inconsistency. Almost without exception, these arguments assume that electoral institutions constrain the choices made by electoral elites but *not* those made by voters. That is, despite their own preferences about public policy, the discipline of periodic elections supposedly forces legislators to worry first about the preferences of voters. They thus are likely to support instrumentally the package of policies that maximizes their chances of reelection.

Voters, on the other hand, are assumed to vote rather straightforwardly their policy preferences, or more precisely to use their policy preferences as a guide to choosing between competing candidates or parties. But this assumption requires voters who are not instrumentally rational, who do not see how their ability to realize their preferences is constrained by political institutions.

Consider the kinds of goods for which scholars assume voters have preferences. Public policies are typically what economists term collective or public goods, that is, nonexcludable goods that cannot be withheld from those who did not pay for them.[14] For example, national defense ensures security from attack to all who live within a country's borders, regardless of whether individual inhabitants of that country have paid for that security or not. This nonexcludable aspect of public goods creates a problem in the provision of such goods: even though individual citizens might value the benefits of national defense more than they value their share of the costs of that defense, in the absence of coercion no citizen has individual incentives actually to pay her share of those costs. That share is so small as to not make a discernible difference in whether defense is actually provided, and if defense is in fact provided by others she will benefit regardless of whether she paid her share of the costs. And why pay when you can get something for free?

To an economist the significance of a collective good is that it must be provided by the public sector, because private firms will have no incentives to produce goods or services for which they cannot charge a

---

[13]Anthony Downs, *An Economic Theory of Democracy* (New York: Harper & Row, 1957), p. 28; Joseph A. Schlesinger, "The Primary Goals of Political Parties: A Clarification of Positive Theory," *American Political Science Review* 69 (September 1975): 840–849; Joseph A. Schlesinger, *Political Parties and the Winning of Office* (Chicago: University of Chicago Press, 1991); Aldrich, *Why Parties?*, pp. 19–21.

[14]Collective goods are therefore to be distinguished from selective or private goods, which are received only by those who pay for the good.

price. But to political scientists collective goods present an additional problem, namely, Why should vote-maximizing politicians provide them either? The institution of mass elections creates an analogous public goods problem for voters, because voting (and its attendant tasks) is costly, a single vote does not make a discernible difference in the outcome of an election, and nonvoters cannot be excluded from enjoying the policy benefits provided by victorious candidates or parties.

Voting in order to receive collective policy benefits is costly, of course, first, because of the opportunity costs involved in researching candidate positions on issues, estimating the effect of those positions on the voter, and then calculating which candidate better serves the voter's interests and, second, because of the opportunity costs involved in actually registering and voting. Importantly, while the information costs of voting can conceivably be borne by a third party, all voters must eventually pay the opportunity costs of voting themselves. There are thus irreducible costs to voting, small though they may be.

Despite the costs of casting an informed vote, voters may very well (and in fact probably do) value the policy benefits that flow from elections more than they value the costs of voting. But individual votes can have only a negligible impact on election outcomes: only under very unlikely conditions will individual voters make or break electoral ties. Moreover, public policies cannot be distributed only to those who voted (anonymously) for the candidates who promised these policy benefits. As a result, instrumentally rational individuals who have preferences about the outcome of an election have very few *incentives* to vote for their preferred candidates.[15] That is, rational individuals will reason that since they will get the benefits (or not) of a candidate's election (or defeat) regardless of whether or not they vote, they should pay the costs of voting only if their vote will make a difference in the outcome of the election. But in large electorates, there is no plausible scenario under which an individual's vote can affect the outcome of an election, and therefore rational individuals will have insufficient incentives to vote on the basis of expected policy benefits (otherwise known as the collective action problem in voting).[16]

[15]I assume throughout that individuals are rational in the sense that they seek to maximize expected utility, where utility is simply that which is preferred by the individual. Norman Frohlich and Joe A. Oppenheimer, *Modern Political Economy* (Englewood Cliffs, N.J.: Prentice-Hall, 1978).

[16]Anthony Downs first alluded to the collective action problem in electoral politics (without naming it as such) in *An Economic Theory of Democracy*. Mancur Olson made the first comprehensive study of the collective action problem in politics in *The Logic of Collective Action: Public Goods and the Theory of Groups* (Cambridge, Mass.: Harvard University Press, 1965); also see Russell Hardin, *Collective Action* (Baltimore: Johns Hopkins University Press, 1982).

More precisely, the collective action problem stems from an individual's consideration of her expected utility from voting for a candidate because of his policy positions. According to the calculus of voting first proposed by Anthony Downs, an individual's decision of whether to vote rests on the following equation:

$$R = p(B) - C,$$

where R = the reward from voting; B = the differential utility of the individual's preferred candidate defeating his opponent, or the collective policy benefit from voting; p = the increase in probability of the preferred candidate winning when the individual's vote is cast; and C = the informational and opportunity costs of voting. The individual's decision rule for voting is to vote if $R > 0$, or $p(B) > C$.[17]

In large electorates, the probability of a single vote affecting the outcome of an election approximates zero. As a result, the collective policy benefit that an individual can expect to receive as a result of voting also approximates zero. In large electorates, therefore, the costs of voting should always outweigh the benefits of voting, and turnout should be nonexistent.[18]

The simple strategic story about policy change thus runs into a significant problem. Assuming instrumental rationality on the part of both electoral elites and voters leads to the conclusion that voters will have very few incentives to vote solely on the basis of their policy preferences. If instrumentally rational voters cannot be motivated with policy promises, then instrumentally rational candidates will have few (if any) incentives to make those promises and to follow through on them. Any arguments for policy change that hypothesize legislative response to voter pressure must therefore take into account this implication of the collective action problem in voting.

The next section develops a theoretical account of how the collective

---

[17]Downs, *An Economic Theory of Democracy*, p. 266; also see William H. Riker and Peter C. Ordeshook, "A Theory of the Calculus of Voting," *American Political Science Review* 62 (1968): 25–42; and William H. Riker and Peter C. Ordeshook, *An Introduction to Positive Political Theory* (Englewood Cliffs, N.J.: Prentice-Hall, 1973).

[18]The collective action problem can also be analyzed in game theoretic terms, in which the problem becomes a prisoners' dilemma: although all voters who favor a particular policy would be better off if they all voted for the candidate who espoused that policy, individually each has stronger incentives to defect from the collective action of voting than to cooperate. Thus, no one votes, and the group's preferred policy is not forthcoming. See John A. Ferejohn and Morris P. Fiorina, "The Paradox of Not Voting: A Decision Theoretic Analysis," *American Political Science Review* 68 (1974): 525–535; Aldrich, *Why Parties?*, pp. 31–33, 46–48.

action problem gets solved for voters. As we shall see, these solutions do raise the possibility that voters' policy concerns may be addressed by vote-maximizing legislators. However, that is certainly not a necessary conclusion. And in the case of women after enfranchisement, it does not appear to be the correct conclusion.

An Extended Electoral Approach

Voters. The fact is that turnout does exist, and therefore there must be a theoretical solution to the collective action problem. One class of solutions seeks to reformulate voters' decision rules in order to eliminate the problem while still preserving instrumental or outcome-oriented rationality as the framework of analysis. Thus John A. Ferejohn and Morris P. Fiorina suggested that there need be only a logical possibility of an individual's vote affecting the outcome to induce individuals to vote, if those individuals are minimizing their maximum regret from action. But this approach implies that voters should vote for themselves since there is clearly a logical possibility that they might be elected to public office by doing so. Yet very few voters pursue this course. Others retain the notion of expected utility maximization but suppose that voters can reasonably assume that very few others will vote, and that therefore their vote may be instrumental to the election. This latter approach remains unsatisfactory for large electorates, however.[19]

A second class of solutions to the collective action problem draws upon the hypothesis that voters receive private or selective benefits directly from the act of voting. In terms of a voter's decision rule, this line of reasoning implies that an additional "consumption" term D must be added to the equation, which, as it does not depend on the outcome of the election, is not discounted by the probability that a single vote will affect that outcome. The revised equation thus reads

$$R = p(B) - C + D.[20]$$

[19]Ferejohn and Fiorina, "The Paradox of Not Voting"; John O. Ledyard, "The Paradox of Voting and Candidate Competition: A General Equilibrium Analysis," in George Horwich and James P. Quirk, eds., *Essays in Contemporary Fields of Economics* (West Lafayette, Ind.: Purdue University Press, 1981), pp. 54–80; John O. Ledyard, "The Pure Theory of Large Two Candidate Elections," *Public Choice* 44 (1984): 7–41; Thomas R. Palfrey and Howard Rosenthal, "Voter Participation and Strategic Uncertainty," *American Political Science Review* 79 (1985): 62–78.

[20]This consumption term has in fact been around as long as the voting equation itself; it simply is useful to separate conceptually the problem and potential solutions to the problem.

If we follow the formulation first proposed by James Q. Wilson, three primary forms of private (or consumption, or selective) incentives may be used to explain political participation: material, purposive, and solidary.[21] Material incentives are tangible benefits that may be valued in monetary terms: cash, wages and salaries, and goods and services that one would otherwise have to purchase on the open market. The receipt of material benefits for voting, while extremely rare today, was prevalent in the United States at the turn of the century through the agency of political machines, and indeed appears to have had strong effects on voter turnout.[22]

Purposive or intrinsic incentives are intangible benefits that derive from the inherent nature of performing an act itself, such as a sense of satisfaction received from having fulfilled one's civic obligation, or having expressed one's candidate preferences.[23] But intrinsic incentives provide a rather weak explanation for voter participation. Theoretically, relying on a purely noninstrumental explanation of voter motivation to solve a problem created by assuming instrumental rationality on the part of voters seems logically inconsistent.[24] In addition, empirical evidence suggests that a strong sense of civic obligation accounts for only a very small percentage of turnout.[25]

A more plausible and theoretically compelling solution is the argument that many voters receive solidary benefits from voting, or benefits received from pleasing others in some definable group.[26] While the concept of solidary incentives has been around for some time, their exten-

---

[21]James Q. Wilson, *Political Organizations* (New York: Basic Books, 1973). Although this typology may sometimes be used to apply to collective goods, I here restrict the discussion to selective goods.

[22]See Steven P. Erie, *Rainbow's End: Irish-Americans and the Dilemmas of Urban Machine Politics, 1840–1985* (Princeton: Princeton University Press, 1988).

[23]Downs, *An Economic Theory of Democracy*, pp. 267–271; Riker and Ordeshook, "A Theory of the Calculus of Voting."

[24]Brian Barry, *Sociologists, Economists, and Democracy* (Chicago: University of Chicago Press, 1970).

[25]Steven J. Rosenstone and John Mark Hansen found that those who felt a strong sense of civic duty were only 6 percent more likely to vote than those who expressed little civic responsibility, and caution that even that 6 percent may be an overstatement. *Mobilization, Participation, and Democracy in America* (New York: Macmillan, 1993), p. 147.

[26]Authors who have relied on solidary incentives to solve the collective action problem include Rosenstone and Hansen, *Mobilization, Participation, and Democracy in America*; Carole J. Uhlaner, "Rational Turnout: The Neglected Role of Groups," *American Journal of Political Science* 33, no. 2 (May 1989): 390–422; Carole S. Uhlaner, " 'Relational Goods' and Participation: Incorporating Sociability into a Theory of Rational Action," *Public Choice* 62 (1989): 253–285; Dennis Chong, *Collective Action and the Civil Rights Movement* (Chicago: University of Chicago Press, 1991), chap. 3; Hardin, *Collective Action*, chap. 7.

sion to the case of large groups has only recently been given a foundation in instrumental rationality. With such a foundation, solidary benefits that flow from group acceptance can be used to solve a problem originally created by assuming instrumentally rational behavior on the part of individual voters.[27]

The basic idea underlying an instrumentally rational story about the benefits individuals receive from identifying with a group is an emphasis on the inherent uncertainty that characterizes the world of social exchange.[28] Our social environment is composed of a complex series of interactions with others, many of whom we do not know beforehand. As rational individuals, we attempt to calculate the consequences of our actions in this social world, and act when we feel that the instrumental benefits from action outweigh the costs of action. These consequences of our actions, it being a social world, typically depend upon the reactions that our actions produce in others. Often we may know the parties to our social exchanges and can predict with some certainty how they will react to our actions. But when we interact with individuals with whom we are not acquainted, as in many social contexts, we will not possess good information on how they will respond to our actions. We will thus be unable to predict with any accuracy how these strangers will respond to our words and deeds, and will therefore be unable confidently to calculate the likely consequences of our actions. Moreover, this information can be quite costly to acquire for every such interaction in which we might want to engage. As a result, we often face a relatively high degree of uncertainty in our interactions with others.[29]

In the terms of rational choice theory, we experience this uncertainty as disutility or as a "bad." Acting inappropriately in the social world can clearly have negative consequences for such typical goals as enhancing one's material and social assets. If on my first day at a new job I tell a joke that my boss finds to be offensive for some reason, I may have jeopardized my future prospects of advancement within only several hours of beginning this job. But how am I to know what my new colleagues and superiors will find offensive, without getting to know each of them individually?

[27]See Russell Hardin, *One for All: The Logic of Group Conflict* (Princeton: Princeton University Press, 1995), for such a foundation.

[28]Economists and political scientists have begun to pay much more attention to the role of uncertainty and information and transaction costs in economic and political exchange (cf. Douglass C. North, *Institutions, Institutional Change, and Economic Performance* [Cambridge: Cambridge University Press, 1990]). The argument in Hardin, *One for All*, extends the significance of information costs more broadly to nearly all forms of social interaction.

[29]Amihai Glazer, "A New Theory of Voting: Why Vote When Millions of Others Do," *Theory and Decision* 22 (1987): 257–270.

As a result of the potential negative consequences posed by our lack of good, cheap information about others, we all recognize the value inherent in reducing our uncertainty and introducing some predictability into our interactions with others. But since acquiring information on an individual-by-individual basis is expensive, we also all search for short-cuts to reduce those costs. Any shortcuts that reduce our disutility from social uncertainty more than they cost us in terms of time and money provide us with net utility or benefits.

One clear shortcut is to coordinate with others on some shared patterns of acceptable behavior. These shared conventions of social interaction provide all members of a group with net benefits because, if coordination is successful, they reduce information costs drastically for members of the network or group. So if young urban professionals can coordinate on certain shared norms of behavior, such as wearing specific kinds of clothes, eating at specific restaurants, working out at specific gyms, and supporting specific political causes such as environmentalism, then the odds are much higher that members of this group will be able to navigate the social world of young urban professional life much more easily than if such coordination did not exist. When members of some group follow the cues of other group members in order to avail themselves of the resulting benefit of cheaply purchased social acceptance, we can say that they *identify* with that group, and call the benefits that they receive *solidary* benefits.[30]

As the foregoing example illustrates, these groups can in fact be quite large if there are mechanisms by which group coordination can be ensured. For example, if a particular magazine is able to position itself successfully as an arbiter of young urban professional fashion, intellectual, and political trends, then subscribers can easily purchase information about currently prevailing group norms (norms that will, of course, in all likelihood be set largely by the magazine itself). And the larger these groups are, the greater the potential benefits for members, because the groups encompass more people whose reactions to certain types of group-endorsed behavior will be predictable. Upon meeting a new acquaintance, if one knows that the individual is a member of one's group, one also now knows that by following group-endorsed norms of behavior, one can expect a predictable (and presumably favorable) response by that individual. The more new acquaintances for whom this is the case, the better.

Individuals who identify with some group and follow group-based

---

[30]This follows the convention in the voting literature. Hardin calls this benefit an "epistemological benefit" because of its role in providing us with information or knowledge. Hardin, *One for All*, p. 77.

cues will therefore be more likely to perform any given action, ceteris paribus, if they believe that others in their group endorse and/or are performing that action also. Indeed, the benefits you receive from acting in concert with others may be enough to motivate action where considerations of collective benefits alone would lead to inaction. So I may not donate money to an environmental group even if I value its goals more than I value the cost of the contribution, because I know that my contribution won't significantly affect the group's ability to realize those goals. But if receiving the Sierra Club magazine at work is likely to facilitate my acceptance by my boss and co-workers, then I have a direct selective (solidary) incentive to pay my dues.

Significantly for our purposes, and given the appropriate circumstances, which will be discussed later, voting can be one of the group-sponsored actions that produces solidary benefits for group members. Voting for any candidate may be irrational if the only benefit a voter considers is one that derives from the outcome of an election. But if an individual who identifies with a particular group believes that voting for a particular candidate or party is the appropriate group-endorsed behavior, then that belief can provide her with sufficient solidary incentives actually to turn out and vote for that candidate.[31]

That is, in a general election in the United States, there are typically three alternatives to choose from with respect to voting: not to vote, to vote for one major party candidate, or to vote for the other major party candidate. The groups with which one identifies in order to win social acceptance may not have any coordinated norm with regard to this choice. If that is the case, then there are no solidary benefits to be won or lost by choosing any of these alternatives. Voters' choices in these cases will thus likely turn on other kinds of benefits, like collective policy benefits. But if one believes that voting for a particular candidate is in fact a group-endorsed action, and that others in one's group are voting

---

[31]In game theoretic terms, the consumption of solidary benefits through the act of voting can be thought of as a coordination game. (Indeed, the generation of group identification itself in this story is a coordination game; if voting becomes a group-sponsored action then voting becomes the object of the group identification coordination game.) I as a member of some group want to make sure that my actions are in accordance with those of other group members in order to realize the solidary benefits that flow from knowing that my actions are the "right" ones within my chosen group. In other words, I receive benefits only if the rest of the group performs some action along with me; I receive no benefits from acting alone without the protection of the group. If both I and my spouse (for example) either vote for the same candidate or stay home together, then we both receive solidary benefits. If we pursue different courses of action, then we receive no solidary benefits. See Hardin, *One for All*, chap. 3, for a relevant discussion. Also see Thomas Schelling, *The Strategy of Conflict* (Cambridge, Mass.: Harvard University Press, 1960).

for that candidate, then one can gain solidary benefits from voting that may very well outweigh the costs of voting. For example, turning out to vote for the group-sponsored candidate may permit one to reap the rewards of social approval the next day at the office.[32]

Some may object that the privacy of the voting booth provides individuals with a (perhaps unusual) protected context in which they do not have to worry about the reactions that their vote will induce in others. Since the introduction of the Australian ballot in the United States, voting has perhaps become an essentially solitary and private act, not a social act whose attendant uncertainty and unpredictability generate the search for solidary benefits. But the world remains a social world, in which the annual event of voting is a relatively publicized and noted event, and in which the topic of whether and how one votes is likely to arise in social contexts. In those contexts one can either volunteer the socially acceptable and truthful response about whether and how one voted, remain silent (which is likely to be interpreted as having acted differently from one's colleagues), or one can lie.

This last alternative might seem to many to be the obvious first best course of action, given that one can reap the solidary benefit of acceptance without paying the costs of voting. And if individuals can in fact lie with absolute certainty that their deceptions will not be revealed, this argument will hold. Lying bears risks, however: one may have a "tell" that alerts others to the fact that one is lying, or one may simply be tripped up by objective evidence contradicting one's story (evidence that will always exist in some fashion when one tells a lie). Lying to a group, if one is caught, can have serious negative consequences. If the probability of being caught multiplied by the consequences of lying is less than

---

[32]Turnout among respondents in the 1980 NES major panel survey rose approximately 3.5 percentage points for each neighbor reported whose political views were similar to the respondent's and who was also expected to vote. In a nationwide 1983 ABC–Harvard survey, 37 percent of respondents and 41 percent of regular voters cited as a reason for voting the statement, "My friends and relatives almost always vote and I'd feel uncomfortable telling them I hadn't voted." Married respondents in a 1990 Social Sanctions Survey administered by Stephen Knack, who reported that if they knew that a friend had not voted, "I would disapprove, and let him or her know," were associated with a 21 percentage point increase in the probability of reporting that their spouse had voted. Married respondents who reported that they would only passively disapprove of nonvoting were associated with only a statistically insignificant 12 point increase in reported spousal voting. Respondents in the same survey who answered yes to the question "Do you have any friends, neighbors, or relatives who would be disappointed or angry with you if they knew you had not voted in this year's elections?" (42 percent of respondents) were significantly more likely to vote than those who answered in the negative. Stephen Knack, "Civic Norms, Social Sanctions, and Voter Turnout," *Rationality and Society* 4, no. 2 (April 1992): 137, 139.

the costs of voting, then the rational individual will lie about voting rather than vote. Given relatively small opportunity costs of voting, however, many may rationally choose to vote with the group rather than lie.[33]

In short, we probably should not attempt to separate voters' turnout decisions from their actual choices made in the voting booth. Some argue that however it is that voters get to the voting booth, they logically will vote their "true" or policy-based candidate preferences once there. Group pressures have no meaning in the privacy of the voting booth. But a voter in a voting booth knows full well that her vote, because it will in all likelihood not affect the outcome of the election, will not require her to bear the opportunity costs of voting against her more preferred candidate on purely policy grounds. On the other hand, voting against the group-endorsed candidate once she is in the voting booth may very well require her to bear later costs in interaction with others. So if the voter has solidary incentives to vote for her less preferred candidate on purely policy grounds, those social incentives may provide her with sufficient incentives to vote for that candidate.[34]

We can formalize quite simply this notion of a benefit that voters receive from participating in an action with other members of a group with which they identify. Because my solidary benefit or utility from acting requires others with whom I can act in solidarity, my benefit is dependent upon the actions of others (or my perceptions of the actions or likeliness of actions by others). If I believe that only a few members of the group with which I identify are voting for a particular candidate, for example, I receive a proportionately small benefit from voting with them because there are very few others from whom I can win acceptance by this action. The more group members that I believe are voting for that candidate, however, the more benefit I receive from voting along with the group. There are many more opportunities for me to win acceptance by group members as a result of my voting.[35]

[33]Glazer, "A New Theory of Voting: Why Vote When Millions of Others Do."

[34]A similar argument is made in Geoffrey Brennan and James Buchanan, "Voter Choice: Evaluating Political Alternatives," *American Behavioral Scientist* 28, no. 2 (December 1984): 185–201.

[35]A similar argument is made in Hardin, *One for All*, pp. 28, 37. For other models in which my utility from action depends upon the number of other people performing that action, also see Thomas Schelling, *Micromotives and Macrobehavior* (New York: Norton, 1978), chaps. 3 and 7; Robert Sugden, "Reciprocity: The Supply of Public Goods through Voluntary Contributions," *Economic Journal* 94 (December 1984): 783; Thomas R. Palfrey and Howard Rosenthal, "Private Incentives in Social Dilemmas: The Effects of Incomplete Information and Altruism," *Journal of Public*

We can thus conceptualize the solidary benefit group members receive from voting with the group as similar in form to the benefit or utility that members of a network (e.g., a telephone network) receive from their subscription to the network.[36] The more subscribers to a telephone network, the more utility I receive from my own subscription to that network, as there exist more possibilities for interaction with members of some group with whom I value communication. Similarly, the more group members who participate with me in some group action or who clearly endorse that action, the more utility I receive from action, as there now exist more possibilities for me to realize the benefit of social acceptance from that action.

In somewhat more formal terms, if D_i is a solidary benefit that derives from individual i's acceptance by other members of some group G, then we assume that:

For member i of group G, where $i = 1, \ldots, n$, if i acts with or in a way endorsed by some other member j, i receives payoff d_{ij}, where $d_{ij} > 0$. If i acts with or in a way endorsed by all members of group G, then i receives payoff

$$D_i = \sum_{j \neq i} d_{ij}.$$

If i acts with or in a way endorsed by some fraction of the group G, and assuming that i values acting with each member of her group equally, then i receives payoff

$$D_i = \frac{p}{n} \sum_{j \neq i} d_{ij},$$

where p represents the number of participating or endorsing group members for any given group action. Group member i's payoff from participation in a group-sponsored action is thus a simple linear function

Economics 35 (1988): 326; Chong, *Collective Action and the Civil Rights Movement*, chap. 6; and Alexander Schuessler, "Expressive Motivation and Mass Participation" (unpublished manuscript, Department of Politics, New York University).

[36]Roland Artle and Christian Averous, "The Telephone System as a Public Good: Static and Dynamic Aspects," *Bell Journal of Economics and Management Science* 4, no. 1 (Spring 1973): 89–100; Jeffrey Rohlfs "A Theory of Interdependent Demand for a Communications Service," *Bell Journal of Economics and Management Science* 5, no. 1 (Spring 1974): 16–37.

of the percentage of the group that participates in or endorses that action.[37]

Given this cumulative utility function from participation in group-sponsored actions, it is easy to see how even small numbers of group voters can induce other group members to vote also. Solidary benefits thus stand in stark contrast to collective policy benefits from voting, where the more that I believe that other group members will vote, the fewer incentives I have to vote also (because the probability that my vote will affect the outcome decreases as more people participate). Solidary incentives, on the other hand, can generate a dynamic whereby group participation leads to more rather than less group participation.

In sum, it is illogical to assume that individuals vote in order to register their preferences on policy alternatives. It is unrealistic today to assume that individuals vote from coercion or for money. Moreover, it is insufficient to argue that individuals vote because of the intrinsic benefits the act of voting brings them. Rather, if we assume that many eligible voters vote because they receive cues during an electoral campaign from others whose opinions matter to them, cues that indicate to them that voting (and, even more strongly, voting in a particular way) in that election is required in order to be an accepted group member, then we can explain the turnout of certain cohesive groups.[38]

---

[37]We might in fact have reason to think that the marginal utility received from another individual joining the group action is not constant across all group members; past a certain threshold we may not care whether one more individual joins the group or not. The curve may therefore flatten out as more group members join the action. But this should not matter for our purposes; straight lines can serve as proxies for many kinds of curves without altering the results. As Schelling notes in his discussion of modeling externalities, straight lines have the virtue of being noncommittal; see *Micromotives and Macrobehavior*, p. 234.

[38]Empirical evidence confirms that group identity is strongly correlated with voter turnout. For a discussion of interdependent voting in the context of spousal reference groups, see Bruce C. Straits, "The Social Context of Voter Turnout," *Public Opinion Quarterly* 54, no. 1 (Spring 1990): 64–73. For discussions of ethnic group voting, see Raymond Wolfinger, "The Development and Persistence of Ethnic Voting," *American Political Science Review* 59, no. 4 (December 1965): 896–908, and Nathan Glazer and Daniel Patrick Moynihan, *Beyond the Melting Pot* (Cambridge, Mass.: MIT Press and Harvard University Press, 1963). Sidney Verba and Norman H. Nie reported that racial group identification influenced participation – "[Blacks] participate less than whites but more than one would expect given their social and economic conditions. And among those blacks who manifest some consciousness of group identification, the rate of participation is as high as that of whites and higher than one would expect given their other social characteristics" – in *Participation in America: Political Democracy and Social Equality* (New York: Harper & Row, 1972), p. 159, as did Richard D. Shingles, "Black Consciousness and Political Participation: The Missing Link," *American Political Science Review* 75 (March 1981): 76–91. Arthur Miller and his colleagues found similar effects for women, the poor, and young people who identified with these respective groups; Arthur H. Miller, Patricia Gurin, Gerald

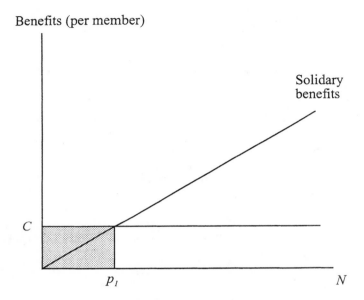

The dynamic of mobilization

Figure 1

Office-Seeking Elites. In large groups, however, the potential for voters to reap the benefits of group acceptance is compromised by both start-up and coordination problems. The start-up problem is depicted in Figure 1, where the diagonal line represents any group member's solidary benefits as an increasing function of the number of other group members participating in a given group-sponsored action. The figure also contains a constant cost function that describes some common opportunity cost of voting.[39] In order for any group member to have sufficient solidary

Gurin, and Oksana Malanchuk, "Group Consciousness and Political Participation," *American Journal of Political Science* 25 (August 1981): 494–511. Uhlaner found a higher Democratic turnout for members of union households after an appeal by union leaders in the 1982 congressional elections; Uhlaner, "Rational Turnout." Finally, Miller and his colleagues recently found that, "even after controlling for relevant demographic variables, retrospective party performance judgments and party identification, group affect had a substantial effect on party evaluations . . . and candidate choice"; see Arthur H. Miller, Christopher Wlezien, and Anne Hildreth, "A Reference Group Theory of Partisan Coalitions," *Journal of Politics* 53, no. 4 (November 1991): 1144. Also see Jeffrey W. Koch, *Social Reference Groups and Political Life* (Lanham, Md.: UPI, 1995).

[39]As with the constant benefit function, we might have reason to think that the

incentives to vote for any given candidate, that is, $D_i > C$, some threshold number of group members must already have endorsed voting for that candidate. On the graph, this threshold is given as p_1, where the number of group members endorsing a particular course of action is sufficient to generate solidary incentives that meet the costs C of voting for other group members. Once this threshold has been met, mobilization should take off essentially on its own by the expansive dynamic of group-based solidary benefits. But until this threshold has been met, no group members will have sufficient solidary incentives to join in the mobilization effort. Solidary incentives alone cannot get the mobilization dynamic started.

Moreover, even if some initial core of group members will vote for a given candidate on nonsolidary grounds, typically it will be difficult for other members of a large group to learn of the existence of such a core in the absence of some organized effort to publicize the existence of this core throughout the group. Group members have to know that voting for a particular candidate is endorsed by other group members. In large groups it is often not possible to discover whether other group members value voting in any given election. In the absence of information on other group members' preferences, group members are still likely to abstain from voting. This is a standard coordination problem: we would all be better off if we were doing the same thing, but in large groups it is difficult to coordinate on a particular thing to do.[40]

This is where office-seeking elites like party leaders and candidates may enter the picture. The untapped potential of solidary benefits that exists in large groups creates room for group electoral mobilization by office seekers who have a personal interest in securing votes.[41] Entrepreneurial office seekers can invest in the creation of organizations that provide material or other nonsolidary benefits to that initial core of group members, p_1, benefits sufficient to induce those members to announce publicly their support for some candidate. For example, one type of material benefit offered to group members in this initial core could be simply patronage positions within the entrepreneur's organization, which confer either monetary or status rewards on these individuals. Such organizations can then be used to distribute information among

cost function is not constant across all group members. Nonetheless, all group members have to pay *some* costs of voting, and we can simplify the presentation by assuming a constant cost function without distorting our results.

[40]Schelling, *Micromotives and Macrobehavior*, pp. 126–129, 224.

[41]The term "office seeker" is used by Joseph A. Schlesinger in order to distinguish simple vote maximizers from those with an interest in policy, or benefit seekers; see "The Primary Goals of Political Parties"; *Political Parties and the Winning of Office*. Also see Aldrich, *Why Parties?*, pp. 19–21.

group members about this initial core of supporters, in a sense offering group members a solidary benefit from voting that may cover their costs of voting. This benefit will be received by members if they in fact vote themselves. This organization of group electoral activity by political entrepreneurs is typically called electoral mobilization.[42]

Indeed, political parties as organizations for office seekers appear to have arisen precisely to solve these start-up and coordination problems in the provision of solidary benefits.[43] In the United States, mass electoral parties arose immediately after the expansion of the electorate for presidential electors between 1812 and 1824. During this period, the number of states using state legislatures rather than popular election to select presidential electors dropped from 50 to 25 percent; by 1828 that percentage had dropped to 10 percent, and in 1832 only one state still relied on its state legislature rather than its adult white male electorate to choose electoral college voters. Predictably, in the absence of any organizations that could initiate and coordinate group voting via solidary incentives, turnout was quite low in the 1824 presidential election; only approximately 26 percent of eligible voters went to the polls.

By the 1828 election, however, a national party had been formed with the aim of stimulating voter turnout; turnout in the 1828 election jumped to 50 percent of the eligible electorate (which had itself expanded in the interim). By 1840, when a second mass party had been formed to compete with the Democrats, over 78 percent of the eligible electorate voted in the presidential election. Moreover, the available evidence strongly suggests that the first parties relied not at all on collective policy benefits to mobilize voters to vote, but rather sought to provide selective solidary benefits on both a small scale, through the use of social events like bonfires, parades, and rallies, and also on a larger scale, through the formation of partisan identities which could be used to identify the political beliefs of new acquaintances.[44] By 1895 95 percent of the daily and weekly papers in the United States claimed loyalty to a party, partisanship was a facet of daily life, and voting turnout rose correspondingly.[45]

[42]Rosenstone and Hansen, *Mobilization, Participation, and Democracy in America*; Uhlaner, "Rational Turnout"; and Uhlaner, "Relational Goods."

[43]Material for the following two paragraphs comes from Aldrich, *Why Parties?*, chap. 4.

[44]Most rational choice scholars today interpret partisan identification as a strategy of voters to reduce information costs. As John Aldrich has noted, this interpretation is inadequate to explain the fervor with which most nineteenth-century partisans clung to their political identities. Ibid., pp. 165–169.

[45]Michael McGerr, *The Decline of Popular Politics: The American North, 1865–1928* (New York: Oxford University Press, 1986), pp. 14–23; Jean Baker, *Affairs of*

Votes without Leverage

Mass parties can be seen as organizations, then, which office-seeking elites build at least in part to solve the collective action problem for voters. They enable voters to receive solidary benefits by capitalizing on already existing social networks and turning these networks to political ends like voting, and/or by creating specifically partisan networks. Organizations like parties are necessary, first, to demonstrate to voters the existence of some group with which they can join in solidarity and, second, to distribute campaign material among the group of partisans to clue them in that the group with which they identify values voting for a particular candidate in a particular election.[46]

Importantly, when parties mobilize voters, we should be extremely skeptical about party elites' responsiveness to voters' policy preferences. As discussed earlier, political institutions constrain legislators and other office-seeking electoral elites to produce policy (or policy promises) in order to maximize votes.[47] Note, however, that electoral elites in the foregoing story *do not need* to make policy promises in order to mobilize votes for themselves and their candidates. Mass electoral organizations like parties may exist because the collective action problem in voting exists, a problem that must be solved if candidates are going to win any votes. But the kinds of benefits that parties use in order to win votes are not necessarily related to policy benefits.

Of course, office-seeking elites *do* on occasion make policy promises to voters. Why do office seekers bother with such policy promises, given the foregoing theoretical story?

Benefit-Seeking Elites. The answer to this question is quite simple,

---

Party: The Political Culture of Northern Democrats in the Mid-Nineteenth Century (Ithaca, N.Y.: Cornell University Press, 1983).

[46]There is much empirical literature on parties' mobilization efforts; studies that have found turnout effects from party mobilization in addition to Aldrich include Harold F. Gosnell, *Getting Out the Vote: An Experiment in the Stimulation of Voting* (Chicago: University of Chicago Press, 1927); Raymond Wolfinger, "The Influence of Precinct Work on Voting Behavior," *Public Opinion Quarterly* 27 (1963): 387–398; Gerald H. Kramer, "The Effects of Precinct-Level Canvassing on Voter Behavior," *Public Opinion Quarterly* 34 (1970): 560–572; David E. Price and Michael Lupfer, "Volunteers for Gore: The Impact of a Precinct-Level Canvass in Three Tennessee Cities," *Journal of Politics* 35 (1973): 410–438; Samuel C. Patterson and Gregory A. Caldeira, "Getting Out the Vote: Participation in Gubernatorial Elections," *American Political Science Review* 73 (December 1979): 1071–1089; Robert Huckfeldt and John Sprague, "Political Parties and Electoral Mobilization: Political Structure, Social Structure, and the Party Canvass," *American Political Science Review* 86, no. 1 (March 1992): 70–86; Rosenstone and Hansen, *Mobilization, Participation, and Democracy.*

[47]Downs, *An Economic Theory of Democracy*, p. 28; Schlesinger, "The Primary Goals of Political Parties"; Schlesinger, *Political Parties and the Winning of Office*; Aldrich, *Why Parties?*, pp. 19–21.

when we consider a third critical group of electoral actors, namely interest group elites or, in Joseph Schlesinger's terminology, benefit seekers.[48] Unlike office seekers, who are interested only in maximizing votes, benefit seekers have a personal (profit) interest in obtaining collective policy goods, and know that vote-maximizing candidates and legislators will not have incentives to provide those goods unless the benefit seeker can provide electoral resources such as votes in return.[49] Office-seeking party elites are thus not the only individuals who may seek to coordinate group voting; interest group elites as well have incentives to make investments of time, money, and organizational resources to coordinate group voting by invoking group identity in electoral campaigns.

Such benefit seekers capitalize on the link between loyalty within a group and power without.[50] If a voter values acceptance by other group members, and if she believes that other group members are going to vote for candidate Y, then the voter will have strong incentives to also vote for candidate Y. If other group members reason similarly, then the group will largely vote for candidate Y. The group will therefore have demonstrated the coordinated group electoral behavior that will win it collective goods from vote-maximizing candidates, even though group members did not vote *because* of those collective goods.

Why would benefit seekers have an interest in obtaining collective policy benefits? Although policies are collective goods, they often contain the potential for the extraction of a small number of private goods in the form of government contracts, administrative positions, and the like.

---

[48]Schlesinger, "The Primary Goals of Political Parties"; Schlesinger, *Political Parties and the Winning of Office*; Aldrich, *Why Parties?*, pp. 19–21, 180–193. The important role of benefit-seeking as opposed to office-seeking elites was also anticipated by Downs, *An Economic Theory of Democracy*, p. 249. A literature also exists on the role of interest group entrepreneurs in solving the collective action problem more generally; see Richard Wagner, "Pressure Groups and Political Entrepreneurs: A Review Article," *Papers on Non-Market Decision Making* 1 (1966): 161–170; Robert H. Salisbury, "An Exchange Theory of Interest Groups," *Midwest Journal of Political Science* 13, no.1 (February 1969): 1–32; Norman Frohlich and Joe A. Oppenheimer, "I Get By with a Little Help from My Friends," *World Politics* 23, no. 1 (October 1970): 104–120; Norman Frohlich, Joe A. Oppenheimer, and Oran Young, *Political Leadership and Collective Goods* (Princeton: Princeton University Press, 1971).

[49]Benefit seekers can also donate money directly to candidates and parties without seeking to coordinate group voting. However, this is typically the case only for groups involving few members, which do not face collective action problems. Those groups which are large require the expenditure of resources merely to solicit funds, and such groups will usually be cash-poor and vote-rich. Jeffrey Berry, *The Interest Group Society* (New York: Harper Collins, 1989).

[50]Uhlaner, "Rational Turnout," p. 392.

Benefit seekers may see the potential to reap private goods for themselves and their associates through the administration of group collective goods.

Probably more importantly, even if a policy contains no possibility for the extraction of private goods, benefit-seeking elites can profit from the status that accrues to group leaders successful in obtaining policy benefits for the group. Voters in fact are likely to have preferences for collective policy benefits, and in most cases are likely to value those benefits much more than they value the costs of voting; voters simply have no incentives to pay the costs for something they can get for free. But if an entrepreneur were to leverage successfully the group's coordinated votes into collective policy benefits valued by the group, then that leader would clearly be preferred by group members over a challenger who had no such success in leveraging policy concessions. Success in obtaining policy concessions desired by the group enhances leaders' stature within (and visibility without) their groups. Group leaders who desire to remain leaders, and who do not exercise dictatorial control over personnel procedures within group-specific organizations, may seek to enhance their job security by using their organizations to leverage group turnout into policy concessions from candidates.[51]

The motivation for group entrepreneurs or benefit seekers to pursue policy concessions implies two important points about the choices they are likely to make when considering whether and how to invest in organizations that can coordinate a group's voting behavior. First, because electoral mobilization is a costly undertaking, the potential benefits to entrepreneurs from mobilizing the group must be balanced against both the personnel and the organizational costs of mobilization. An entrepreneur will choose to make the investment in mobilization if the expected utility to the entrepreneur from legislators' policy concessions outweighs these costs of mobilization. In other words, as will become important in the case of women in the 1920s, if there is no reason to expect policy concessions from legislators, there is no reason for benefit seekers to continue to invest in a group's electoral mobilization.

Second, because their goal is to secure policy concessions from candidates, benefit seekers will seek to ensure either that they will have the personal authority to negotiate with candidates over these concessions, and to issue sanctions against or endorsements for candidates as the result of those negotiations, or that their organizations themselves will

---

[51]Frohlich and Oppenheimer, "I Get By with a Little Help from My Friends"; Uhlaner, "Rational Turnout," p. 406. This point obviously applies with most force to the (possibly quite small) circle of group members responsible for choosing leaders of the group.

possess procedures for developing a legislative agenda for the group and for issuing statements of opposition to or support for candidates on the basis of their positions on that agenda. Again, as will become important in the case of women in the 1920s, benefit-seeking entrepreneurs should require it to be the case that at least one of these alternatives exists before investing in a group's electoral mobilization.

If legislators believe that group leaders can produce group votes, and if group leaders demand policy concessions from legislators in return, then office-seeking legislators will clearly have incentives to make policy concessions to such benefit seekers. Of course, these policy concessions bring costs as well: given their need to remain responsive to the pressures of electoral politics, it is reasonable to assume that legislators value the ability to move freely in their policy positions. Public concessions to groups' issue preferences reduce the maneuverability of legislative elites and are thus costly for legislators in the form of votes lost either directly or indirectly.[52] The potential benefits for legislators from making concessions to an interest group may thus very well be outweighed by other considerations such as competing group claims and the costs to legislators from reducing their flexibility of action.

But most importantly for our purposes, if candidates do *not* believe that group leaders can influence the turnout of a particular group, then candidates have no incentives to make policy concessions to that group, *even if* the group is being coordinated to vote by, for example, an office-seeking organization like a political party. This is true because, as discussed previously, voters are highly unlikely to be mobilized by appeal to their preferences on collective goods; rather, mobilization *becomes* linked to collective goods because group leaders have incentives to seek collective goods for their group. Candidates and party leaders do not share these incentives, because they cannot: they must always place the goal of vote maximization first. Making costly policy concessions to a group without the return of coordinated group votes would be simply irrational for office seekers.[53]

In other words, it is a *necessary though not sufficient* condition of group-specific policy benefits that a benefit-seeking organization is pursuing an electoral strategy in return for policy concessions. If benefit-seeking group leaders are not pursuing an electoral strategy of any kind, we should not expect legislators to make any policy conces-

[52]Schlesinger, "The Primary Goals of Political Parties," p. 849; Uhlaner, "Rational Turnout," p. 407.

[53]I do not attempt to investigate the question of when candidates' benefits of movement will outweigh their costs of movement, as my concern is primarily to contrast the case where candidates have incentives to move in issue space with the case where they do not.

sions to the group: there are clearly costs to making policy concessions, and legislators would be bearing those costs without receiving any benefits in return.[54]

Is there any empirical evidence to support this theoretical conclusion? Scattered evidence exists to suggest that policy benefits in the United States have flowed much more frequently to independently organized than to unorganized voters, and typically only after the organization of the former by interested benefit-seeking elites.[55] However, these studies tend to lack variation in the independent variable, namely whether mobilization was carried out by benefit-seeking or office-seeking elites (presumably if a group is capable of mobilization, then some type of elite is seeking to mobilize it). In these studies groups were mobilized by benefit-seeking elites; in no cases were these groups mobilized by office-seeking elites alone. This lack of variation in the independent variable may result from the advantage that benefit seekers appear to have over office seekers in discovering unmobilized social networks and in turning those networks into interest group organizations (as will be discussed later). In any case, only with such variation will we be able to test the argument that benefit-seeking mobilization is a necessary condition of group-specific policy change.

As we will see in the following chapters, women actually provide a very neat test of this hypothesis because they present something of a natural experiment: after female enfranchisement, women's benefit-seeking organizations first pursued and then dropped a strategy based on electoral mobilization; women were then mobilized to vote as a group solely by the office-seeking parties until the late 1960s, at which time

---

[54]Thomas Ferguson has also come to a similar theoretical conclusion in his work; see *Golden Rule: The Investment Theory of Party Competition and the Logic of Money-Driven Political Systems* (Chicago: University of Chicago Press, 1995), chap. 1 and appendix. Ferguson concentrates primarily on the policy influence of firms that face few collective action problems in donating money to office seekers, but he also discusses periods when benefit-seeking entrepreneurs have been successful in organizing voters in mass "secondary associations" which win concessions from office seekers.

[55]Ibid., pp. 23, 29, 82–84, 87; Aldrich, *Why Parties?*, pp. 290–291; Hansen, *Gaining Access*; Lizabeth Cohen, *Making a New Deal: Industrial Workers in Chicago, 1919–1939* (Cambridge: Cambridge University Press, 1990); John M. Allswang, *A House for All Peoples: Ethnic Politics in Chicago, 1890–1936* (Lexington: University Press of Kentucky, 1971); J. David Greenstone, *Labor in American Politics* (New York: Alfred A. Knopf, 1969), chaps. 1 and 2; Richard Oestreicher, "Urban Working-Class Political Behavior and Theories of American Electoral Politics, 1870–1940," *Journal of American History* 74, no. 4 (March 1988): 1257–1286; Steven Fraser, *Labor Will Rule: Sidney Hillman and the Rise of American Labor* (New York: Free Press, 1991).

women's benefit-seeking organizations once again sought to leverage women's votes into policy. We can thus see whether policy concessions to women as a group correlate with this periodization better than with other potential explanatory variables. In addition, we can check the robustness of our argument by investigating the relationship between this independent variable and other dependent variables such as women's status within the party organizations themselves.

To preview the argument of subsequent empirical chapters, this explanation works very well for explaining the waves of policy and party concessions for women as a group, better, in fact, than any of the existing explanations. But this explanation itself raises a different, although related, question, namely, What determined the decisions of women's organizations either to pursue or not to pursue an electoral strategy? Given the negligible likelihood of policy concessions in the absence of such a strategy, why not seek to mobilize women's votes if such votes were in fact mobilizable, that is, if women shared a cohesive enough group identification to permit effective appeals to solidary benefits? This question will be addressed in the next section.

EXPLAINING STRATEGIES OF MOBILIZATION: THEORETICAL APPROACHES

Existing Explanations

What determines the decisions of benefit-seeking group organizations to pursue (or not) an electoral strategy? In the case of women during the 1920s, again two classes of explanations have been given: one relies on nonstrategic factors and another on too simple a strategic story. More specifically, the former class includes authors who have suggested variants on the story of ideological constraints that prevented the leaders of women's organizations from seeking the electoral mobilization of women.[56] The latter class includes scholars who have argued that since women's leaders could have expected to have more lobbying success with women's votes than without them, clearly those leaders must not

---

[56]For the "gender sameness" ideological argument, see Sara Alpern and Dale Baum, "Female Ballots: The Impact of the Nineteenth Amendment," *Journal of Interdisciplinary History* 16, no. 1 (Summer 1985): 63; and Nancy F. Cott, *The Grounding of Modern Feminism* (New Haven: Yale University Press, 1987), p. 112. For the "gender difference" ideological argument, see Paula C. Baker, *The Moral Frameworks of Public Life, 1870–1930* (New York: Oxford University Press, 1991), p. 148; Muncy, *Creating a Female Dominion*, p. 127; and Kristi Andersen, *No Longer Petitioners: Women in Partisan and Electoral Politics after Suffrage* (Chicago: University of Chicago Press, 1996), pp. 22–23, 30–31.

have believed that women constituted a distinct electoral group that *could* be mobilized.[57]

While it may seem empirically that interest group elites make the decisions they do as a result of ideological beliefs, we might inquire into the causal mechanism producing such decisions. Ideologies are rarely so specific as to produce precise decision-making rules, leaving open the question of why interest group elites would make any particular decision at any given point in time. One plausible source for such specific decisions lies in the pressures generated by political competition well defined by the rules of an electoral game. Actors in this game (e.g., candidates, voters, interest group leaders) are easily identifiable and have goals that are clearly specified for them by the rules of the game. Interest group leaders may have goals other than the pursuit of policy benefits for their group, but if they miss opportunities to pursue such benefits effectively, they can be sure that others will rise to challenge their leadership by taking advantage of those opportunities. Group leaders who refuse to pursue the electoral mobilization of their group, in the face of the apparent viability of such mobilization, over time should be replaced by others who can more successfully secure benefits for the group by threatening electoral retaliation on uncooperative legislators.

This line of reasoning appears to be incorporated into simple strategic explanations that infer from the absence of group electoral mobilization the conclusion that the group in question was not likely to respond to mobilization appeals on the basis of solidary incentives. If the group *were* likely to respond to such appeals, then logically interest group leaders should be making them. However, this is a faulty inference. The inference assumes a model of perfect electoral competition in which, if an electoral group exists, benefit-seeking group leaders have every opportunity to leverage the group's votes into policy concessions. But just as many (if not most) economic markets do not reflect the conditions of perfect competition, so too may political "markets" be only imperfectly competitive.

In particular, just as the foregoing section discussed the implications of the collective action problem in voting for legislators' responses to voters' policy preferences, this section will explore the implications of solutions to that problem for the competition between benefit-seeking organizations and office-seeking organizations for voters' loyalties. It turns out that solving the collective action problem in voting by using solidary group benefits leads to imperfect competition between these organizations. That is, the first organization to begin mobilizing a group

[57]See, e.g., Naomi Black, *Social Feminism* (Ithaca, N.Y.: Cornell University Press, 1989), pp. 249–250; Cott, *The Grounding of Modern Feminism*, p. 112.

on such a basis can amass significant advantages over later competitor organizations; the bigger the head start of the first organization the greater will be this competitive advantage.

Imperfect Competition in Electoral Markets

When individuals decide to vote for a particular party or candidate because they believe that others want them to, and moreover when the *more* individuals they believe they can please by voting, the greater their incentive to vote for that party or candidate, we can say that voters' preferences are interdependent: they depend upon the preferences of others. And just as interdependent preferences in economic markets lead to imperfect competition between firms, so too do they lead to the same result in electoral markets.

Recall the costs of mobilization for entrepreneurs interested in coordinating any given group's voting behavior. Just as benefits to group members increase with the number of other group members thought to endorse voting for a particular candidate, so too does the marginal cost of mobilization for entrepreneurs decrease with the number of group members already mobilized. This is so because once an entrepreneur has secured material or other benefits for the initial core of endorsing group members, and has an organization in place that can distribute information to the group, then electoral mobilization should essentially take off on its own momentum. The more group members that join the mobilization effort, the more attractive the effort becomes to other group members, without the entrepreneur having to spend any significant additional resources.

This implies that competition between entrepreneurs to mobilize any group will be imperfect or monopolistic. That is, if an entrepreneur is already engaged in mobilizing a group, that entrepreneur can mobilize much more cheaply than can an entrepreneur considering mobilizing the group behind another candidate or simply through a different organization. Indeed, the costs to the later entrepreneur rise in direct proportion to the number of group members already mobilized by another organization. To see this point, consider Figure 2. For an entrepreneur who happens to be the first entrant to a group's market in mobilization, the size of the initial costs of mobilization will be given by the small shaded area on the graph in Figure 2. That is, an entrepreneur will have to pay some number of group members, given by p_1, some amount of nonsolidary benefits sufficient to cover those group members' costs of candidate endorsement.[58]

---

[58]This argument assumes some common cost of either voting or endorsing a can-

Benefits (per member)

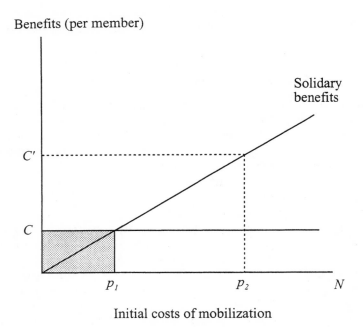

Initial costs of mobilization

Figure 2

But a second entrepreneur who enters the market in a group's mobilization after some initial mobilization activity has covered the baseline costs of voting for group members and thus, after the self-generating mobilization dynamic has begun, will face much higher initial costs than the first entrepreneur to enter the market. As depicted in Figure 2, if a second entrepreneur enters a market in a group's mobilization after some first entrepreneur has already mobilized (for example) p_2 group members, that second entrepreneur will have to offer a *nonsolidary* benefit of amount C' to group members to attract an initial core of size p_2 before he can make offers of *solidary* benefits to group members that meet the existing offer (C') of the first entrepreneur's organization. The costs to the second entrepreneur will thus be represented by the much larger area in Figure 2 bounded by p_2 and C'.

In short, once the initial fixed costs of mobilization are covered, an organization can offer group members more expected utility from voting

---

didate, which may not be the case. However, this point would not significantly affect the argument I am making here.

with very small marginal costs of mobilization, as that utility is simply a function of the number of group members already mobilized. If an organization mobilizing a group by appeal to group solidarity has enough of a head start in initiating the mobilization of that group, later organizations seeking the group's votes may not be able to compete effectively with the first organization. Start-up costs for the later competitor may be much higher than those experienced by the existing organization, and may eventually drive the later competitor from the market for the group's mobilization.[59]

It is therefore a flawed inference to conclude that if an identifiable group exists that *could* be coordinated to vote via solidary benefits, then benefit-seeking entrepreneurs will pursue such coordination in the quest for policy concessions. Benefit-seeking elites will clearly *not* pursue such coordination if they are significantly disadvantaged by the existence of competitor organizations, for example, office-seeking organizations or parties, already engaged in the coordination of the group's votes. What matters for the ability of benefit-seeking organizations to avoid this situation is the timing of their entry into a group's market in electoral mobilization, relative to the timing of office-seeking organizations' entry into that same market. In other words, the *chronological sequence* of entry into such markets matters for the ability of benefit-seeking organizations to pursue the coordination of a group's votes.

What should we expect to be the case with respect to this chronological sequence? As already discussed, many empirical studies show that benefit-seeking group elites have in fact been able to coordinate various groups of male voters and through such coordination win policy benefits for those groups. Just within the period of the 1920s we see men's unions, farmers' organizations, and immigrant associations initiating these groups' electoral coordination *as* groups. What are the circumstances that likely led to the initiation of the electoral coordination of these groups by benefit-seeking rather than office-seeking elites?

---

[59]For a discussion of this phenomenon in economic markets, see William W. Sharkey, *The Theory of Natural Monopoly* (Cambridge: Cambridge University Press, 1982), pp. 45–48. A classic example of a natural monopoly is a local telephone network, where the good being provided is access to the network, and where the value of that access to subscribers increases as more individuals join the network. Because of these consumption "externalities," access to the network is a public or collective good. Artle and Averous, "The Telephone System as a Public Good," pp. 89–100; Rohlfs, "A Theory of Interdependent Demand for a Communications Service," pp. 16–37. Suppliers of indivisible public goods experience decreasing average costs as demand for the good rises rather than increasing average costs. Public goods are thus natural monopolies. See also Frohlich et al., *Political Leadership and Collective Goods*, pp. 66–72.

Votes without Leverage

The Sequence of Entry in Electoral Markets

Here we must engage in hypothetical analysis: under what conditions will benefit-seeking elites have the opportunity to initiate group electoral coordination before purely office-seeking elites? First, we may start with a proposition that follows from our previous assumptions concerning the motivation of benefit- and office-seeking elites.

1. Political entrepreneurs, either benefit or office seeking, with both information about a group's capacity for coordination and the organizational resources necessary to locate and reach group members, will have incentives to initiate a group's electoral mobilization.

As discussed earlier with reference to solidary benefits, a potential market in group mobilization is created when a group begins to develop shared expectations concerning appropriate group behavior. Individuals cannot receive solidary benefits from voting for a particular party or candidate unless they believe that others expect them to vote for that party or candidate. But such expectations do not develop overnight. In order for these expectations to reduce individuals' uncertainty about the likely responses of others to their actions, individuals need to be confident that others will in fact respond favorably to their actions. As scholars who have studied coordination problems have noted, there appear to be increasing returns to coordination over time: through repeated interaction with others who accept a norm of group conduct, individuals become confident that relying on this norm is an efficient way to both reduce information costs and secure acceptance by others.[60] This means that both benefit-seeking and office-seeking entrepreneurs are likely to want to capitalize on existing norms of group identification rather than to create new norms from scratch.[61] Of course, this implies that both benefit-seeking and office-seeking entrepreneurs have an interest in information about the existence of such norms. And given the motivation we ascribe to benefit-seeking elites, information about the existence of such a norm would create incentives to act on that information, if those elites could also secure the necessary organizational resources.

---

[60]Cf. North, *Institutions, Institutional Change, and Economic Performance*, pp. 94–99.

[61]Even at the time of the formation of the first mass parties in the United States, national party elites sought to capitalize on existing local and state electoral organizations by offering them benefits in return for affiliating with the new parties. See Aldrich, *Why Parties?*, chap. 4. As new social neworks developed, both benefit- and office-seeking elites would have competed to mobilize these groups as partisans or as members of independent interest groups.

With respect to organizational resources, the coordination of a large group's electoral behavior requires organization in order to generate the snowballing effect of solidary benefits. Even potential entrepreneurs with knowledge of a group's shared norms of group behavior will not have incentives to seek electoral mobilization if they do not have access to either the financial resources necessary to create a new organization or control of an existing group organization that could be turned to the coordination of the group's votes. But where motivated entrepreneurs possess both information and organizational resources, we should see them seek to initiate a group's electoral mobilization.

Now we must justify hypotheses about the conditions under which benefit-seeking elites will have informational and organizational advantages over office-seeking elites with respect to a group's electoral coordination.

2. Group members will likely have more information than nonmembers on the development of shared expectations of appropriate behavior within any given group; benefit-seeking group elites will thus likely have an informational advantage over office-seeking party elites who are not group members in initiating group electoral mobilization.

Clearly the first entrepreneurs to gain knowledge of a group's shared expectations of appropriate behavior will have an advantage over potential competitors in initiating the group's electoral mobilization. To the extent that office-seeking party elites are drawn from groups already mobilized into electoral politics, they are unlikely to be members of groups that have not yet fully developed as groups, much less mobilized as voting groups into electoral politics. They are thus likely to be at an informational disadvantage relative to group entrepreneurs in discerning the existence of potential markets in group mobilization, and thus in capitalizing on that information.

3. Benefit-seeking elites who already control group-specific organizations will likely be able to target group members for the purpose of electoral mobilization more efficiently than the office-seeking elites who control geographically based political parties; benefit-seeking group elites may thus also have an organizational advantage over office-seeking party elites in initiating a group's electoral mobilization.

Even if party elites have information regarding the development of a potential market in group mobilization, parties are still at an organizational disadvantage relative to group-specific organizations in initiating group mobilization. Because parties are geographically rather than demographically organized, they are better equipped to engage in geographical rather than group mobilization.[62] Empirical studies of party canvasses have demonstrated that party and candidate organizations typically select the citizens whom they will seek to mobilize by targeting neighborhoods with high percentages of their likely supporters. This information may be obtained from previous election returns, from voter registration rolls, from primary participation, or from neighborhood surveys conducted by the campaign organizations. Party organizations use the direct contact of the canvass to convince supporters to display their support visibly, thereby informing others in their geographic context of their political preferences.[63] The effect of these canvassing efforts on overall turnout levels appears to be due primarily to the influence that neighbors have on one another through their relatively frequent social interaction.[64]

The efficient mobilization of an identity group, however, requires both the identification of group members and the creation of an organization that can effectively reach those members with group-specific information, while not wasting resources on nongroup members. Unless groups may be identified exclusively by geographic boundaries, parties will be less efficient than existing group organizations in identifying and communicating with group members. Party organizations would have to create separate, group-based organizations within their geographic organizations in order effectively to mobilize a group to vote, while group-specific organizations are already organized to coordinate the group effectively.

This is not to say that group-specific organizations will necessarily be immediately ready to begin the task of electoral mobilization as soon as benefit-seeking elites have the information that the group has the capacity to be coordinated in such mobilization. If the leaders of these group organizations exercise authoritarian control over organizational decisions, then coordinating the group's votes in pursuit of a legislative agenda may be simply a matter of executive fiat. However, group entrepreneurs not possessing sufficient personal authority to dictate such an

---

[62]John H. Aldrich, "Presidential Campaigns in Party- and Candidate-Centered Eras," in Mathew D. McCubbins, ed., *Under the Watchful Eye: Managing Presidential Campaigns in the Television Era* (Washington, D.C.: CQ Press, 1992): 64–67.

[63]Price and Lupfer, "Volunteers for Gore"; Huckfeldt and Sprague, "Political Parties and Electoral Mobilization."

[64]R. Robert Huckfeldt, "Political Participation and the Neighborhood Social Context," *American Journal of Political Science* 23, no. 3 (August 1979): 579–592; Christopher B. Kenny, "Political Participation and Effects from the Social Environment," *American Journal of Political Science* 36, no. 1 (February 1992): 259–267.

agenda within these organizations will seek to develop procedures for developing that agenda and for authorizing group leaders to act on its behalf. On the other hand, because it is likely that leaders of these organizations have an informational advantage over party elites with respect to the group's capacity for coordination, group elites may have all the time they need to make requisite organizational changes in order to pursue group electoral mobilization.

4. The likely initiation of group mobilization by benefit-seeking group entrepreneurs may give those entrepreneurs significant competitive advantages over party entrepreneurs who later have an interest in contesting that market in mobilization.

As discussed previously, the earliest entrant to any given market in mobilization on the basis of group identity will have cost advantages over later entrants to that market. To the extent that benefit-seeking group entrepreneurs are able to initiate group mobilization as a result of informational and organizational advantages, party entrepreneurs will bear higher costs of mobilization if they should later contest that market.

The actual timing of group and party efforts to mobilize a new group into electoral politics may vary from case to case depending upon intervening factors. Group entrepreneurs may not have enough of a temporal advantage over party entrepreneurs to deter the latter completely from contesting the group's market in mobilization. On the other hand, they may in fact have such an advantage: if group entrepreneurs have enough of a head start over the parties in initiating the group's mobilization, group entrepreneurs should be able either to deter party organizations from even contesting the group's market in mobilization or to force the latter to leave that market. At the very least, benefit-seeking group entrepreneurs should not be at a disadvantage with respect to the parties in contesting group markets in mobilization.

5. Group entrepreneurs should be able to use their capacity to coordinate the group's electoral behavior as leverage in negotiations with candidates over policy concessions to the group.

As discussed previously, where benefit-seeking group entrepreneurs can successfully initiate group electoral mobilization, and can thus deter party elites from seriously contesting a group's market in mobilization, those entrepreneurs can then threaten to transfer and/or withhold votes from any given candidate in order to win policy concessions from that candidate. This leverage over candidates should exist even when a group's policy preferences are much closer to one candidate or party than the other, and/or when a group has consistently supported one party in previous electoral campaigns. That is, even if it is not credible for an entrepreneur to threaten to switch his group's votes to the competing candidate, the entrepreneur can still threaten to *withhold* his group's votes from the clearly favored candidate.

Although the foregoing seems compelling on purely theoretical grounds, is there any evidence to support these predictions? In fact, the patterns of electoral mobilization of several groups contemporaneous with women in the 1920s appear to conform to the chronological sequence predicted by our theoretical arguments. To take just one brief example, the case of immigrant mobilization in Chicago during the New Deal years is consistent with these hypotheses. As several scholars have noted, this electoral mobilization of previously nonvoting "new" immigrants was in large part due to the efforts of ethnic entrepreneurs to extract concessions from the parties, particularly from the Democratic Party.

Ethnic entrepreneurs in Chicago began organizing these new immigrants around the turn of the century and earlier into ethnic nationality and benevolent associations that capitalized on immigrants' strong group identities. In their earliest incarnations, these nationality associations facilitated ethnically differentiated support networks among new arrivals to the United States. These networks helped serve the need of new arrivals to find housing, jobs, assistance in learning English and attaining American citizenship, and other services in their new country of residence, and were not initially oriented toward facilitating immigrants' participation in electoral politics. After all, most new arrivals could not vote in the first place.

In 1906 local Chicago nationality associations merged into the United Societies for Local Self-Government, which by 1919 reportedly comprised 1,087 distinct ethnic organizations, representing a membership of 258,224 immigrants.[65] With this merger the first step was taken to begin appealing to ethnic group members on the basis of a broader identity than their nationality. Moreover, these new arrivals were gradually registering to vote throughout the first two decades of the century, often helped by the nationality associations themselves. In other words, a large mobilizable group was slowly developing among this population.

Eventually, the leaders of these nationality associations came to see the potential benefits inherent in seeking policy concessions for their constituency, specifically in the area of repealing prohibition and immigration restriction legislation. And by the late 1920s, a sufficiently

[65]Allswang, *A House for All Peoples*, pp. 118–119.

large percentage of the immigrant community could vote to make an electoral strategy a worthwhile endeavor for such leaders. For the 1928 presidential election ethnic group leaders from the United Societies, in cooperation with foreign language newspapers, in fact initiated the electoral mobilization of immigrants as a means to realize policy concessions on these issues from candidates. Significantly, this mobilization appears to have been made on the basis of group identity rather than policy preferences. Thus, in 1928, foreign language newspapers and the United Societies supported Democratic presidential candidate Al Smith for his stance against prohibition. The message they disseminated among the immigrant population, however, was that Smith was "one of us": "*Dziennik Chicagoski* enthusiastically informed Chicago's Poles that the Smith candidacy was 'a big moment in your lives.' The Republicans were against 'all Catholics, foreigners, and Negroes,' but Smith was 'a friend of the Poles.' "[66] In 1931, *Dziennik Zwiazkowy* informed its readers that a vote for Democratic mayoral candidate Anton Cermak, former head of the United Societies, was a vote to " 'Help your own kind.' Nothing could be more meaningful to the ethnic voter."[67]

As Lizabeth Cohen has argued, these ethnic organizations were the primary means by which immigrants were mobilized to support the Democratic Party in the 1930s, and also the means by which policy concessions were leveraged from the party's elites: "Ethnic politicians established such entities as the Polish Democratic Club of the 7th Ward or the Lithuanian Democratic League to help their constituencies exact their due from the party and the new agencies of government. . . . Ethnic organizations proved to be crucial conduits providing new members and resources" to the Democratic Party.[68] Importantly, these partisan ethnic organizations were created by ethnic entrepreneurs outside of the regular party hierarchy and only *after* the establishment of ethnic political organizations independent of the parties. Moreover, this pattern of independent group mobilization appears to have been true of other ethnic groups more generally.[69]

The chronologies of the electoral mobilization of other contempora-

---

[66]Ibid., p. 163.
[67]Ibid., p. 157.
[68]Cohen, *Making a New Deal*, p. 362.
[69]See Wolfinger, "The Development and Persistence of Ethnic Voting," p. 898: "Typical loci of immigrant politicization were . . . the leaders of nationality associations, usually men who were the first to achieve some economic success. Such relationships set the pattern for ethnic politics. Each nationality group in a city had leaders who bargained with politicians, trading their followers' votes for money, favors, and jobs." See also Erie, *Rainbow's End*.

neous groups also are consistent with the foregoing hypotheses.[70] Benefit-seeking group entrepreneurs in these cases appear to have possessed both informational and organizational advantages that enabled them to be the first entrants to new markets in group electoral mobilization. These benefit seekers then appear to have had competitive advantages over office seekers in coordinating the groups' mobilization.

INSTITUTIONS AND THE SEQUENCE OF ENTRY IN ELECTORAL MARKETS

A significant characteristic of the foregoing hypothetical chronological sequence is the extent to which it depends upon available information and organizational forms. That is, when we set out to hypothesize why benefit-seeking groups in many cases seem to have an advantage over office-seeking groups in initiating a group's electoral coordination, the likely suspects for explaining those advantages were the group-specific information and organizations available to benefit-seeking group elites. The fact that informational and organizational resources seem to be important to these advantages is significant because of recent research on the importance of institutional context in allocating incentives to invest in information and organizational forms.

As with economic markets, political markets are structured by institutional rules that satisfy participants' need to reduce uncertainty and cut information costs by establishing regularized patterns of interaction. For example, electoral laws create a stable framework within which parties and interest groups can compete for the support of voters. As with economic organizations like firms, political organizations learn how best to maximize votes at the minimum cost in part by seeking out easily available public information, such as dates and times for elections, the location and characteristics of election districts, and the provisions of campaign finance laws, and in part by what economist Douglass C. North has called "learning by doing":

Learning by doing in organizations, as the term implies, means that an organization acquires coordination skills and develops routines that work as a consequence of repeated interaction. The kinds of knowledge, skills, and learning that the members of an organization acquire will reflect the payoff – the incentives – imbedded in the institutional constraints.[71]

[70]Cf. Hansen, *Gaining Access*; Greenstone, *Labor in American Politics*; Oestreicher, "Urban Working-Class Political Behavior and Theories of American Electoral Politics, 1870–1940"; Fraser, *Labor Will Rule*.
[71]North, *Institutions, Institutional Change, and Economic Performance*, p. 74.

The Logic of Policy Change

Learning by doing results in the acquisition by organizations of "tacit knowledge" specific to a particular institutional context.[72] For political organizations, that tacit knowledge might consist in learned wisdom concerning the optimal internal governance procedures to mesh non-policy appeals to voters with policy lobbying of legislators, the relative merits of direct mail versus membership organizations, or the best marketing strategies to attract a given electoral group.

One consequence of these learning and coordination effects discussed by North is the phenomenon of increasing returns to institutions: the longer that an organization pursues profit opportunities under a given set of institutional constraints, the more profit that organization will realize for a given level of effort. Conversely, an exogenous change in a market's institutional context will result in a costly period of adaptation for affected organizations, as they seek out new forms of tacit knowledge appropriate to their new institutional context.

The preceding argument has been consistent with North's theoretical framework: instrumentally rational individuals respond in predictable ways to the opportunities and constraints posed for them by political institutions. In democracies, one of the most important institutions is obviously that of elections, which may take different forms depending upon a particular country's institutional history. As we have seen, electoral institutions in the United States have created predictable strategic problems for voters, office-seeking elites, and benefit-seeking elites. In particular, the predicted sequence of entry for organizations in a group's electoral market was entirely dependent upon an institutional context of elections.

But if we now return to our original puzzle of women in electoral politics in the 1920s, it is immediately obvious that women in general and women's benefit-seeking elites in particular would have faced different strategic problems from every other group between 1867 and 1920, because they faced a different institutional context: disfranchisement. This is precisely the period during which, according to women's historians (and probably not coincidentally), female-specific organizations and activities in the public sphere proliferated, signaling the development of female-specific norms of appropriate behavior. Given that electoral politics was not an avenue of opportunity open to women's benefit-seeking elites with incentives to pursue policy concessions for women, it stands to reason that the foregoing series of predictions concerning the chronological development of markets in group electoral mobilization will not hold.

And if women's benefit-seeking elites made investments in specific

[72]Ibid., p. 77.

kinds of organizations appropriate to the context of disfranchisement, the transition to the context of enfranchisement would not have been particularly speedy. As discussed earlier, if the institutional environment that constrains political entrepreneurs is altered, organizations that have adapted to one set of institutional rules will have to be restructured in order to take advantage of the new set of rules. More specifically, the removal of the laws preventing women from voting would have necessitated just such a period of adaptation for women's organizations.

If we use the same model of strategic interaction developed in this chapter to explain policy change, but assume an initial institutional condition of disfranchisement, we can make the following predictions about the sequence of entry of organizations into the postsuffrage market for women's electoral mobilization.

1. Political entrepreneurs, either benefit or office seeking, with both information about a disfranchised group's capacity for coordination and the organizational resources necessary to locate and reach group members, will *not* have incentives to initiate the group's electoral mobilization.

The rationale for this prediction is obvious: because a disfranchised group cannot vote, it is simply impossible to initiate the group's electoral mobilization. However, and not so obviously, even a disfranchised group can still influence the policy decisions of vote-minded legislators by coordinating to influence the voting decisions of enfranchised citizens. Given that disfranchised citizens are likely to know and interact with enfranchised citizens, if coordinated the former group can seek to use their interactions with the latter group as a way to provide solidary benefits to the latter if they vote for policy benefits for the disfranchised. A disfranchised group that shares strong expectations of appropriate group behavior thus still presents an opportunity of sorts to benefit-seeking group elites. The significant point is that this opportunity is not an *electoral* opportunity.

2. When the group does enter the electoral system, group members are no longer likely to have more information than nonmembers on the development of shared expectations of appropriate behavior within the group. Benefit-seeking group elites will thus no longer have an informational advantage over office-seeking party elites who are not group members in initiating group electoral mobilization.

The coordination of nonvoting citizens to influence the decisions of voting citizens who must then act to influence the decisions of vote-minded legislators is clearly a convoluted and difficult endeavor. Influencing legislative decisions is a much more straightforward process if a group can vote. Logically, at least some leaders of nonvoting groups' organizations will focus on attaining the concession of suffrage as a priority before pursuing other policy benefits for the group. If a disfranchised group develops shared expectations about appropriate group behavior sufficient to permit coordination by group elites, then group entrepreneurs are likely to pursue such coordination in order to attain suffrage for the group. But the very process of coordinating the group through collective action to win suffrage implies that by the time the group does enter the electorate, it will be highly visible not only to benefit-seeking group elites but also to office-seeking party elites. Moreover, such presuffrage mobilization will demonstrate to the latter group exactly how and how well the group can be coordinated in collective action.

3. Because benefit-seeking group elites will have to adapt existing presuffrage organizations to the requirements of electoral mobilization, office-seeking party elites will likely also have an organizational advantage over group elites in initiating the group's electoral mobilization.

Benefit-seeking group elites in a presuffrage context will logically seek suffrage as a proximate goal to obtaining broader policy benefits for their group. Benefit seekers for disfranchised groups will thus be led by the structure of their situation to streamline their organizations, or to support the streamlining of a single organization, to pursue the goal of suffrage exclusively. As a consequence, these suffrage-seeking organizations are not likely to possess procedures designed to develop a broader legislative agenda that could be supported by the organizations' memberships. Nor are leaders of these presuffrage organizations likely to possess either the personal or the procedural authority to negotiate with electoral elites over a legislative agenda.

If suffrage is finally won, this implies that the benefit-seeking elites who had been pursuing suffrage must have been successful in coordinating the group's mobilization. These elites' organizations will thus be the logical choice to pursue the group's electoral mobilization as a means to leverage other policy concessions from office-seeking elites. But because these organizations are likely to have focused exclusively on suffrage, they are therefore not likely to possess procedures to develop a legislative agenda that can be agreed upon by organizational leaders. These procedures will have to be developed and implemented, and then only after suffrage is guaranteed. This period of organizational adaptation will prevent the suffrage-seeking organization from immediately seeking the electoral mobilization of the group upon the group's enfranchisement.

Party organizations, on the other hand, will face no such delay in pursuing the opportunity presented by the entrance of a mobilizable group into the electoral arena. Because the parties are functioning electoral organizations, all party entrepreneurs need to do is tap visible group members to help mobilize the group into party clubs and organizations by offering those members jobs with the party, greater visibility, leadership status, and possibly political appointments. As discussed previously, those group members can then publicize throughout the group the existence of an initial core of group supporters of the party in order to jump-start the dynamics of group mobilization via appeals to group solidarity. To the extent that these group members operating within the party organizations can successfully convey the impression to potential group voters that they are in fact representing a course of action valued by group members, these party workers should face few difficulties in initiating group mobilization.

4. The likely initiation of group mobilization by office-seeking party entrepreneurs may give those entrepreneurs significant competitive advantages over group entrepreneurs who later have an interest in contesting that market in mobilization.

As discussed previously, the earlier an entrepreneur can initiate a group's mobilization, the cheaper that mobilization will be. With only a relatively small number of paid organizers and canvassers, an entrepreneur can offer enough solidary benefits to those group members who either place a very high value on their group identity, have large nonsolidary benefits from electoral participation, or bear very low costs from participation to register and/or vote with the entrepreneur's organization. With each successive registration and/or election, the entrepreneur will be able to attract more group members to register and/or vote with the group because of the increased solidary benefits the entrepreneur can offer to more reluctant group members. At the same time, the growing group following of the entrepreneur's organization will also bring increased solidary benefits to the initial joiners of the organization.

A second organization that enters the group's market in mobilization, however, will not be so fortunate. In order to mobilize any group members strictly on the basis of solidary benefits, the second organization will have to first match the registration or membership of the existing organization. To do so will require the provision of material incentives to an equally large fraction of the group as supports the existing organization, a task that will grow prohibitively expensive the longer the time elapsed between the entrance of the first and that of the second organization into the group's market in mobilization.

In other words, the longer it takes group entrepreneurs from a previously disfranchised group to adapt to their changed institutional environment, the more difficult it will be for those entrepreneurs to compete with the parties in their group's electoral mobilization. If the parties have enough of a head start over independent group organizations in initiating the group's mobilization, party entrepreneurs should be able to either deter group entrepreneurs from even contesting the group's market in mobilization or force the latter to leave that market.

5. Until the threat of competition from group entrepreneurs is negligible, party entrepreneurs will have incentives to make concessions to a group's policy preferences. However, if independent group organizations stop competing with the parties for the group's electoral loyalties, party entrepreneurs will no longer have any incentives to make further concessions to the group's issue preferences.

If benefit-seeking entrepreneurs from a newly enfranchised group do attempt to adapt group organizations to compete with the parties for mobilization of the group's votes, there may be a period of uncertainty regarding the outcome of competition between these organizations. After all, if party entrepreneurs for some reason do not successfully appeal to a shared group identity, or if group entrepreneurs can somehow find the resources to overcome the disadvantages inherent in a late entrance to the group's market in mobilization, then the playing field between these competitors will be somewhat leveled. Thus, during this initial period of uncertainty, party elites will have incentives to negotiate on policy concessions with those entrepreneurs who are contesting the group's market in mobilization.

If in fact entrepreneurs from a newly enfranchised group cannot overcome their competitive disadvantages, then the parties will no longer need to fear those entrepreneurs' influence in electoral politics. And because party elites and candidates should view policy concessions as inherently costly, in the absence of entrepreneurial pressure candidates will have few incentives to make such concessions. Candidates can simply rely on their organizational resources to coordinate the group's electoral mobilization by using group members to appeal to shared group norms of behavior, in which case the group's unrepresented preferences will remain unrepresented.

Moreover, while those group members who were tapped by the parties to help mobilize the group may attempt to lobby within the parties for concessions to the group's policy preferences, these party appointees can at any time simply be dismissed and replaced with more docile party functionaries. Group entrepreneurs engaged in group mobilization *within* these office-seeking organizations will have no leverage over office-seeking elites, for the latter control the means of mobilization and can find other group members to work with those means.[73] Further, office-seeking elites in one party need fear no competition from their rivals in other parties with respect to policy concessions for the group, for no party stands to gain by making such concessions. Group members cannot be induced to vote by policy promises, and benefit-seeking group elites who *do* have incentives to seek such promises will have been frozen out of the market in group mobilization by the early action of the parties.

To conclude, groups that enter the electoral system with strong shared norms of group identification after having previously been disfranchised are at a serious disadvantage in terms of seeing their preferences represented by competing candidates. *Because of their previous electoral exclusion,* enfranchised groups are likely to be mobilized by parties, not by independent group organizations. And because parties are controlled by vote-maximizing electoral elites who are reluctant to make policy concessions, the group's electoral mobilization will not induce party bosses or candidates to move toward endorsing the group's previously unrepresented preferences. By the logic of electoral mobilization outlined here, disfranchisement has significant downstream consequences for later attempts by enfranchised groups to attain electoral representation.

TESTING THE ARGUMENT

The following chapters present the evidence for these five hypotheses regarding a disfranchised group's market in electoral mobilization, looking at the case of women between approximately 1920 and 1970. In addition, these chapters will discuss the competing hypotheses that purport to explain the events in question, and will argue that the hypotheses presented here more fully explain the facts at issue.

The next chapter examines the development of a market in women's electoral mobilization in New York State between 1909 and 1920, paying particular attention to the strategies of women's groups and major party elites. New York is the appropriate place to begin the chronolog-

---

[73]This argument highlights the importance of a hierarchical organizational structure to exchanges in the electoral market. For an economic analogy that highlights the theoretical significance of firm hierarchy to exchanges in economic markets, see Oliver Hart, "An Economist's Perspective on the Theory of the Firm," *Columbia Law Review* 89 (1989): 1757–1774.

ical story of women's politics during the 1920s, for two reasons. First, its passage of statewide female suffrage in 1917 was widely perceived to be the turning point in the campaign for constitutional female suffrage, with the result that after 1917 both the National American Woman Suffrage Association and the major party organizations began discussing plans for the postsuffrage national electoral mobilization of women. Second, New York State was the first (and last) site of head-to-head competition between those organizations to mobilize women's votes, in a 1920 U.S. senatorial campaign.

3

Testing Competing Hypotheses: Pre- and Postsuffrage in New York State, 1909–1920

Chapter 2 presented a new explanation for the surprising failure of women's organizations in the second half of the postsuffrage decade, and for some time after that, to continue to secure congressional policies designed to benefit women and children. On purely theoretical grounds, this explanation appears to be sounder than existing accounts of those events. But it remains to be seen whether the explanation is actually more convincing on empirical grounds as well. This chapter begins the process of searching the empirical record to see whether the second set of hypotheses discussed in Chapter 2 more completely explains the facts at issue than its competitors.

In order to preserve the chronological sequence of events, we will hold in abeyance the first question addressed in the preceding chapter, namely whether it is correct that the presence of an independent electoral threat produced policy concessions for women in the first half of the 1920s. First, we will examine the sequence of events leading up to the private decision by the NLWV in 1923 to rescind its policy of selective candidate endorsements in furtherance of its policy objectives. That decision was preceded by a provisional suspension of candidate endorsements in late 1920. The withdrawal of the league from targeted electoral activity was particularly consequential, as historians tell us that no other women's organizations in the Women's Joint Congressional Committee (WJCC) lobbying coalition ever engaged in electoral activity like candidate endorsements. Why would league leaders voluntarily have refrained from making such endorsements, given the damage that decision was likely to inflict on any lobbying efforts?

As discussed previously, there are three existing explanations for the decisions made by former suffrage elites with respect to women's electoral mobilization in the postsuffrage years. In Chapters 1 and 2, we classified those explanations as "ideological" or "simple strategic" based on their theoretical assumptions. Here, for the purpose of hypothesis testing, we group them rather on the basis of their testable implications. Thus the first two explanations for former suffrage elites' postsuffrage decisions may be called gender "sameness" stories. The first of these relies on an ideology of gender "sameness" as an explanation for the actions of former suffrage elites: pursuing the electoral mobilization of women as a group in the postsuffrage years was not an option for former suffrage leaders ideologically committed to the development of a society in which gender differences bore no political relevance.[1] A more strategic version of this hypothesis, which nonetheless makes similar predictions, concludes from their lack of electoral activity that former suffrage elites did not believe that women in fact constituted a distinctive electoral group.[2] Under this version of the gender "sameness" hypothesis, efforts to mobilize potential female voters as distinct from potential male voters would simply have been doomed to failure.

The third explanation for the lack of electoral activity by former suffrage leaders in the postsuffrage years again relies on ideology: former suffrage leaders were constrained by an ideological tradition of nonpartisanship, which would have precluded the mobilization of women as a group in partisan electoral contests.[3] During the presuffrage years, so the story goes, this ideological tradition was developed by politically active women in opposition to what was perceived as exclusively male partisanship. Prohibited from voting and thus denied significant participation in the political parties, women developed a uniquely female style of political participation, which was issue- rather than party-driven. When women entered the electorate, women's elites were evidently caught in an ideological bind: pursuing a policy of electoral mobilization in support of an issue agenda would necessarily involve supporting partisan candidates. Rather than make a traumatic break with women's presuffrage ideological traditions, former suffrage elites chose to abstain from any electoral involvement that would necessitate siding with one party's candidate against the others.

The explanation suggested in the previous chapter, on the other hand,

---

[1]See, e.g., Sara Alpern and Dale Baum, "Female Ballots: The Impact of the Nineteenth Amendment," *Journal of Interdisciplinary History* 16, no. 1 (Summer 1985): 63; and Nancy F. Cott, *The Grounding of Modern Feminism* (New Haven: Yale University Press, 1987), p. 112.

[2]See, e.g., Naomi Black, *Social Feminism* (Ithaca, N.Y.: Cornell University Press, 1989), pp. 249–250; and Cott, *The Grounding of Modern Feminism*, p. 112.

[3]Scholars who have made this argument include Paula C. Baker, *The Moral Frameworks of Public Life, 1870–1930* (New York: Oxford University Press, 1991), p. 148; Robyn Muncy, *Creating a Female Dominion in American Reform, 1890–1935* (New York: Oxford University Press, 1991), p. 127; and Kristi Andersen, *No Longer Petitioners: Women in Partisan and Electoral Politics after Suffrage* (Chicago: University of Chicago Press, 1996), pp. 22–23, 30–31.

argues that the decision of league elites in the mid-1920s to refrain from mobilizing women as an electoral group was more likely due to competitive disadvantages incurred by the league as a result of organizational investments made during the context of disfranchisement. By this account, former suffrage elites may very well have been *willing* to mobilize women as a distinct group in partisan electoral contests, and have *believed* that women in fact constituted a distinct electoral group, yet nonetheless have been deterred from such mobilization by the party organizations' competitive advantages.

In order to assess these competing explanations, we need to derive from each hypotheses that can be tested using the available evidence. The following represent the testable hypotheses predicted by each explanation, concerning both the pre- and the postsuffrage history of women's organizations and the major party organizations. Because both the ideological and the simple strategic versions of the gender "sameness" explanation imply quite similar testable hypotheses, they have here been treated as a single account.

1a. If the supposition about suffrage elites' belief in gender "sameness" is correct, either as a matter of ideology or as a matter of their perceptions about reality, then we would not expect to see the vote being sought as an instrument to secure the distinctive policy preferences of women. To the extent that suffrage elites either privately or publicly sought woman suffrage on those grounds, as opposed to seeking suffrage as a natural right of citizens, the gender "sameness" account is undermined.

1b. If the supposition about suffrage elites' belief in gender "sameness" is correct, we would also not expect to see women being mobilized to support suffrage as *women* rather than as individual citizens. To the extent that women were mobilized by suffrage leaders as a distinct group, via appeals to gender solidarity, the gender "sameness" account is again undermined.

2. If the supposition about a suffrage ideology of nonpartisanship is correct, then we would not expect to find in suffrage documents either a history of involvement in electoral campaigns, or statements of policy that sanctioned the participation of suffrage organizations in electoral campaigns. If that history shows a record of suffrage organizations' involvement in electoral campaigns and/or statements of policy which clearly sanction candidate endorsements, then this explanation is weakened.

3a. If the supposition about competitive disadvantages is correct, then *if* women's leaders in the presuffrage years believed women to be a distinct group sharing a norm of gender identification sufficient to permit group coordination, we should expect those leaders to have been the *first* to have sought such coordination. If party leaders rather than women's leaders were the first to initiate the coordination of women in the presuffrage years, then the competitive disadvantages account is weakened.

3b. If the supposition about competitive disadvantages is correct, then we would also expect to see presuffrage women's organizations that pursued the coordination of women focusing only on the attainment of suffrage, rather than on the pursuit of a broad legislative agenda to benefit women as a group. If those organizations rather pursued a wide variety of legislative benefits for women in the presuffrage years, then the competitive disadvantages account is again undermined.

4a. If the gender "sameness" supposition is correct, then in the post-suffrage years we would not expect to see former suffrage elites either lobbying on behalf of women as a group or expressing the sentiment that women constituted a distinct electoral group with distinguishable policy preferences. If we do see either of these events in the historical record, then the gender "sameness" account is again undermined.

4b. If the gender "sameness" supposition is correct, then we would also not expect to see major party elites behaving as if women were a distinct and significant electoral group, for example, by creating separate women's organizations or mobilizing women by gender-specific appeals. If we do see any of these events in the historical record, then the gender "sameness" account is once again undermined.

5. If the supposition about a suffrage ideology of nonpartisanship is correct, then we would expect to see former suffrage organizations, if they remained in existence in the postsuffrage years, proscribing involvement in partisan electoral campaigns. If former suffrage organizations rather encouraged such involvement as women entered the electorate, then again this account is undermined.

6a. If the supposition about competitive disadvantages is correct, then we would expect to see suffrage organizations undergoing a period of organizational transformation before they could initiate the electoral mobilization of women. If suffrage organizations rather were able to begin the electoral mobilization of women immediately upon women's enfranchisement, then the competitive disadvantages account is weakened.

6b. If the supposition about competitive disadvantages is correct, then we would also, not coincidentally, expect to see major party elites able to initiate the electoral mobilization of new female voters *be-*

Votes without Leverage

fore similar actions by suffrage organizations. If the suffrage organizations were able to commence the electoral mobilization of women before the parties, then the competitive disadvantages account is undermined.

All these hypotheses concern elite beliefs and behavior, and all can thus be tested using the ample documents that recorded those beliefs and behavior. Specifically, this chapter examines the records left by the suffrage organizations, the NLWV, the New York State League of Women Voters (LWV), and the New York State major party organizations. New York State was the only site of direct competition between the NLWV and the major party organizations. It thus provides us with the best records of the progression of events which might (or might not) have led to competitive advantages for the parties. The next chapter will expand the search for evidence beyond New York State and over time, and will also examine the limited records which allow us to analyze mass beliefs and behavior in at least a partial way.

PRESUFFRAGE ORGANIZATIONS AND GENDER "SAMENESS"

It is relatively easy to disprove through suffrage histories the claim that suffrage elites did not seek the vote at least in part as a tool with which to pursue the policy interests of women as a group. As historians have documented, the mid-nineteenth-century United States saw an increasing number of female activists seeking to improve the lot of women through public policy.[4] Despite the fact that women could not vote, these female reformers tried to sway legislators' decisions through various means of moral persuasion.[5] Elizabeth Cady Stanton and Susan B. Anthony were among those who sought to change public policy

---

[4]Histories of nineteenth-century female reformers include Baker, *The Moral Frameworks of Public Life*; Lori Ginzberg, *Women and the Work of Benevolence: Morality, Politics, and Class in the Nineteenth-Century United States* (New Haven: Yale University Press, 1990); Nancy Hewitt, *Women's Activism and Social Change: Rochester, New York, 1822–1872* (Ithaca, N.Y.: Cornell University Press, 1984).

[5]For examples of women using these nonelectoral means to influence policy before suffrage, see S. Sara Monoson, "The Lady and the Tiger: Women's Electoral Activism in New York City before Suffrage," *Journal of Women's History* 2, no. 2 (Fall 1990): 109; Melanie Gustafson, "Partisan Women: Gender, Politics, and the Progressive Party of 1912" (Ph.D. dissertation, New York University, 1993), pp. 90–91; Theda Skocpol, *Protecting Soldiers and Mothers: The Political Origins of Social Policy in the United States* (Cambridge, Mass.: Belknap Press of Harvard University Press, 1992), p. 363; Elisabeth S. Clemens, "Organizational Repertoires and Institutional Change: Women's Groups and the Transformation of U.S. Politics, 1890–1920," *American Journal of Sociology* 98, no. 4 (January 1993): 783.

through these nonelectoral means, working to effect marriage, divorce, and wages and working hours reform. But as Stanton and Anthony concluded, vote-minded legislators were not particularly concerned about the policy preferences of a nonvoting group. As the two later wrote of the efforts of nonvoting female reformers to change laws by petitioning reelection-minded legislators, "They forgot that women were a disfranchised class, and that legislators give no heed to the claims of such for protection."[6]

Occasionally women's organizations would win, through these nonelectoral means, policy reforms that benefited women, but those policies lacked security inasmuch as they lacked a voting constituency. Stanton and Anthony were particularly impressed by the fact that measures enacted in New York State in 1860 giving women equal guardianship rights were repealed in 1862 and 1871: "Had woman held the ballot – that weapon of protection – in her hand to punish legislators, by withholding her vote from those thus derelict to duty, no repeal of the law of 1860 could have possibly taken place."[7]

Stanton and Anthony were not alone in taking the lesson of women's nineteenth-century attempts to influence policy to be that women needed the vote in order to have any real efficacy in securing public policy reform. The early history of the suffrage movement in the United States, even prior to the formation of suffrage organizations themselves, reflects this focus on the vote as the means by which other legislative reforms benefiting women could be won. A Massachusetts women's rights convention in 1851, for example, proclaimed that the vote was the "cornerstone" of the quest for reform benefiting women:

While we would not undervalue other methods, the Right of Suffrage for Women is, in our opinion, the corner-stone of this enterprise, since we do not seek to protect woman, but rather to place her in a position to protect herself.[8]

Similarly, at the seventh annual National Woman's Rights Convention of 1856, the convention resolved that

the main power of the woman's rights movement lies in this: that while always demanding for woman better education, better employment, and better laws, it has kept steadily in view the one cardinal demand for the right of suffrage; in a democracy the symbol and guarantee of all other rights.[9]

[6]Elizabeth Cady Stanton, Susan B. Anthony, and Matilda J. Gage, *History of Woman Suffrage*, vol. 1 (New York: Fowler & Wells, 1881), p. 490.
[7]Ibid., p. 749.
[8]Ibid., p. 825.
[9]Ibid., p. 634.

Votes without Leverage

Organizationally, the national suffrage movement can be dated to 1869 with the formation of the National Woman Suffrage Association (NWSA) by Stanton and Anthony. As clearly articulated by its two founders, the NWSA was formed to implement their belief in the primacy of the ballot over further lobbying for legislative reform: "While we would yield to none in the earnestness of our advocacy of these [policy] claims, we make a broader demand for the enfranchisement of women, as the only way in which all her [sic] just rights can be permanently secured."[10] And the documents that record the history of this organization and its successor, the National American Woman Suffrage Association (NAWSA, formed by merger of the NWSA in 1890 with another national suffrage organization, the American Woman Suffrage Association [AWSA], and presided over by Stanton and Anthony as its first two presidents), contain numerous references to the vote as a means to advance women's specific interests as a group in economic and sexual equality.[11]

In addition to seeking the vote as a means to secure policy benefits for women as a group, many suffrage leaders also relied upon the mass mobilization of women in order to achieve their goal of winning woman suffrage. Scholars of this period have argued that after 1867, the development of a norm of gender identification accelerated in the United States, as women became the sole group denied the suffrage. The last three decades of the nineteenth century witnessed the multiplication of exclusively female organizations, including the female suffrage organizations. These latter did not fail to take advantage of the apparent development of norms of female solidarity. As illustrated by the suffrage campaign in New York State, coordinating women by appeal to a norm of gender solidarity became a key element of suffrage strategy.[12]

Prior to approximately 1909, New York State suffragists appeared to believe that the intellectual and moral force of the arguments for suffrage

---

[10]*The Revolution*, December 6, 1869, in Ellen Carol DuBois, ed., *Elizabeth Cady Stanton; Susan B. Anthony: Correspondence, Writings, Speeches* (New York: Schocken Books, 1981), p. 100.

[11]See, e.g., Stanton et al., *History of Woman Suffrage*, vol. 1, pp. 15, 460–461, 488–492, 499, 513–517, 747–749; Ida H. Harper, ed., *History of Woman Suffrage*, vol. 5 (New York: J. J. Little and Ives, 1922), pp. 346–363.

[12]Evidence of the existence of such a norm is given by the appeals made to it by suffrage leaders. For more direct evidence on the existence of women's networks in New York State, see Naomi Rosenthal, Meryl Fingrutd, Michele Ethier, Roberta Karant, and David McDonald, "Social Movements and Network Analysis: A Case Study of Nineteenth-Century Women's Reform in New York State," *American Journal of Sociology* 90, no. 5 (1985): 1022–1054; Anne Firor Scott also explores the existence of women's "networks" in *Natural Allies: Women's Associations in American History* (Urbana: University of Illinois Press, 1991).

themselves would be enough to win legislative support for suffrage, even in the absence of any kind of mobilization. After persistent legislative failure based on moral persuasion alone, however, New York suffragists came to see the necessity of winning the support of the voters on whom legislators depended for their political survival:

We can petition, and our petitions will be laughed at; we can beg, and be treated with contumely; we can plead, and the result will be a roar – of laughter. Until we have sufficient *power* in every assembly district to make it worthwhile for candidates bidding for the suffrage of the dear electors to take us into account, we must continue to labor in vain. We can demonstrate with logic and sentiment and pathos the justice of our cause; but, we shall not win unless we work – and we certainly shall not convince the politicians until we fight them with their own weapons. . . . When the legislators are aware of the fact that the women intend to quit petitioning and set to work on the electorate, they will suddenly see a light that has hitherto been obscured to their vision.[13]

Earlier suffragists had come to see the wisdom of seeking suffrage as a means of creating incentives for male legislators to support female-backed policy reform. But suffrage still had to be won, and by nonvoting women at that. Ultimately, suffrage leaders came to focus on the mobilization of male voters in support of female suffrage as the best tactic to create incentives for vote-minded legislators to support that policy.

But how to mobilize male voters? Even if any norm or norms of male group identity existed, men could not have been mobilized by female political elites on the basis of such an identity or identities. The constraints of gender roles at the time left little room for female leaders of organizations whose membership was largely or exclusively male. However, female political elites could (and did) capitalize on the multitude of relationships that individual women maintained with voting men, and which presumably were often highly valued by the latter (recall the discussion of spousal turnout in Chapter 2). If enough women could be convinced to attempt to persuade their male family members, friends, and neighbors to support suffrage, male voters could be mobilized indirectly.[14]

In order to mobilize men through their individual relationships with

---

[13]*TWV*, October 1911, p. 12.

[14]After the attainment of suffrage, former suffragists would look back on the tactics of the suffrage campaign and contrast the "indirect method" of influencing policy by creating sympathy for their cause among voting men with the "direct method" of exercising their own votes. Lillian Feickert, in Felice D. Gordon, *After Winning: The Legacy of the New Jersey Suffragists, 1920–1947* (New Brunswick, N.J.: Rutgers University Press, 1986), p. 38; also see Carol Nichols, *Votes and More for Women: Suffrage and After in Connecticut* (New York: Haworth Press, 1983), p. 34.

women, however, women themselves had to be mobilized in some way to pursue this task. And here suffrage elites revealed their evident belief in the existence of a norm of gender identification. In New York State, the program for suffrage organizations became the mass mobilization of women by appeals to gender solidarity, followed by the exhortation that these women should seek to convert their male family members and acquaintances to support the suffrage cause.

The course of the suffrage drive in New York State clearly reflects this strategic program. In 1909 the existing suffrage organization of New York City was reorganized to mirror the geographical divisions of the electoral system, and was renamed the New York City Woman Suffrage Party (WSP); the state suffrage organization would follow suit in 1915. This development was undertaken in order to implement New York suffragists' new strategy of women's mass mobilization.[15] One of the first actions of the WSP through its own newspaper was to make a public appeal to a norm of gender identification: "This is the day of organization, and it is the time when women must stand by women. Working together, actuated by a common desire, united as to policy, 'failure is impossible.' "[16] The following year, the Suffrage Party's newspaper urged its readers to attend the national suffrage convention en masse in order to signal the potential for collective action by women: "We call upon you to show a united front significant of the growing solidarity of women."[17]

Tactically, these appeals to gender solidarity were developed through a series of assemblies of women at all levels of the suffrage organization. For the election district organizations, these meetings took the form of exclusively female social gatherings, as described in this report from the 25th Assembly District in Manhattan: "a series of afternoon parlor meetings is being held to develop interest in the various election districts. In preparation for each, the election district is thoroughly canvassed, and printed invitations distributed from house to house. . . . At these informal gatherings tea is served, literature distributed, and a social time enjoyed."[18] Such meetings provided female attendees with the benefit of

---

[15]As Ellen Carol DuBois has shown, mass mobilization on the basis of gender solidarity was pioneered in New York by suffragists affiliated with "militant" suffrage organizations; the New York State Woman Suffrage Party soon followed suit. "Working Women, Class Relations, and Suffrage Militance: Harriot Stanton Blatch and the New York Woman Suffrage Movement, 1894–1909," *Journal of American History* 74, no. 1 (June 1987): 56–57.

[16]*TWV*, September 1910, p. 8.

[17]*TWV*, October 1911, p. 18.

[18]*TWV*, May 1911, p. 6.

solidarity through joining with their female friends and neighbors in the suffrage campaign.

Assembly district leaders could then call upon their election district captains to muster their women to larger mass meetings, as then could borough and city leaders. These monthly mass meetings at all levels of the party's organization further served to publicize the collective and united action of women to nonparty members: "Our cycle of meetings carrying out our own organization plans and perfecting our basis of activity, supply recruiting [efforts with] centers of activity and inspiration. Solidarity, concerted action and better crystallized programmes of procedure grow out of these district, borough and city conventions."[19]

By the time of the 1915 campaign for state female suffrage, suffrage leaders were ready to direct women mobilized by appeals to gender solidarity to use their personal influence over individual men to win the latter's support of suffrage. At the New York State Woman Suffrage Association convention which closed 1914, the association's president Gertrude Foster Brown argued that,

If we can work enough this year to get at all the voters in the state, we are sure to win this campaign. We need meetings, as many as we can have, but more than that we need the personal touch. It is that that makes canvassing so valuable. The man will stand and listen to a speaker if it happens to be convenient, but to draw out his view point and meet particular objections, a personal word is necessary. To reach all the voters in the state in this way, our organizers, speakers and leaders are not enough. We need a veritable army of women – an army of peace. We need every woman who believes in suffrage as an actual worker for suffrage, not necessarily to go out and take much time from her private duties, but to use every opportunity, to talk to every one she comes in contact with in the ordinary course of her life.[20]

Similarly, at the same convention Carrie Chapman Catt related that the first year of the 1915 campaign had revealed that "the most valuable service must be given by local workers; the direct constituents of legislators and the friends and neighbors of the voters to whom we must make final appeal. To arouse such women to activity was the aim of the organization department."[21]

At the height of the 1915 campaign, the appeal to individual women to convert the men with whom they were engaged in ongoing relation-

[19]*TWV*, October 1912, p. 7.
[20]*TWV*, November 1914, p. 14.
[21]Ibid., p. 18.

ships was made explicit. In March 1915, for example, *The Woman Voter* exhorted its readership that

This is a time when every woman who believes in equal suffrage must work. The leaders, splendid as they are, cannot win this State alone. It requires more than the consecrated services of a few and the sympathy of the others. Do not regard the suffragists as "they" and the campaign as "theirs." Make this battle *yours* and think in terms of "we." Be on the firing line.[22]

Two months later suffrage party members were urged to "Go and carry that conviction to those who have the power to decide our question at the polls . . . the leaders of the movement know of only one way to reach all the voters, and that is by seeing all the voters face to face. . . . There is a lot of religion in the woman's cause, and every canvasser should feel herself a missionary carrying the gospel to those whose minds are closed."[23] The same issue contained the assertion that "Every member of the Woman Suffrage Party, every believer in votes for women, every suffrage worker in every one of the 63 Assembly Districts of Greater New York must join our canvassing crusade if the work of the Organization Committee is to be a success."[24]

The point of mobilizing women by appeal to solidarity, in spite of the circumstance of female disfranchisement, was to draw upon women's individual relationships with voting men in order to use solidary benefits as a way of persuading male voters to support suffrage. Men could be mobilized indirectly to support suffrage, in other words, through the individualized efforts of women drawn to the suffrage campaign by direct appeals to gender solidarity. Thus WSP leaders in New York State exhorted their followers to proselytize among voters:

"Do you never see any man during the seven days of the week? Do you never have a word with your butcher, your grocer, your plumber? Is it impossible for you to hand them suffrage leaflets? Can you not ask them to vote for the amendment?" I maintain that if every suffragist spoke of suffrage to every man with whom she came in contact within the next three months, the campaign would be ours. . . . The next time I saw this woman she had signed up her furnace man and her grocer, and was giving literature to the wash woman for her husband . . . never lose a chance to speak of suffrage to every man whom you meet. . . . The circle of voters that could be reached by the women who are suffragists is big enough to win as a majority.[25]

---

[22]*TWV*, March 1915, p. 7.
[23]*TWV*, May 1915, p. 11.
[24]Ibid., p. 17.
[25]*TWV*, August 1915, p. 17.

Women were even instructed to answer the telephone with "Votes for Women" rather than "Hello" in order to maximize their ability to convert male acquaintances.

During the successful 1917 New York State referendum campaign, the suffrage strategy was again twofold. First resources were to be devoted "to the women of the State, to a thorough canvass and propaganda that shall be so far reaching that no woman shall be able to say she has never heard of suffrage. Then to the half million voters who have already placed themselves on record [in the 1915 referendum] as believing in equal rights we intend to add as many more by education and argument."[26] The women recruited in the first stage of the campaign by appeal to gender solidarity would each be responsible for converting one male voter known to them already: "The new slogan for enrollment is 'women first,' and the plan is to enlist women in every walk in life, to interest them to become workers wherever possible, and to induce every woman to be responsible for at least one voter of the *right* kind when our referendum is again submitted."[27]

During the 1917 campaign massive suffrage parades were used extensively in order to reach women with public displays of gender solidarity, the better to provide solidary benefits to potential mobilizers of male voters. A final parade just before the 1917 referendum, in fact, was billed as a "Woman's Parade" rather than merely a suffrage parade, and all women in the state were invited to march regardless of their opinion on suffrage. During the parade, all of the 1,006,503 names of the enrolled women in the New York State Woman Suffrage Party were marched down Fifth Avenue, and "pledge" blanks were distributed to the women watching this spectacle of women, enabling them to register their support of their sisters while their feelings of solidarity were at their strongest.[28]

The women mobilized by such appeals were then to bring the suffrage campaign into their own homes:

In the last campaign we won the endorsement of enough groups and parties to have enfranchised us. Now we must reach the individual voter. He can be reached only by personal effort, at his work and in his home. He should find

[26]*TWV*, January 1916, p. 11.
[27]*TWV*, February 1916, p. 19.
[28]*TWV*, September 1917, p. 29. On the New York suffragists' parades as a tactic to reenforce gender solidarity, also see Carrie Chapman Catt, *Woman Suffrage and Politics: The Inner Story of the Suffrage Movement* (New York: C. Scribner's Sons, 1923), pp. 286–287; Cott, *The Grounding of Modern Feminism*, pp. 26–28; and Michael McGerr, "Political Style and Women's Power, 1830–1930," *Journal of American History* 77, no. 3 (December 1990): 874–880.

that the "Suffragettes" are not strange women, but they are the women of his own household. The first task then of the great new campaign is to increase our organization among the women themselves, until behind the door of every house in the State and City there is a suffragist. Our canvassers should not only go from house to house, but they should *be* in every house. The new campaign must grow more and more intensive. . . . All the officers of the Woman Suffrage Party, State and City branches, agree now on the outlined policy: to increase the force of women workers in order to carry on a most intensive work among the voters.[29]

As examples to suffrage workers of how the two-staged process should work, *The Woman Voter* published reports like the following:

Having secured more than the number of women's enrollments assigned, the 15th Assembly District is now turning its attention to the men of the district. . . . At another meeting of suffragists and workers in a largely Italian district, a big brown-eyed Italian woman took the speaker by the hand and said: "I am so glad to know you; I can go home now and talk to my husband and tell him the rich ladies don't want the vote for themselves only; they want it for the poor women and the women who work in the factories. You couldn't talk to him but I can, now I know what you want me to say."[30]

The following from a worker in the failed Iowa referendum campaign was also published as support for the new plan of work: "I am firmly convinced that the women must be reached first and through them the men. No man whose wife is indifferent to the question can be expected to be an enthusiastic suffragist or cast his vote for the cause."[31]

In sum, leaders of suffrage organizations, both nationally and in New York State, certainly did not behave as though women did not constitute a distinct group and could not be mobilized to collective action via appeals to gender solidarity. Quite the contrary. Both the reasons given to seek the goal of woman suffrage and the means used to attain that goal suggest a willingness to treat women as a group sharing distinctive interests and norms of behavior.

PRESUFFRAGE ORGANIZATIONS AND "NONPARTISANSHIP"

The evidence with respect to a suffrage ideology of nonpartisanship, an ideology that would have proscribed a policy of electoral mobilization,

[29]*TWV*, May 1916, p. 11.
[30]*TWV*, April 1917, pp. 23–24.
[31]*TWV*, July 1916, p. 16.

is similarly not particularly supportive of this explanatory account. A review of suffrage documents reveals that working for or against candidates in order to achieve legislative reform was well within the traditions of political action established by suffrage organizations.[32] The latter on occasion strategically sought involvement in electoral politics in pursuit of realizing the suffrage agenda. For example, in 1872 the NWSA had campaigned for the Republican Party because of its historic reference to women in its platform;[33] in 1890 and 1897 NAWSA conventions featured discussions of the virtues of remaining sufficiently nonpartisan to worry both parties at the polls;[34] and in 1909 the Illinois State NAWSA affiliate reported to the annual convention on its work in electoral campaigns to elect prosuffrage candidates.[35]

Moreover, NAWSA policy itself explicitly sanctioned the use of candidate endorsements as a means to further the suffrage cause. For instance, in 1912, 1914, and 1915 NAWSA annual conventions reaffirmed the organization's position that not a candidate's party but rather his position on suffrage should determine female voters' support of that candidate.[36] In 1918 the National Association itself engaged in several campaigns to defeat antisuffragists, under the following authorization passed at the 1917 annual convention:

Resolved, that if the 65th Congress fails to submit the Federal Amendment before the next congressional election, the Association shall select and enter into such a number of senatorial and congressional campaigns as will effect a change in both houses of Congress sufficient to insure the passage of the Federal Amendment.[37]

As these examples of organizational action and policy reveal, suffrage leaders did not appear to have a problem with participation in partisan electoral campaigns. They did seem to be concerned that they not appear to have been "captured" by one party or another, but this concern seems to have been the product of strategic rather than ideological motivations.

---

[32]Melanie Gustafson also makes this point, and argues that this was the case for other women's organizations in the presuffrage years also. "Partisan Women," pp. 25, 31, 61–78.

[33]Elizabeth Cady Stanton, Susan B. Anthony, and Matilda J. Gage, *History of Woman Suffrage*, vol. 2 (Rochester, N.Y.: Charles Mann, 1881), p. 516.

[34]Ibid., pp. 173, 280.

[35]Harper, *History of Woman Suffrage*, vol. 5, p. 262.

[36]Ibid., pp. 342, 426, 454.

[37]*TWC*, December 22, 1917.

Votes without Leverage

Neither the gender "sameness" nor the ideology of nonpartisanship stories appears to be supported by the evidence from suffrage histories and documents. What about the supposition of competitive disadvantages? Recall that the first hypothesis predicted by that theoretical account is that if presuffrage women's leaders believed a norm of gender identification to exist, then women's leaders rather than party leaders should have been the first to make appeal to that norm. As discussed in Chapter 2, we would typically expect members of a coalescing group to be the first to initiate a group's mobilization on the basis of group solidarity. Membership in a developing group gives group members privileged access to valuable information concerning the group's receptiveness to mobilization appeals.

As the previous sections have documented, suffrage leaders both appeared to believe in the existence of such a norm, and did indeed seek to make appeal to that norm in New York State. But also because women could not vote, appeals to a norm of gender solidarity during the suffrage movement were not made in the service of mobilizing women's electoral participation. Rather, those appeals were designed to mobilize an army of female persuaders, an army that would be deployed primarily within families and small circles of acquaintances to convince male family members and friends to support woman suffrage with their votes. This tactic was eventually successful. But its very success in publicly appealing to a norm of gender identification *before* the attainment of woman suffrage likely served to remove any advantage held by women's leaders in the possession of information concerning women's potential for eventual electoral mobilization.

In New York State, for instance, the successful campaign for the 1917 referendum appeared to demonstrate the wisdom of a strategy for attaining suffrage that relied on the mass mobilization of nonvoting women into an army of suffrage proselytizers. As suffrage elites came to see, the most efficacious way to accomplish their goal was not to rely on abstract arguments, but rather to mobilize individual women into supporting suffrage and then to deploy these women on a mission to use their personal connections to swing male voters into support of woman suffrage. This strategy was eventually successful: a norm of gender identification evidently existed that could facilitate women's mobilization, and suffrage elites had been the first to recognize and capitalize through mass mobilization on the existence of that norm. Under normal circumstances – that is, where women could vote – these elites would have been drawing upon that norm to mobilize women in electoral contests, and they would thus have been in a position to deter potential competitors for women's electoral loyalties.

Instead, the exclusion of women from the vote implied that their mass mobilization in order to *get* the vote would bring the existence of their norm of group identification to the attention of party elites well before their eventual attainment of suffrage. As a result, party elites would have been acutely aware of the potential for women's eventual electoral mobilization several years before female enfranchisement.

Another hypothesis predicted by the competitive disadvantages account is that suffrage organizations would focus on suffrage only during the presuffrage years, rather than on the pursuit of broader public policy objectives. This hypothesis also receives considerable support in the historical record. The constitution of the NWSA stated clearly that its only aim was the pursuit of woman suffrage.[38] The leaders of the AWSA, formed only a few months later to pursue suffrage on primarily a state-by-state basis, proclaimed similar sentiments: the focus of the organization would be to secure the ballot for women, "everything else being held for the time in abeyance. . . . Suffrage is not the only object, but it is the first, to be attained . . . we must take one thing at a time."[39] And as other women's organizations pursuing legislative goals came to the same conclusion, they allied with the developing suffrage movement.[40]

This is not to say that the leaders and subleaders of these organizations did not continue to *care* about legislative issues other than suffrage or that, by inference, the members and supporters of these organizations did not care about policy issues either. Both the NWSA and the AWSA, before and after their merger into the NAWSA, allowed individuals to make resolutions from the floor of their annual conventions endorsing specific policy reform measures, and the NAWSA even appointed specific committees to monitor the progress of reform in areas such as women in industry, child welfare, women's civil rights, and peace.[41] But no legislative work toward securing these goals was ever performed by the NAWSA or its state affiliates, with one exception: state affiliates that were "not strong enough to attempt a [suffrage] campaign" were allowed to work for the removal of legal discrimination against women and other policy reforms in their states.[42] But every other resource of the suffrage organization and its state affiliates was to be directed only toward the attainment of suffrage, as reaffirmed by NAWSA President

[38]Stanton et al., *History of Woman Suffrage*, vol. 2, p. 401.
[39]Ibid., pp. 802–803.
[40]Scott, *Natural Allies*, pp. 165–166.
[41]For examples of the former, see Stanton et al., *History of Woman Suffrage*, vol. 2, pp. 420, 542, 818–819.
[42]Harper, *History of Woman Suffrage*, vol. 5, pp. 10, 163.

Carrie Chapman Catt in 1904: "To help working women was the motive that determined me to devote my life to obtaining woman suffrage. How hard it is that women must spend so many years just to get the means with which to effect reforms! But we who believe that behind them all is the ballot are chained to the work for that until it is gained."[43] Because of this exclusive focus on suffrage, the NAWSA's and the New York State WSP's internal decision-making structures were skeletal to non-existent.[44]

In other words, the institutional fact of women's disfranchisement in the nineteenth-century United States created strong incentives for those interested in policy reform benefiting women to focus first on securing woman suffrage.[45] In the estimation of the founders of the suffrage organizations, it was simply wasted effort for women's elites to continue to lobby legislators on behalf of a group that could neither reward nor punish legislators for their actions. Rather than spend scarce and valuable organizational resources on developing and pursuing a legislative agenda with nonelectoral means, these women's leaders chose to found organizations that focused all their resources on the single-minded pursuit of suffrage.

The ultimate goal of those who initiated the woman suffage movement, then, was the pursuit of women's distinctive policy concerns through the medium of electoral politics. Under "normal" circumstances (i.e., where women could vote), the steps for achieving that goal would have been clear: Stanton and Anthony would have created an organization that would have enabled them to coordinate women's voting by appeal to solidary incentives, while giving them the authority to develop a legislative agenda and then to pursue specific policy reforms through lobbying and targeted electoral intervention.

Without suffrage, however, there was simply no point in developing within the NWSA, the AWSA, their successor the NAWSA, or these organizations' state affiliates any organizational procedures that would have constituted an apparatus for developing policy priorities and linking those priorities to electoral targets. Because women did not possess suffrage, they could not pursue policy reforms that furthered their interests as a group with any efficacy. The vote was a proximate goal, which required attainment before the ultimate goal of policy reform

---

[43]Ibid., p. 98.

[44]See, e.g., Harriet Burton Laidlaw, "The Conventions," *TWV*, February 1913, p. 10.

[45]See also Gustafson, "Partisan Women," p. 24; Maureen A. Flanagan, "The Predicament of New Rights: Suffrage and Women's Political Power from a Local Perspective," *Social Politics* 2, no. 3 (Fall 1995): 309–310.

could be attempted. Suffrage leaders, therefore, did not need to and therefore did not seek to resolve the organizational questions of developing a legislative agenda that could be supported by women's elites and their followers. As noted earlier, the only mechanisms within the NAWSA that bore any relationship to public policy reform were a few committees that simply monitored progress in these areas. Instead, NAWSA existed solely to coordinate suffrage mobilization campaigns in the states and the U.S. Congress, and the national organization consisted exclusively of a handful of national officers and a committee on which sat a representative of each state affiliate.

As an organization that existed solely to coordinate the timing and partial funding of state mobilization campaigns, NAWSA was an entirely appropriate adaptation to the presuffrage context faced by women's leaders. As those leaders learned in the years prior to 1869, any efforts expended on policy reform in the absence of woman suffrage were largely wasted, and they streamlined their organizations to eliminate such costly and unrewarding efforts. Yet while this structure worked remarkably well when all local units were affiliated in agreement on one issue (e.g., suffrage), it would require extensive alteration in order to induce agreement within the organization on a more diverse legislative agenda, as would be required in the postsuffrage years.

POSTSUFFRAGE ORGANIZATIONS AND GENDER "SAMENESS"

For the postsuffrage period, our three stories concerning why the league might not have participated fully in electoral politics during the 1920s again make divergent predictions. First, the supposition of a suffrage ideology of gender "sameness" implies that, after the attainment of suffrage, we would not expect to see former suffrage elites either lobbying on behalf of women as a group or expressing the sentiment that women constituted a distinct electoral group with distinguishable policy preferences. The evidence for the national suffrage organization and its New York State affiliate does not support this hypothesis, however.

The first step taken by WSP leaders in New York State was to announce immediately after the 1917 referendum victory their intention to remain in existence in order to pursue a number of legislative goals, including legislation designed to benefit women and children.[46] Similarly,

---

[46]*TWC*, December 1, 1917, p. 1.

only a few weeks after the state convention, NAWSA leaders discussed the organization of former suffrage auxiliaries in enfranchised states into a "National League of Women Voters."[47] NAWSA's policy at that time was to allow state suffrage auxiliaries to disband once state suffrage referenda had been passed and the auxiliaries' goal had been achieved. However, with the suffrage victory in New York State, national suffrage leaders felt that the suffrage tide had turned, and that they could begin advance planning for their postsuffrage activities.[48] As first proposed by Carrie Chapman Catt in December 1917, the NLWV was to have as a central goal the pursuit of legislation of interest to women.[49]

One year later, a call was issued to former suffrage leaders in enfranchised states to participate in the creation of the proposed organization at the 1919 annual NAWSA convention. The call stated plainly that an important purpose of the new organization would be "to discuss and adopt a national charter of Women's Civil Rights; to discuss and adopt a charter of Children's Rights . . . and other lines of political action."[50] As the 1919 NAWSA convention neared, the organization's newsletter proclaimed that the proposed league would seek to represent women as an electoral group with distinct interests:

This is nothing less than a national union of women citizens comprehensive of the interests of the women voters of the country, as well as of the non-voters. . . . Does this mean to form a new party exclusively of women? If a party is, as the dictionary says, "a body of persons united for some purpose," it does. The proposed coalition also seems to be a party in so far as it aims to be a "part or portion" of the government.[51]

The editorial in *The Woman Citizen* also noted that a mission of legislative reform specifically to benefit women was not ideologically hostile to the traditions of the suffrage movement, whose leaders had in the early years of the movement supported a broad program of legislative goals.[52]

At the 1919 NAWSA convention itself, the league was chartered as

---

[47]Louise M. Young, *In the Public Interest: The League of Women Voters, 1920–1970* (New York: Greenwood Press, 1989), p. 22.

[48]There was an organizational precedent for the league; the National Council of Women Voters had been founded in January 1911 with the goals of educating women voters in citizenship, securing legislation of interest to women, and aiding in the further extension of suffrage in the United States. This organization had no affiliation with the National Association, however. *TWV*, August 1913.

[49]*TWC*, December 1, 1917, p. 1.

[50]*TWC*, December 14, 1918, p. 584.

[51]*TWC*, March 15, 1919, p. 857.

[52]Ibid., p. 858.

a component of NAWSA.[53] In the new league's original statement of principles, a belief in the distinctiveness of women as a political group was clear: "[women] should study public questions, not as good citizens only, but as WOMEN citizens; that there are matters for which women are peculiarly responsible; and that organization of women is necessary in order to give these matters the emphasis in government that their importance demands."[54]

It seems clear that the postsuffrage organizations created by the former suffrage associations were based on neither an ideology of "gender sameness" nor a belief that in fact women did not constitute a distinct group. And the leaders of these postsuffrage organizations were not alone in rejecting these beliefs. If the gender "sameness" supposition is correct, then we would also not expect to see major party elites behaving as if women were a distinct and significant electoral group, for example, by creating separate women's organizations or mobilizing women by gender-specific appeals. But the evidence with respect to the New York State parties is similarly not supportive of the gender "sameness" account.

As discussed earlier, during the course of the New York State suffrage campaign, elites in the two major state political parties could not have failed to notice the growing coordination of women by appeal to their identification with other women. The frequent mass meetings and parades staged by suffrage party leaders to demonstrate to women the developing solidarity of women would have displayed this fact to male party elites as well. And upon the heels of the 1917 referendum, the major political parties lost no time in seeking to use that norm of gender identification to facilitate women's electoral mobilization themselves.

The clearest evidence that this in fact occurred is that both major parties in New York State created entirely distinct women's organizations in order to mimic the success that the suffrage organizations had had in mobilizing women as a group.[55] Apparently believing that men would not be effective in mobilizing potential female voters to the polls in support of party candidates, male party elites created new positions

---

[53]Proceedings of the Fiftieth Annual Convention of the National American Woman Suffrage Association, March 25, 1919, Papers of the National League of Women Voters, 1918–1974, microfilm edition (Frederick, Md.: University Publications of America, 1985), Pt. II, Reel 1, Frame 5 (emphasis added).

[54]*Principles and Policy of the National League of Women Voters* (Washington, D.C.: National League of Women Voters, 1920).

[55]Nancy Cott characterizes the parties' women's organizations as "curious," given her own assessment that a "woman vote" was an "interpretive fiction." "Across the Great Divide: Women in Politics before and after 1920," in Louise A. Tilly and Patricia Gurin, eds., *Women, Politics and Change* (New York: Russell Sage Foundation, 1990), p. 172.

within the party organizations to tempt leaders of women's organizations to work for the parties. These new positions were billed as leadership opportunities in what would be exclusively female party organizations, mobilizing only female voters, and using gender-specific campaign appeals to do so. These mobilization efforts by the parties would substitute *partisan* female leaders as the authoritative source of cues for group-based electoral behavior, rather than *independent* female leaders:

We seek to draw into the active service of the Republican party those women who have earned and justified their leadership in the long accustomed services of women. Women who have thus won their way know and are known to women throughout their states and throughout the country, just as our party leaders are known. Through these women we shall reach others, and so bring to the women in the cities and in the villages, in the counties and at the crossroads, our purposes.[56]

Only a few days after the November 1917 suffrage referendum, New York's Republican Governor Whitman tapped the president of the New York City Federation of Women's Clubs, Mrs. John Francis Yawger, to serve as the "Associate Chairman" of a "Women's Republican State Committee," that would be formed in every county and every election district in the state, "under the guidance of George A. Glynn, Chairman of the Republican State Committee."[57] (In 1920, following guidelines formulated by the Republican National Committee, a "Republican Women's State Executive Committee" composed of sixteen women was created by the men's state committee to direct the women's state organization.)[58]

As part of this "associate" organization of the Republican Party, county chairmen were to see to the creation of duplicate organizations of women in their jurisdictions. For example, the New York County Republican Committee created a "Women's Republican County Executive Committee" of thirty-six women, the same number as the men's Republican County Executive Committee. The thirty-six women would be appointed by the male county chairman, and would serve as the "associate leaders" in the Assembly districts from which they were appointed, "the associate leader to be a woman with her own staff of lieutenants and election district workers of her own sex."[59]

These "associate" Assembly district leaders then arranged for the se-

[56]*TWC*, February 15, 1919, p. 784.
[57]"Office for Mrs. Yawger," *NYT*, November 15, 1917, p. 6.
[58]"Names Women Workers," *NYT*, May 19, 1920, p. 15.
[59]"Republicans Admit Women as Partners," *NYT*, December 21, 1917, p. 11.

lection of women in each election district to serve as "captains" of a team of canvassers recruited to contact women door-to-door prior to enrollment days. The chair of the Women's Republican County Executive Committee in New York City, Helen Varick Boswell, described the progress of the women's organization in April 1918:

"From the talk I have had with the women associated with men as leaders of the different Assembly District organizations, I find that despite the short time we have been at the work, the districts are from 50 to 90 per cent organized. Complete organization, in our terminology, contemplates not only the election of a leader, but the selection of a Captain for every election district . . . [and] at least five helpers [for every election district Captain] to aid in the house to house canvass that we expect to make prior to enrollment." Miss Boswell told her leaders that the task confronting them between now and May 25, when the newly enfranchised women will have their opportunity to enroll with the party of their choice for participation in the Fall primaries, would be to persuade as many as possible in their districts to enroll under the Republican emblem.[60]

When time came for the house-to-house canvass for the May registration, the female election district captains were armed with pamphlets "setting forth the excellences of the Republican Party and urging women to be sure to enroll under the eagle," and sent out by Boswell on their mission of persuasion.[61] These appeals were clearly based on references to women's norm of gender identification, calling women's attention to their wartime role and asking for their loyalty to the party, which "has carried the flag as it has kept step with the music of the Union which it made": "The test of all time of the womanhood of the world is upon us. It is the women who are carrying the supreme burden of this war and noble and magnificent beyond expression is their conduct. . . . I am convinced that the women of America can be depended upon and that they believe in those things for which the Republican Party stands."[62]

The Democratic state party in New York kept up with the Republican organization's efforts to initiate women's mobilization. On December 11, 1917, the Democratic State Executive Committee voted to increase its membership from twenty-one to thirty-six, with the stipulation that the fifteen new members be women, and directed the state chairman to appoint the fifteen women members of the committee.[63] (By April of the following year the state committee had decided to appoint twenty-one women members to the executive committee so that men and women

[60]"Republican Women Keen," *NYT*, April 18, 1918, p. 12.
[61]"Women Urged to Enroll," *NYT*, May 10, 1918, p. 5.
[62]"Hays, in Plea, Urges Women to Enroll," *NYT*, May 16, 1918, p. 24.
[63]"Will Put Women on State Committee," *NYT*, December 12, 1917, p. 10.

would have equal numerical representation.)[64] The state committee also organized a "Plan and Scope Committee . . . to bring about a full enrollment of women in the Democratic Party," chaired by William Farley.[65]

As part of that plan the county committees were urged to organize to mobilize prospective female registrants into the Democratic Party. The most important such committee, the New York County Committee or Tammany Hall, created its own special committee in February 1918 to report on "A comprehensive and detailed plan for the organization of women voters in the county," chaired by Acting Mayor Alfred E. Smith. The report, adopted the following week by Tammany's executive committee, recommended the appointment of an "Auxiliary County Committee" of women until after registration days. This Tammany "Auxiliary" would consist of as many women from each election district as there were men on the county committee, a number determined by each election district's Democratic gubernatorial vote in the previous gubernatorial election.[66] Moreover, the Tammany executive committee, as an unofficial body composed of a certain number of representatives from each election district, voted to double its number of members with women, the women to be elected by the members of the county committee in each election district (which at this time was still composed only of men).[67] The Democratic Executive Committee of the Bronx created a similar plan for its election districts.[68]

Like the Republicans, the Democrats used their women's organization to appeal to potential female registrants in gender terms, for example, making explicit reference to women's roles as wives, sisters, and mothers: "President Wilson and the Democratic Party are responsible for the conduct of the war. The women of our land have a right to demand that their husbands, their brothers, and their sons who are fighting gallantly at the front shall be returned to their homes at the earliest possible moment consistent with victory."[69]

As *The Woman Citizen* noted in 1918, "Republicans and Democrats alike are becoming urgent in their efforts to get New York women to make their party alignments and to come early and avoid the rush, on

[64]"Hunt for Candidate to Oppose Hearst," *NYT*, April 8, 1918, p. 8.
[65]"Democrats Discuss Women," *NYT*, April 14, 1918, p. 18.
[66]"Tammany Women on Par with Men," *NYT*, February 22, 1918, p. 1.
[67]"Women Now Eligible for Tammany Ranks," *NYT*, March 1, 1918, p. 20; "Tammany Welcomes Women in Council," *NYT*, May 8, 1918, p. 7.
[68]"Widen Vote for Women," *NYT*, January 28, 1918, p. 14; "Women Leaders in Bronx," *NYT*, March 13, 1918, p. 7.
[69]"Democrats Call on Women to Enroll," *NYT*, May 16, 1918, p. 24.

enrollment days. No sort of stimulating device seems likely to be spared by the individual politician in his ambition to convince woman that she can save her country only by enrolling with his party."[70] Reporting on the Republicans' canvass, *The Woman Citizen* noted that

The woman's division of the New York County Republican Committee has inaugurated a drive for a record breaking enrollment of the Republican women in that county. May 25 is the day appointed by the board of elections for the enrollment of women in the primaries. It is expected that women Republican district leaders and helpers to the number of 4,000 will work on this enrollment campaign. The plan calls for a house to house canvass, thus establishing a personal acquaintance with the new voters. The county organization of women leaders is practically completed and the canvass under their direction will start at once. In some districts the work is already well under way, and seventy five per cent of the women have been personally interviewed by the Republican women captains.[71]

The argument about gender "sameness" predicts that former suffrage elites would not have sought to pursue a distinct legislative agenda for women in the postsuffrage years. Yet both New York and national league elites publicly proclaimed their intention to do just that. The gender "sameness" account also predicts that other electoral elites, such as major party elites, would not have treated women as a distinct electoral group. Yet again, elites in both major parties in New York State did just that.

POSTSUFFRAGE ORGANIZATIONS AND "NONPARTISANSHIP"

The supposition of a suffrage ideology of nonpartisanship predicts that if suffrage organizations continued in existence after the attainment of suffrage, then those organizations should have proscribed participation in partisan electoral campaigns. But the evidence with respect to both the NLWV's New York State affiliate and the NLWV itself does not support this hypothesis.

When leaders of the WSP in New York State announced their intention to remain in existence after the successful 1917 suffrage referendum, in order to pursue, among other legislative goals, policy benefits for women and children, they also plainly announced their intention to campaign against candidates who opposed the extension of such policy ben-

---

[70]*TWC*, May 4, 1918, p. 447.
[71]*TWC*, May 11, 1918, p. 467.

efits.[72] As WSP leaders noted, this decision did not break tradition with an ideology of "nonpartisanship":

The Woman Suffrage Party has, since its beginning, opposed individuals in all political parties who are against woman suffrage. It will be remembered that the Woman Suffrage Party of New York City did pioneer work in campaigning against anti-suffragists for office. This policy will be continued and will undoubtedly be more effective with thousands of voters behind it.[73]

In December 1918 the state suffrage party reaffirmed its intention to participate in electoral campaigns when necessary, voting to "oppose candidates for public office, irrespective of their political affiliations, when the records and policies of such candidates are at variance with the objects set forth in the Party's constitution."[74]

Similarly, as first proposed by Carrie Chapman Catt in December 1917, the NLWV was to use women's votes for or against candidates as necessary to further NAWSA's and the league's legislative goals: "In view of the further fact that woman's task of securing the suffrage is not finished and will not be until she gets nation-wide suffrage, she would be too stupid to vote at all if she did not use her vote to delete such opposition to suffrage wherever it may be found."[75]

At the 1919 NAWSA convention chartering the NLWV as a component of the suffrage organization, the latter's constitution was revised to reflect the new organization's potential use of women's votes to secure league and NAWSA policy objectives:

The object of this Alliance [League] shall be to secure the vote to the women citizens of the United States by appropriate National and State legislation and *to increase the effectiveness of women's votes in furthering better government.*[76]

This same convention also specifically reaffirmed the National Association's willingness to participate in electoral campaigns by ratifying the following resolution:

Resolved, That the National Association shall not affiliate with any political party nor endorse the platform of any party nor support or oppose any political candidate *unless such action shall be recommended by the Board of Directors*

[72]*TWC*, December 1, 1917, p. 1.
[73]*TWV*, January 1916, p. 8.
[74]*TWC*, December 21, 1918, p. 616.
[75]*TWC*, December 1, 1917.
[76]Proceedings of the Fiftieth Annual Convention of the National American Woman Suffrage Association, March 25, 1919, Papers of the National League of Women Voters, Pt. II, Reel 1, Frame 5 (emphasis added).

in order to achieve the ends and purposes of this organization as set forth in the constitution. Nothing in this resolution shall be construed to limit the liberty of action of any member or officer of this association to join or serve the party of her choice in any capacity whatsoever as an individual . . . the National Board shall be empowered to enter any state to carry on work without the authority of that state if necessary.[77]

As a component of the NAWSA, the NLWV was thus authorized to endorse or oppose candidates in pursuit of its legislative agenda.

Some confusion has perhaps arisen on this point because of the league's avowed refusal to endorse or oppose candidates on the basis of their partisan affiliation, as was advocated by Alice Paul's Congressional Union and later National Women's Party. League officers argued (correctly) that American political institutions precluded assigning responsibility for party positions to individual legislators, who could often ignore stated national party positions. Of course, this policy had nothing to do with whether the league would endorse or oppose candidates on the basis of their issue positions, which was the clear policy of the NLWV.[78]

New York's WSP was the first state affiliate of the NAWSA to become a state League of Women Voters, in April 1919;[79] by December 1919 state league elites had developed rudimentary criteria for supporting or opposing candidates and had decided that at least one statewide candidate for office met their rudimentary criteria for opposition. The state league in convention voted to declare itself " 'as opposed to [U.S.] Senator [James] Wadsworth's nomination or election' and committed to do 'everything in our power to defeat him.' "[80]

In January 1920 the state league publicly announced its intention to campaign against Wadsworth, issuing a pamphlet to league workers for distribution that set forth the league's case against the senator's renomination by the Republican Party.[81] In February 1920, the newly created full NLWV voted to join the New York State league in its campaign to defeat Wadsworth.[82] This action was taken despite the fact that the new

[77]Ibid., Frame 3 (emphasis added).
[78]This, I believe, is the correct interpretation of the 1920 letter cited by Andersen as evidence for the NLWV's disavowal of candidate endorsements, in which Carrie Chapman Catt writes to Edna Gelhorn, "I do not think we can make a rule that no candidates are to be worked against, but what I am trying to make clear was that we are not going to endorse candidates *as between the parties.*" Cited in Andersen, *No Longer Petitioners*, pp. 2–30 (emphasis added).
[79]*TWC*, April 26, 1919, p. 1025.
[80]*TWC*, December 6, 1919.
[81]*TWC*, January 17, 1920, p. 727.
[82]*TWV*, February 21, 1920, p. 895.

1920 league constitution proclaimed that the league "as an organization
... shall be allied with and support no party," clearly indicating that
endorsing or opposing candidates was not interpreted to violate that
policy.[83]

The state and national leagues began to distribute anti-Wadsworth
material in New York the summer before the fall Republican State Convention, seeking to prevent his renomination.[84] Defeated there, the
leagues' attempt to mobilize women against Wadsworth began in earnest
in October 1920, under the slogan "Wadsworth's place is in the home."
In letters sent out to former suffrage workers, the leagues asked them to
participate in a strategy of gender mobilization reminiscent of the suffrage campaign:

1) Vote against him yourself; 2) See that his record is known and understood
in your family, your neighborhood, your town; 3) Get nine women to form with
you a committee of ten. Get each of the ten to form other committees of ten
each and so on as far as you can stretch it, and ask every woman to get ten
men and women outside the working committees to vote against him.[85]

The national league's newspaper added its voice to the campaign by
asking for campaign contributions, telling its readership that "The non-
partisan campaign against Senator Wadsworth is of especial interest to
women because he has been their particular enemy. He is bound to block
whatever women want."[86]

The supposition of a suffrage ideology of nonpartisanship hypothesizes that upon women's enfranchisement, former suffrage organizations
would not participate in electoral campaigns either as a matter of custom
or as a matter of organizational policy. But the evidence for both the
NLWV and its New York State affiliate does not support this hypothesis.
Both organizations clearly possessed policies sanctioning the mobilization of female voters in electoral campaigns, and both organizations
attempted such mobilization in 1920.

---

[83]Papers of the National League of Women Voters, Pt. II, Reel 1, Frame 142. At
a meeting following the 1920 convention, the National Board of Directors voted to
distinguish this case from that of a league officer presenting herself as a candidate
for election in a partisan campaign. The latter case was thought to identify the league
too closely with a given party, and the board recommended to state leagues that they
seek to avoid this situation although, significantly, even this case was said not ex-
pressly to violate the league's constitution. Papers of the National League of Women
Voters, Pt. 1, Reel 1, Frame 76.

[84]"Women to Keep Up Wadsworth Fight," *NYT*, July 24, 1920, p. 12.

[85]*TWC*, October 2, 1920, p. 475.

[86]*TWC*, October 9, 1920, p. 504.

POSTSUFFRAGE ORGANIZATIONS AND
COMPETITIVE DISADVANTAGES

As was the case with the presuffrage period, neither the supposition of a belief in gender "sameness" nor the supposition of an ideology of "nonpartisanship" appears to be supported by the available evidence from the postsuffrage period. The evidence discussed with respect to these stories is, however, compatible with the supposition of competitive disadvantages. That account also makes specific predictions for the post-suffrage period. First, if the supposition of competitive disadvantages is correct, then we would expect to see suffrage organizations undergoing a period of organizational transformation before they could initiate the electoral mobilization of women.

It certainly appears to be true that the NAWSA was simply not organizationally equipped to pursue its new objective of securing broader legislative benefits for women and children after the attainment of suffrage. The organizational form adopted by the NAWSA and its state affiliates like the New York WSP to address their presuffrage environment was ill-suited to the tasks they faced upon women's enfranchisement. Specifically, while NAWSA and WSP leaders envisioned the role of these organizations in their changed environment as including seeking legislation of interest to voting women by endorsing or opposing candidates, they did not possess the channels of authority through which the crucial decisions about which pieces of legislation to support and which candidates to endorse or oppose could be made. Altering the suffrage organizations' existing structures and procedures to address their changed role was not an impossible task, merely one that required time: time for elites to assemble information, present ideas, argue, marshal their supporters within the organization, organize the membership to vote on proposals, and so forth. In fact, it would take almost three years before the new incarnations of the NAWSA and its affiliate the New York State WSP, namely the NLWV and its affiliate the New York State League of Women Voters, were ready to begin a remobilization of women by appeals to gender identity in an electoral campaign.

In 1917 the WSP in New York State announced its new organizational mission, but the decision-making processes that would permit the development of a specific legislative program and the targeting of candidates to support or oppose based on their legislative records were simply nonexistent. Moreover, the resolution of these organizational questions was dependent upon the actions taken by the NAWSA, which only a few weeks after the WSP's announcement initiated discussions about a "National League of Women Voters."[87] As a result, the New York State auxiliary essentially went into a holding pattern, refraining from any explicitly electoral activity until the organizational issues raised by mobilizing female voters in support of a legislative agenda were settled by the national association.[88]

Instead, the former state suffrage association limited itself to such innocuous tasks as general voter and civic education for women. These activities did not involve the mobilization of women by appeal to gender identification to support some desired legislative end, as had the suffrage drive and as would later electoral campaigns. And when during the 1918 elections new female voters reportedly looked to the New York City WSP for guidance in their voting decisions, the party sent them away empty-handed: "Hundreds of women flocked to our various headquarters seeking information. . . . Some of them were disappointed because we did not advise them how to vote."[89]

Despite its inactivity in the 1918 elections, the state suffrage party continued to maintain that it would eventually participate in electoral campaigns as a way to pursue policy benefits for women. But at the close of 1918 the party was still waiting upon the national association to propose what those benefits would be, and how they would form criteria by which candidates would be supported or opposed.

There had not been enough time between New York's suffrage victory in November 1917 and the NAWSA's convention in December 1917 to organize Carrie Chapman Catt's proposed NLWV. Moreover, the skeletal national organization that existed in between conventions was merely a handful of officers and state leaders who were not authorized to create a new organization. Further progress toward creating the league thus awaited the NAWSA's next annual conference. The next step toward the league was therefore not taken until December 1918, when an official call was issued to representatives from former suffrage organizations in the fifteen full suffrage states to attend a NAWSA convention in March 1919 for the purpose of creating an organization of voting women within the association.

While the *goals* and the proposed *tactics* of the league appeared ideologically consistent with the history of the mother organization, the machinery to implement these goals and tactics in the new context of electoral politics was innovatory. Indeed, the March 1919 convention saw the creation of an entirely new organizational structure to

---

[87]Young, *In the Public Interest*, p. 22.
[88]*TWC*, January 12, 1918, p. 128.
[89]*TWC*, September 14, 1918, p. 306.

develop a legislative agenda and to link that agenda with electoral action.

Carrie Catt had posed the question of fundamental organizational change to the 1919 convention, asking the assembled delegates,

Shall we merely unite for the one purpose of hastening the final day of the century-long struggle for the enfranchisement of women, or shall we frankly change our policy, recognizing that in this period more great issues are pressing for attention than at any other period of the world, and therefore unitedly use our votes and our utmost influence to "keep God's truth marching on"?[90]

Catt had also acknowledged that such a mission, even if not inconsistent with the organization's ideology, would still require major alterations in the organization's structure:

It must be remembered that no League of Women Voters can be possible on the lines suggested unless the NAWSA is willing to amend its time-honored policy in response to what seems a new time and new conditions. It must be further remembered that to make these amendments involves the most fundamental changes in our internal policy ever proposed. It will doubtless arouse sharp differences of opinion, and action should be taken only after careful and sincere reflection.[91]

In the end, control of the league's legislative program was given in part to seven newly created national standing committees, each responsible for studying a particular legislative area thought to be of interest to female voters.[92] These committees would be composed of the chairs of corresponding legislative committees at the state level, which would also be newly created. The national standing committees were to draw up legislative recommendations, which would then be voted upon and amended if necessary by the full league in convention, and then approved by the league council, composed of the league state chairs.

Based on this national legislative program, each state would receive its marching orders, or would be "assigned the legislation necessary to bring its state's code of laws up to the standard."[93] Local leagues would not possess legislative committees, and would instead be given carefully

---

[90]Carrie Chapman Catt, "A Nation Calls," speech to 1919 NAWSA Convention, Papers of the National League of Women Voters, Pt. II, Reel 1, Frame 20.

[91]Ibid.

[92]These committees were given the following legislative responsibilities: women in industry, child welfare, citizenship, elections, social morality, unification of laws (in the various states, regarding women's civil rights), and food supply and demand. Papers of the National League of Women Voters, Pt. II, Reel 1, Frame 18.

[93]*TWC*, May 3, 1919, pp. 1044–1045.

defined topics to discuss and publicize, the goal being to arouse and educate women around unifying legislative initiatives.[94]

The national league's board of directors, along with the national league in annual convention, would decide whether to support or oppose candidates for national office based on their legislative platform or record.[95] State and local leagues could make similar decisions for state and local candidates for election based on those candidates' legislative agendas.

This organizational overhaul in 1919 demonstrates the kinds of changes NAWSA and its state affiliates had to make before they could seek to mobilize women in support of a legislative agenda. And although several basic issues were resolved at the 1919 convention, many more organizational questions remained. At the first meeting of the league's governing council in June 1919 (when membership in the league was still limited to twenty-six states), questions of electoral strategy and organizational structure were still being argued.[96] For instance, NAWSA's previous involvement in electoral politics had been limited to senatorial campaigns selected for their potential to alter the balance of power in the Senate. With the federal suffrage amendment now through Congress, should the national league still focus on senatorial and/or congressional campaigns? Should the NLWV endorse a presidential candidate? Would the national league's endorsement decisions be binding upon state and local leagues? What would be the criteria by which state and local leagues would decide to endorse or oppose candidates? For the time being, these questions were left unresolved.

The New York State Woman Suffrage Party was the first state affiliate of the NAWSA to become a state League of Women Voters, in April 1919.[97] The state's LWV thus was not created until eighteen months had passed after woman suffrage had become the law in New York State. Criteria for making candidate endorsement decisions were not developed until December 1919.[98] An electoral campaign against a candidate targeted for defeat using those criteria was not begun until the late summer of 1920.[99]

By the fall of 1920, then, the former suffrage organization in New York State had begun a new campaign to mobilize women by appeal to their norm of gender solidarity, this time as voters in electoral politics. But this campaign of electoral mobilization was not undertaken until

[94]Ibid.
[95]*TWC*, March 29, 1919, p. 940.
[96]Young, *In the Public Interest*, pp. 35–36.
[97]*TWC*, April 26, 1919, p. 1025.
[98]*TWC*, December 6, 1919.
[99]"Women to Keep Up Wadsworth Fight," *NYT*, July 24, 1920, p. 12.

approximately three years after women had achieved the right to vote in New York State. Because of their organizational adaptations to the context of disfranchisement, neither the national nor the New York State suffrage organizations were prepared to begin such mobilization any earlier.

If the supposition of competitive disadvantages is correct, then we would also expect to see major party elites able to initiate the electoral mobilization of new female voters *before* similar actions by suffrage organizations. As earlier documented, this too was the case in New York State. Recall that both parties in New York State began to create distinct women's organizations as early as December 1917. By the spring of 1918 both parties had at least partially implemented plans to have teams of women in each of New York's six thousand election districts, their job being to convince the women in their district to join with other women in enrolling in one party or the other. The parties' efforts appeared to generate substantial returns; in the May 1918 registration alone, 679,618 women enrolled in one of the two major parties in New York State, 375,093 or approximately 60 percent as Republicans.[100] In the general registration for the 1918 fall elections the parties were able to increase substantially their female enrollments, to approximately 1.2 million women.[101] If women registered as Republicans in roughly the same proportion as they did in the special May registration days, it is not unreasonable to assume that roughly 720,000 women had registered as Republicans in New York State by the close of 1918. The Democrats would have thus registered approximately 480,000 women by that time.

1919 saw another enrollment drive by the Republicans, particularly in New York City where the party's women's division focused on mobilizing female immigrants: "The Republican party of New York City has begun an aggressive campaign to Americanize the foreign-born women who will be entitled to vote when their husbands have become citizens of this country. . . . The Republican club houses are being used as social centre houses in many districts, and the use of these clubs by the foreign-born women will be encouraged during the coming months."[102] For the fall registration days the Republicans once again initiated a canvass directed at women.

---

[100]*TWC*, July 27, 1918, p. 165.

[101]In 1918 women accounted for approximately 41 percent of the total registration in New York City. "Registration over the Million Mark," *NYT*, October 14, 1918, p. 24. Extrapolating that percentage to the statewide total registration, we obtain the figure of 1,195,959. "2,916,974 May Vote in New York State," *NYT*, October 27, 1918, p. 7.

[102]*TWC*, March 22, 1919, p. 908.

Doubling the enrollment of Republican women of the state of New York this fall is the task Mrs. [Mary] Livermore has set out to accomplish as chairman of the Women's Executive Committee of the Republican State Committee. . . . a series of sectional conferences was initiated to bring out the best Republican thought in the state on the question of getting out a strong woman enrollment and vote. . . . then came a "barn-storming" tour through central and western New York.[103]

By December 1919, the Republicans had women's organizations in "virtually every county in the State."[104]

To prepare for the fall 1920 campaign, the Republican state women's organization first used the occasion of the special spring primaries (held in presidential election years to elect delegates to the party conventions and the personnel of the party committees) to launch a mobilization drive among women:

We have in every way possible tried to make the Republican women of the State conversant with the meaning of primaries and the necessity of voting at them. For the past few weeks we have been emphasizing in our weekly bulletins just how to go about this matter. These bulletins reach 2,800 organization leaders. Through them the contents are disseminated among the members. We have a woman Vice Chairman of the county organization in every county except five. Every county except one has the women organized in some form of political association. It is through these organizations that we reach the woman in her home. House to house canvasses are made, instructions mailed and the press utilized to draw the attention of the women to the duty that is expected of them.[105]

The next step in the 1920 campaign was to mobilize women in support of the party's nominees for office, including former antisuffragist Senator Wadsworth. To that end the Republican Party's female workers sent out an appeal to the female voters of the state asking them to lay aside suffrage considerations and vote for Wadsworth's reelection.[106]

All of the foregoing party mobilization efforts were undertaken before the commencement of similar efforts by the NLWV and the state LWV. The New York State LWV acknowledged its competition in October 1920, noting that "with speech, editorial, letter and literature; with desperate appeal along every avenue known to campaigning, the Republican workers are pleading, entreating, begging, beguiling all Republicans and

[103]*TWC*, September 20, 1919, p. 404.
[104]"Republican Women Dine Chairman Hays," *NYT*, December 4, 1919, p. 18.
[105]Mary Livermore, Chairman, Republican State Women's Executive Committee, in "Priming the Feminine Voter for the Primary," *NYT*, April 4, 1920, p. 2.
[106]*TWC*, October 2, 1920, p. 474.

persons of Republican sympathy, to vote for Wadsworth in order that Harding may have a Republican Senator from New York. . . . Will women surrender before this most specious of fallacies as men have done over and over again?"[107]

However, if the theoretical account discussed in Chapter 2 is correct, the years of mobilization efforts undertaken by New York State's parties would have provided those organizations with significant advantages over the LWV in the fall of 1920. The Republican Party now had some degree of influence with those potential female voters who recognized Republican Party female leaders as the source of authoritative cues concerning the coordination of women's collective action. Given the number of women registered with the Republican Party and plausibly following those cues, the league must have found it quite difficult to attract women to its anti-Wadsworth campaign by arguing that theirs was a "women's" campaign. All a potential female voter would have had to do was to compare the number of women on record as supporting the Republican Party versus the number of women on record as supporting the league. While the Republican Party could boast an enrollment of at least 720,000 women in the spring of 1920, the New York League of Women Voters could have claimed no more than 25,000 women as members.[108]

Since the Republican Party, the Democratic Party, and the New York State LWV were direct competitors for the mass of women who could be mobilized by an appeal to gender identity, this put the LWV at the bottom of the list in terms of the utility it could offer to prospective female voters. Any woman who valued her identity as a politically active woman, and who was the target of all three organizations' appeals on the basis of that identity, would rationally seek to maximize the benefit she received from voting by voting with the largest group of politically active women in her election district. To do otherwise would place her action at odds with the mass of women with whom she identified, and whose opinion of her actions was a valued good. To do otherwise, in short, would have been irrational.

Upon women's entrance into the New York electorate in 1917, then, suffrage elites no longer had an informational advantage over party elites in their knowledge of the existence and the strength of that norm of gender identification; state party elites clearly believed that women shared a norm of group identification strong enough to facilitate their electoral mobilization by appeal to that norm. Moreover, the parties

---

[107]*TWC*, October 9, 1920, p. 504.

[108]The Pennsylvania League of Women Voters was the largest postsuffrage NAWSA affiliate, and claimed 25,000 members. Young, *In the Public Interest*, p. 51. In 1923, the New York State League of Women Voters reported a membership of 19,065. Papers of the National League of Women Voters, Pt. II, Reel 4, Frame 453.

were not hampered by an organizational structure inappropriate to electoral mobilization in support of or opposition to candidates: this was, after all, the task that parties were originally designed to solve. State party elites were thus able to implement their plans for the electoral mobilization of women much more quickly than were suffrage elites, having only to appoint women at the various levels of the party organizations to its new women's division. These appointments were largely made by the spring of 1918, only a few months after the state's passage of the suffrage referendum. The party organizations thus had a significant head start over the New York State WSP in initiating women's electoral mobilization.

CONCLUSION

At an NLWV board meeting held in New York immediately after the 1920 election, the following motion was made and carried:

> Moved by Mrs. Marie Edwards that we recommend that as far as possible we do our League work along the constructive lines of our general program and unless an emergency arises our advice is, *that for the present we keep out of local political struggles or endorsements of candidates. Carried.*[109]

The NLWV had provisionally repealed its long-held electoral policy of positive or negative endorsements of candidates. It was neither a final nor a public repeal, as will be discussed in later chapters. But it would not be reversed in the years to come.

What explains the league's 1920 decision? Of our three explanatory stories, only one so far appears to have its subsidiary hypotheses supported by the evidence. In the presuffrage period, the historical record reveals suffrage elites from the earliest stages of the suffrage movement stating publicly that they sought the vote as tool with which to advance the policy interests of women. They may also have believed that the vote was a natural right of citizens, but there is a consistent history of suffrage elites declaring that women needed the vote to protect their interests as a group, rather than or at least in addition to women being entitled to the vote as adult citizens. In addition, women were mobilized during the suffrage movement itself precisely as a distinct group sharing a norm of gender identification. Suffrage documents also reveal that suffrage elites never proscribed the endorsement of candidates in partisan electoral contests as a tool with which to attain their goals. Indeed, suffrage elites

---

[109]Papers of the National League of Women Voters, Pt. I, Reel 1, Frame 94 (emphasis added).

and organizations campaigned against antisuffrage candidates well before the ratification of the Nineteenth Amendment. Finally, suffrage documents reveal that, although women's organizations rather than party organizations did indeed initiate the mass mobilization of women, that mobilization was exclusively in the service of attaining suffrage. No procedures existed within suffrage organizations to facilitate the development or pursuit of a broader legislative agenda during the presuffrage years, despite the clear interest of suffrage elites in that broader agenda.

Postsuffrage documents reveal that upon the attainment of suffrage, former suffrage elites did in fact begin to discuss pursuing the distinct legislative interests of women. There is simply no question but that the postsuffrage NLWV and its state affiliates were created to develop and pursue a legislative agenda that promoted women's interests as a group. Only later did league leaders abandon that organizational mission. Postsuffrage records also reveal the New York State major party organizations discussing the mobilization of women as a distinct group and creating organizations to implement that mobilization.

Postsuffrage documents also reveal that the electoral mobilization of women in support of or against candidates for office in order to further that legislative program for women was in fact a central goal of the newly created NLWV and its state affiliates. The NLWV and the New York State LWV even attempted such mobilization in 1920.

Finally, postsuffrage documents reveal that the New York State parties were able to begin the electoral mobilization of women much earlier than were the NLWV or the state LWV. While the parties in New York State created women's organizations in early 1918 and immediately began campaigns of mobilization among women, the state LWV at that point was still awaiting the organizational transformation of the NLWV, which would permit it to begin the mobilization of women for electoral contests. The NLWV and the state LWV would not begin the electoral mobilization of women until the fall of 1920.

The next chapter extends our testing of these stories to the national level of party competition and through the 1920s. It also goes beyond the documentation of elites' beliefs and actions, analyzing the limited evidence available on women's and men's electoral behavior.

4

The National Race to Mobilize Women, 1917–1932

By the end of 1920, the National League of Women Voters had privately and provisionally repealed its candidate endorsement policy. The evidence discussed in the preceding chapter was not particularly consistent with existing stories about why this decision might have been made by league elites. That evidence appeared to be more consistent with the hypotheses discussed in Chapter 2. But the evidence itself is rather thin. Elite beliefs and behavior are relatively well documented; mass beliefs and behavior are not. Organizational forms can easily be recovered from the historical record; the interaction between organizations and their constituencies cannot.

Granted, if the hypotheses discussed in Chapter 2 do not explain the chain of events related in the previous chapter, then those events remain largely unexplained. But it would be reassuring to have more evidence either in support of the account presented in Chapter 2 or in direct contradiction of that account. In particular, it would be helpful to find direct evidence of mass beliefs and behavior to support the evidence found in the records left by party and suffrage elites.

One way to amass more evidence is to extend the scope of investigation of elite records beyond New York State and over time. The dependent variable remains the same, namely the status of the national league's endorsement policy. That policy, as will be documented in this chapter, remained suspended until 1923, when a more permanent prohibition on candidate endorsements was enacted by league elites. Despite later reconsiderations of this prohibition, the prohibition would remain in force throughout the 1920s. Why did league elites continue to maintain their provisional repeal of the league's endorsement policy throughout this period?

As in the preceding chapter, competing stories seek to account for the league's lack of electoral activity: an account about league elites' belief in the lack of any relevant distinctions between men and women, an account about a suffrage ideology of "nonpartisanship" constraining league elites from participating in partisan electoral contests, and an account about the competitive disadvantages incurred by the league as a result of its organizational adaptation to disfranchisement. And as in the preceding chapter, we can search the existing historical record of party and suffrage elites' beliefs and actions in order to test these stories, broadening our search to the national level and over time.

Specifically, the hypotheses we can test in this chapter are the following:

1a. If the supposition about suffrage elites' belief in gender "sameness" is correct, either as a matter of ideology or as a matter of their perceptions about reality, then throughout the 1920s but *particularly* after 1923 we would expect to see neither a clear record of lobbying activity by the league on behalf of women as a group nor league elites declaring a belief in the existence of women as a distinct electoral group. If league elites' actions or statements do appear to reflect a belief in women as a distinctive electoral group, particularly after 1923, then this explanatory account is undermined.

1b. If the supposition about suffrage elites' belief in gender "sameness" is correct, then throughout the 1920s but *particularly* after 1923 we would also not expect to see the national parties treating women as a distinct group. If national party elites' actions or statements do appear to reflect a belief in women as a distinctive electoral group, particularly after 1923, then this explanatory account is undermined.

2. If the supposition about a suffrage ideology of nonpartisanship is correct, then we would expect to see a strong prohibition against candidate endorsements made by league elites as women entered the electorate. If any change occurred in this policy, we would expect that change to be in the direction of a weakening of the prohibition as women lost the ideological distinctiveness associated with disfranchisement. If change occurs in the opposite direction, for example if the league began by sanctioning candidate endorsements and only gradually moved away from such a policy, then this account is undermined.

3a. If the supposition about competitive disadvantages is correct, then we would expect to see national major party elites acting upon information about the mobilization potential of female voters *before* similar actions by suffrage organizations. If the suffrage organizations were able to commence the electoral mobilization of women before the national parties, then the competitive disadvantages account is undermined.

105

3b. If the supposition about competitive disadvantages is correct, then we would also expect to see investments by party elites in the electoral mobilization of women actually paying off over time. That is, the party organizations should have been reaping the rewards of increasing returns from the coordination of female voters, unhampered by competition from independent women's organizations.

This last hypothesis bears further discussion. There are two different ways to test this hypothesis: one is to look at party elites' *beliefs* about the behavior of female voters, another is to look at the actual behavior of female voters. With respect to party elites' beliefs, to the extent that elites in the dominant national party recorded any opinions as to the electoral behavior of women, these opinions should reflect an *increasing* satisfaction with the results of mobilization efforts among women. If national Republican elites rather expressed decreasing satisfaction with the electoral mobilization of women, then the account about competitive advantages is undermined.

Elite records provide us with some indirect information about the beliefs and actions of the mass of female voters. In a competitive electoral environment, we would not expect electoral elites to be consistently wrong over time about voters' beliefs and likely actions. But the argument made in Chapter 2 rests on very specific assumptions about voters' utility functions. It would be nice to have a direct test to see whether those assumptions are correct. But reliable survey data do not exist for this period, nor were ballots recorded separately by sex.

Fortunately for the researcher, certain localities, outside of New York State, did record partisan registration data separately by sex. While they are not the ideal data with which to test our arguments, we can ask more specific questions of these data to see whether they are consistent with our hypotheses. In particular, the account discussed in Chapter 2 predicts that female registration behavior should be unique in the following way. Potential female voters, like potential male voters, would have been likely to compare the utility offered them by competing electoral organizations by looking primarily at the number of other individuals in their communities who would respond favorably to their affiliation with a particular organization. For both male and female voters, if one party held a significant numerical advantage over its local competitor, that dominant party could in most cases offer more utility to potential voters.

But even the dominant party would have faced competition from more specialized occupational and demographic organizations for *male* voters. Locally dominant parties would have faced no such competition from women's organizations specifically for *women's* votes. If, then, our account about voters' utility functions is correct, then we would expect

106

to see a stronger bias toward the locally dominant party demonstrated by registering women, relative to that of men, in any given geographical area. If we in fact do see this, across different localities, then our hypothesis about the causal mechanism generating competitive advantages for the parties is lent additional support.

THE NLWV, THE NATIONAL PARTIES, AND GENDER "SAMENESS"

The NLWV, 1920–1930

The supposition of gender "sameness" predicts that after the attainment of woman suffrage, NLWV elites would not continue to treat women as a distinct group, either because they did not believe that women in fact shared interests, beliefs, and/or norms distinguishable from those of men, or because they did not want to encourage the maintenance of such distinct interests, beliefs, and/or norms. But the history of the NLWV in the 1920s reveals quite a different story. Specifically, throughout the 1920s league elites continued to develop that part of the league's organizational mission that envisioned the league as representing the policy preferences of women. And the records of the league's lobbying activity contained in league papers, Republican administration documents, and newspaper accounts reveal no diminution of league efforts after 1923. Indeed, if anything, league lobbying efforts were particularly intense during the Hoover administration, as league elites sought to save the Sheppard-Towner maternal and infant health bill from expiration. Moreover, throughout the 1920s, league elites on several occasions directly expressed the belief that women constituted a distinct electoral group with distinguishable policy preferences.

A brief history of league activity during the 1920s will document these arguments. In 1920 the league presented the national conventions of both major political parties with a "Woman's Platform" of legislative demands; the league also took the lead in forming the Women's Joint Congressional Committee (WJCC) in November 1920, composed of the major women's organizations in the country and designed to help the league's efforts to pass congressional legislation benefiting women as a group.[1] Between 1920 and 1924 extensive documentation exists of both league and WJCC efforts to lobby executive and legislative elites in support of measures believed by women's leaders to be favored primarily by women.[2]

---

[1]"Woman's Platform Filed," *NYT*, May 11, 1920, p. 3; "Women Organize Committee to Forward Bills in Congress," *NYT*, November 23, 1920, p. 1.

[2]Press Release, NLWV, July 5, 1920, Warren G. Harding Papers, microfilm edition,

Votes without Leverage

In addition to the indirect evidence afforded by the league's lobbying activity, direct evidence exists that league elites believed women to constitute a distinctive electoral group with policy preferences. In an interview conducted at the Republican National Convention in June 1920, league official Marie Edwards had the following to say about the league's "Woman's Platform":

We have here certain planks that we think women can appreciate the need for much more quickly than men. As women we are urging them. . . . we remind [party elites] that the great mass of women voters are unaffiliated as yet, and we try to make them understand that they are not going to affiliate blindly. . . . We shall present our planks to the Democrats through Democratic women and to Republicans through Republican women, and we shall remind each party that if it doesn't incorporate them and the other does, they may furnish a very strong talking point for that other party's campaign orators, when it comes to persuading women.[3]

Ohio Historical Society, Columbus, Ohio, Reel 76, Frame 261; Papers of the National League of Women Voters, 1918–1974 (Frederick, Md.: University Publications of America, 1985), Pt. II, Reel 1, Frame 58; Papers of the National League of Women Voters, Pt. II, Reel 1, Frame 158; Katherine Ludington to Warren G. Harding, July 21, 1920, Warren G. Harding Papers, Reel 36, Frame 151; "Cox and Leaders Plan Hot Finish," *NYT*, October 5, 1920, p. 2; Warren G. Harding Papers, Reel 106, Frames 693–1060; Women's Committee on Sheppard-Towner bill to Warren G. Harding, March 5, 1921, Warren G. Harding Papers, Reel 179, Frame 314; "Summons Women to War on Bossism," *NYT*, April 13, 1921, p. 9; "Will Press Harding for Anti-War Move," *NYT*, April 15, 1921, p. 16; NLWV Resolutions, adopted April 15 and July 22, 1921, in Warren G. Harding Papers, Reel 192, Frames 889–890; *NYT*, August 18, 1921, p. 4, "Women Stand by Primary," *NYT*, April 17, 1921, p. 23; Ann Webster to General Sawyer, September 7, 1921, Warren G. Harding Papers, Reel 211, Frame 334; William F. Snow to General Sawyer, September 6, 1921, Warren G. Harding Papers, Reel 211, Frame 335; "Summons Women to War on Bossism," *NYT*, April 13, 1921, p. 9; *NYT*, June 19, 1921, II p. 10; Ann Webster et al. to Warren G. Harding, January 17, 1922, Warren G. Harding Papers, Reel 211, Frame 337; Ann Webster to Warren G. Harding, February 9, 1922, Warren G. Harding Papers, Reel 211, Frames 341–342; Maud Wood Park to Warren G. Harding, September 28, 1922, Warren G. Harding Papers, Reel 192, Frame 938; Papers of the National League of Women Voters, Pt. II, Reel 4, Frame 432; Harriet Taylor Upton to Calvin Coolidge, October 9, 1923, Calvin Coolidge Papers, microfilm edition, U.S. Library of Congress, Washington, D.C., Reel 136, File 538; "Women Voters for World Court Union," *NYT*, October 23, 1923, p. 8; Mina Kerr to C. Bascom Slemp, November 22, 1923, Calvin Coolidge Papers, Reel 100, File 202; Belle Sherwin to Calvin Coolidge, November 26, 1923, Calvin Coolidge Papers, Reel 61, File 79–B; Belle Sherwin et al. to Calvin Coolidge, December 12, 1923, Calvin Coolidge Papers, Reel 61, File 79–B; Charles W. Holman, "What Women Are Asking of Congress," *Farmer's Wife* (October 1923), p. 142, in Calvin Coolidge Papers, Reel 121, File 395.

[3]"Women Organize to Press Demands," *NYT*, June 7, 1920, p. 6.

The following year the NLWV president, Maud Wood Park, claimed that the league's policy positions were representative of "the woman's point of view," which in turn was related to women's "special responsibility for human life."[4] In a speech to the 1921 NLWV convention, Park elaborated on this "woman's point of view" and its relationship to the role of the league:

The great majority of women earnestly desire such things as proper care and well rounded education for all children, the safeguarding of girls in industry, the promotion of social hygiene, the removal of civil and legal discriminations on the ground of sex. It is therefore well for them and well for the community that women of all parties have an opportunity to come together in an organization devoted solely to the interests of women as voters and there take counsel together for the accomplishment of their common aims, which are far more likely to be attained if a program is outlined by an inclusive group of women than they would be if left solely to the initiative of political parties.[5]

At their 1922 convention league delegates again heard from President Park an address on women's distinctive legislative viewpoint as an explanation of why the league should remain a league of *women* voters instead of becoming simply a league of voters.[6] The following year Park once again spoke publicly about the role of the league in advocating measures of special interest to "women, with their special knowledge of problems of maternity and the home."[7]

In 1924 the league again presented a "Woman's Platform" to the major party conventions;[8] league lobbying activity in support of "women's" bills between 1924 and 1928 is also again well documented.[9]

Direct evidence also exists that league elites continued to consider women to be a distinctive electoral group even after the 1924 elections. For example, in 1925 anniversary celebrations were held by the league in recognition of the attainment of constitutional female suffrage five years previously. Carrie Chapman Catt had originally suggested that

[4]*NYT*, August 18, 1921, p. 4.
[5]Papers of the National League of Women Voters, Pt. II, Reel 1, Frame 275.
[6]Ibid., Reel 2, Frames 459–460.
[7]"Discuss Woman Voter," *NYT*, January 31, 1923, p. 5.
[8]C. Bascom Slemp to Laura Morgan, January 28, 1924, Calvin Coolidge Papers, Reel 61, File 79–B; "Dry Action Divides the Women Voters," *NYT*, April 29, 1924, p. 21; "Women Will Press for World Court," *NYT*, May 26, 1924, p. 3.
[9]"Women Working for New Laws," *NYT*, November 29, 1925, IX p. 8; "Women Progress under Suffrage," *NYT*, August 22, 1926, VIII p. 10; "Women Put Issues to Candidates," *NYT*, September 26, 1926, p. 2; "Women Will Fight for Direct Primary," *NYT*, July 8, 1927, p. 2; "Mrs. Catt Asks War on Spoils System," *NYT*, October 5, 1927, p. 12.

after five years women would no longer need the league to push for measures of special interest to women, that those measures would by then largely have been passed. But five years into woman suffrage, no league elites were prepared to disband the organization. Mary Garrett Hay told the *Times* that the league was still necessary to ensure that women's interests were voiced in the policy process: "We should not give up the responsibility as women of standing together whenever the principle of the rights of women is at stake. We should continue to protest when discriminations are visited on women. We won the vote by hard work, so let us now stand together in winning our rightful place in church, schools, business and politics."[10] Carrie Chapman Catt agreed, noting that she could not say that the policy and candidate preferences of women were being given appropriate consideration by political elites: "Most politicians were reluctant converts to woman suffrage and returned to their former attitude of resistance. Granting the vote did not mean to many an old time party leader that women would have in consequence a say about nominations, party policies or platforms, and he 'stands pat' to see that they confine their political liberty to voting the ticket and platform which has been picked out by a few of the party elect in a hotel bedroom. This is no more acceptable to the woman of spirit and intelligence than it is to the man similarly equipped."[11]

In 1928 delegates to the league's (now biennial) convention again developed a women's platform of legislative demands to be presented to those in charge of writing the parties' platforms. Before announcement of the platform planks, NLWV President Belle Sherwin reiterated the league's role in pushing the parties to consider the legislative preferences of women growing out of their distinctive societal role: "Women are adamant where issues touch the home and the child. There is no compromise, never a backward step."[12]

During the Hoover administration, those league officials responsible for the organization's lobbying activity in Washington were primarily consumed with securing a reauthorization for the Sheppard-Towner program in maternal and infant health. The documentation of this (ultimately failed) effort is quite extensive, and reveals a league certainly no less interested in securing this policy for women than the league of 1921.[13]

---

[10]"Women Celebrate Their Suffrage Day," *NYT*, August 27, 1925, p. 3.
[11]Ibid.
[12]"Says Women Teach Men New Politics," *NYT*, April 30, 1928, p. 20; "5 Planks Offered by Women's League," *NYT*, May 28, 1928, p. 4.
[13]Belle Sherwin to Herbert Hoover, August 15, 1929; "Asks Hoover Support for Maternity Bill," *NYT*, September 18, 1929, p. 14; Belle Sherwin to Herbert Hoover, December 10, 1929; "Fights New Infancy Bill," *NYT*, February 23, 1930, p. 17;

Also during the Hoover administration, league elites continued to directly express their belief that women constituted a distinct electoral group. For example, in 1929 President Sherwin wrote Hoover that "there is no question but what this measure [Sheppard-Towner] is the one of greatest interest to women all over the country. They are keenly aware of its possibilities, and will be deeply distressed if federal assistance is withdrawn and the fine programs under way are halted." Sherwin went on to ask Hoover to endorse Sheppard-Towner's reauthorization legislation in his first message to Congress, claiming that, "There is no recommendation which the President elect could make to the Congress which would be more enthusiastically supported by a great body of citizens. The enactment and continuance of maternity and infancy legislation is naturally of special interest to women citizens who regard the Children's Bureau as their particular stake in government."[14] The following year, league representative Caroline Slade publicly declared that women had "first used the vote for what they considered most important – the problems concerning maternity and infancy," and argued that repeal of the program would represent a significant setback for female voters.[15]

The National Parties, 1917–1928

NLWV elites clearly seemed to believe that women constituted a distinct electoral group, sharing interests, beliefs, and norms distinguishable

Caroline Slade to Herbert Hoover, April 26, 1930; Caroline Slade to Walter H. Newton, May 1, 1930; "Women Voters Hit Charge of Futility," *NYT*, May 1, 1930, p. 32. Also representatives of thirteen member organizations of the WJCC to Herbert Hoover, June 11, 1930; Lawrence Richey to Ray Lyman Wilbur, June 14, 1930, enclosing telegram from Caroline Slade; Mrs. Roscoe Anderson (NLWV official) to Herbert Hoover, June 18, 1930; Caroline Slade to Herbert Hoover, January 19, 1931; Caroline Slade to Herbert Hoover, February 26, 1931; representatives of thirteen member organizations of the WJCC to Herbert Hoover, March 2, 1931; representatives of thirteen member organizations of the WJCC to Theodore Joslin, November 21, 1931; Belle Sherwin to Herbert Hoover, February 29, 1932, Presidential Subject Papers, Box 370; Clare H. Treadway to Herbert Hoover, February 25, 1930; Gertrude Ely to Herbert Hoover, March 17, 1930; Harriet Taylor Upton to Walter Newton, April 8, 1930; Caroline Slade to Herbert Hoover, March 24, 1930, enclosing draft bill, Presidential Subject Papers, Box 195; Belle Sherwin to Herbert Hoover, December 10, 1929, Presidential Subject Papers, Box 178; Martha Van Rensselaer to Lawrence Ritchie, September 11, 1930, Presidential Subject Papers, Box 97; Herbert Hoover Papers, Herbert Hoover Presidential Library, West Branch, Iowa.

[14] Belle Sherwin memorandum, January 28, 1929, enclosed in Irvine L. Lenroot to Herbert Hoover, February 4, 1929, Campaign and Transition Papers, Box 43, Herbert Hoover Papers.

[15] "Women Voters Ask Arms Cut Action," *NYT*, April 30, 1930, p. 6; "Vote Full Support to Arms Reduction," *NYT*, May 3, 1930, p. 8.

from those of men. Our inference to this conclusion from the limited evidence available is strengthened, however, if it can be shown that other electoral elites shared this belief. Specifically, did national party elites appear to think about women as a distinct electoral group? The easiest way to answer this question is to consider the organizations created by those elites to respond to the enfranchisement of women, evidence about which is readily available from newspaper accounts and the records of the parties themselves (more extensive records are available for the Republican Party, as the Republicans held the presidency during the 1920s and thus many party documents were preserved in those presidents' papers). Those organizations were distinct in their personnel, being staffed exclusively by women, in their organizational mission, namely the electoral mobilization of women (and only women), and in the means which they used to accomplish that task, namely campaign appeals explicitly designed to tap an assumed norm of gender identification.

The first to act in response to impending female enfranchisement were the Democrats, whose national committee in late 1917 created a women's version of the DNC, staffed by appointed female members from the fifteen full suffrage states.[16] In January 1918 the executive committee of the Republican National Committee (RNC) likewise recommended the creation of a "Republican Women's National Executive Committee," which was appointed the following September.[17]

These national women's party committees formulated plans for national partisan organizations of women, in every state down to the precinct, and presented them to the national committees in early 1919. The Republican plan, ratified by the national committee on January 10, 1919, read as follows:

[16]"Republicans Plan to Enlist Women," *NYT*, January 23, 1918, p. 10; "Democrats Choose Mrs. J. S. Crosby," *NYT*, February 28, 1918, p. 5. A nationally oriented Woman's Democratic Club already existed, as did a later coalition of clubs, the Women's National Democratic League, incorporated in 1912. The DNC had also created a small subcommitee known as the "Women's Bureau" shortly after the 1916 presidential campaign, a move that grew out of the "Women's Campaign Committee," which had operated during that campaign. *TWC*, January 5, 1918, p. 108.

[17]"Republicans Plan to Enlist Women," p. 10; "Adams Drops Out, Hays Elected," *NYT*, February 14, 1918, p. 3; "Report of Republican Women's National Executive Committee, September 3, 1918–June 8, 1920," Warren G. Harding Papers, Reel 54, Frames 978–983. The Republican Party had previously sanctioned the formation of the National Woman's Republican Association in 1888; this organization campaigned for the party during presidential election years. The Republicans had also established a "Women's Bureau" as a subcommittee of the Republican National Committee in 1916. Melanie Gustafson, "Partisan Women: Gender, Politics, and the Progressive Party of 1912" (Ph.D. dissertation, New York University, 1993), pp. 2, 156, 164, 354, 376.

"The Chairman of each State Central Committee shall appoint in consultation with the Woman's National Executive Committee, a State Executive Committee of women numbering from five to fifteen members to act with the State Central Committee. The Woman's State Executive Committee shall arrange the appointment of sub-chairmen in each of the political units throughout the state in consultation with the chairmen of the regular organizations within those units. The local chairmen in turn shall see to the selection of a leader of the women in each precinct or election district." This plan was adopted unanimously by the Committee and immediately a printed copy of it, together with a letter of explanation, was sent to each member of the Republican National Committee and to each State Chairman.[18]

The precinct leaders in turn were later asked to draft "the minimum of five and the maximum of fifteen volunteer women who will assist us in the campaign."[19] The Republican National Committee also sent out regional field organizers to help states and congressional districts set up these women's organizations.[20]

The Democratic plan, adopted by the national committee in February of 1919, was remarkably similar. The newspaper account of the plan read as follows:

A plan for an Associate National Committee of Women . . . was adopted. Members of this auxiliary committee are to be appointed by the Chairman of the National Committee on Nominations or by the committeemen of the respective States until some other method is adopted. The plan also contemplates the election or appointment of a woman as Vice Chairman of every State and county committee, and in each Congressional district, and the selection of committeewomen in each State Senatorial district, town, ward, or precinct, as associates of the male officials in those subdivisions.[21]

By May 1919, a conference of state women leaders held in Washington by the Republican Party was attended by women from all states except Mississippi and Texas, demonstrating that state organizations of women were at least well under way only a few months after the Republican National Committee's directive.[22] By June 1920, the Republican Women's National Executive Committee could report that

[18]"Report of Republican Women's National Executive Committee," pp. 3–4; "Republicans Urge Woman's Suffrage," *NYT*, January 11, 1919, p. 3.
[19]Ruth Hanna McCormick and Christine Bradley South to Warren G. Harding, August 1920, Warren G. Harding Papers, Reel 39, Frame 508.
[20]"Report of Republican Women's National Executive Committee," p. 10.
[21]"Elects Cummings Party Chairman," *NYT*, February 27, 1919, p. 8.
[22]"Republican Women Settle Working Plans," *NYT*, May 24, 1919, p. 3.

thirty-eight states had at least partially completed women's state organizations, with the exceptions being some states in the South and in New England. The committee reported further that in all of the thirty-eight states

a woman acting as Associate Chairman, Vice-Chairman of the State Central Committee or representing a State Executive Committee of women appointed for this purpose, is directly responsible and devoting all of her time to this work. . . . in nearly all of the above thirty-eight states a representative of our committee has made a thorough canvass of the active women in the state and aided the State Chairman in selecting the right woman. . . . in 1,700 Counties and in over 30,000 precincts we now have a woman as well as a man leader on the job. Most of these thirty-eight states are straining every effort to have a one hundred per cent county and precinct organization before the National Convention convenes.[23]

The Democrats also made speedy headway in initiating state organizations of women, holding like the Republicans a national conference of state women leaders in May 1919, which was attended by women leaders from every suffrage state.[24] The Democratic National Committee also appointed female vice chairmen to all of its campaign committees active in congressional elections,[25] took steps in September 1919 to double its executive committee's membership from seventeen to thirty-four, with the new members appointed all to be women, and at the same time created a special subcommittee to work on the organization of women for the 1920 elections.[26]

Not only the permanent party organizations but also the campaign organizations for potential presidential nominees set up women's divisions prior to the national conventions in June 1920.[27] And the construction of women's organizations by the national parties continued during and after their national conventions. In June 1920 the Republican National Convention increased the membership of the Republican National Executive Committee from ten to fifteen members, with seven of the newly enlarged committee to be female appointees.[28] Shortly thereafter

[23]"Report of Republican Women's National Executive Committee," p. 10.

[24]"Sees Third Run for Wilson If League Fails," *NYT*, May 29, 1919, p. 1; "Ranks Wilson with Lincoln," *NYT*, May 30, 1919, p. 3; Felice D. Gordon, *After Winning: The Legacy of the New Jersey Suffragists, 1920–1947* (New Brunswick, N.J.: Rutgers University Press, 1986), pp. 80–81.

[25]"Will Elect Women Vice Chairmen," *NYT*, May 25, 1919, p. 3.

[26]"Democrats Plan for Women's Vote," *NYT*, September 28, 1919, p. 7.

[27]"Women Loom Large in Nation's Politics," *NYT*, March 28, 1920, II p. 1.

[28]"Recommend Putting Women on the Executive Committee," *NYT*, June 9, 1920, p. 2.

the Republican presidential nominee sent letters to the party's state chairmen and national committeemen requesting them to accelerate the process of creating women's organizations in the states.[29] Likewise, at the Democratic National Convention the DNC voted to double its membership by adding one woman from each state, "the women to be elected this year by the delegates to the present convention and thereafter in the same manner as the men."[30] The Women's Bureau was retained by the convention as a subcommittee of the national committee.[31]

These women's organizations were, as the foregoing makes clear, distinct in their personnel from the men's party organizations. Only women staffed the women's organizations and only men staffed the men's organizations. The women's organizations also had a clearly defined directive, namely to mobilize women; female party elites had no authority to mobilize men. Throughout the 1920 presidential campaign, for example, every campaign plan announced by the women's division of the national Republican organization was directed solely at potential female voters. Whether through officially sanctioned women's Republican club meetings,[32] women's "parlor meetings" or "Home and Harding" meetings,[33] specially trained female campaign speakers,[34] or publicity specifically written for and distributed exclusively to women,[35] the Republican campaign among women was directed at appealing to their norm of distinctiveness from men. The reverse also held true: the male party committees continued to retain the task of mobilizing men, and men only.

The one exception to the tendency of Republican Party elites to lump all women together into a distinctive group is a classic example of the

---

[29]See, e.g., Warren G. Harding to Allan B. Jaynes, Republican National Committeeman from Arizona, and Albert B. Sames, Chairman of Arizona Republican State Committee, August 25, 1920, Warren G. Harding Papers, Reel 33, Frames 575, 646.

[30]"Committee Votes for Full Hearing," *NYT*, June 26, 1920, p. 2; "Women Prominent in Day's Session," *NYT*, June 30, 1920, p. 2.

[31]"To Keep Women's Bureau," *NYT*, July 5, 1920, p. 2.

[32]"Republican Women Settle Working Plans," *NYT*, May 24, 1919, p. 3.

[33]"Plan 'Parlor Meetings,'" *NYT*, September 22, 1920, p. 15; "G.O.P. Women Plan Parlor Meetings," *NYT*, September 26, II p. 20.

[34]"Women to Go on the Stump," *NYT*, August 11, 1920, p. 4.

[35]McCormick and South to Harding; "'Woman Republican' Bows," *NYT*, August 27, 1920, p. 14; "Thinking Women Want Republican Success," in *TWC*, October 23, 1920, p. 571; "Her Whims as Voter," *NYT*, October 1, 1922, VIII p. 3; Florence Riddick Boys, Woman's Publicity Editor, Republican National Committee, to George Christian, October 12, 1922, Warren G. Harding Papers, Reel 195, Frame 64; "Why Women Should Vote for Harding and Coolidge," by Herbert Hoover, noted in "How to Win a Vote for Hoover," Women's Division of the Republican National Committee, 1928, Nathan William MacChesney Papers, Box 12, Herbert Hoover Library, West Branch, Iowa.

exception that demonstrates the rule. While gender was apparently considered to be a strong norm of group identification by party elites, race was considered an even stronger norm during this period. African American women were therefore not considered to be the jurisdiction of the party's women's division. Like the segregation of white women in the women's division, this segregation of African American women in a different mobilization operation made electoral sense: since most women's organizations were themselves segregated at the time, the network of connections that would allow white women easily to mobilize other white women did not necessarily exist in the case of African American women. The primary organizational avenues used by party elites to mobilize African American women were thus predominantly African American churches and community organizations.[36]

The parties' organizations for white women, however, appear to reveal a conviction held by major party elites that women were a distinct group that could not be mobilized by male partisan elites. Other organizational forms to facilitate the mobilization of women could have been chosen by elites within the two major parties, ones that did not so completely segregate the sexes, or that were not so comprehensive at every level of party organization. But they were not chosen, and that decision is indicative of the strength of party elites' belief in the existence of a norm of gender identification.

More direct evidence about such beliefs can be found in the public speeches and private correspondence of party elites during the 1920 campaign. For example, upon ratification of the woman suffrage amendment to the Constitution, Republican presidential nominee Warren G. Harding wrote a letter to Republican national committeemen and state committee chairmen in which he referred to women as a "new element in the electorate," surmised that most women would not have a party affiliation, and opined that "the encouragement, and the treatment accorded them will determine the allegiance of many."[37]

The women who were selected to staff the Republican Party's women's organization were somewhat more blunt. The former suffrage leader appointed by nominee Harding to run the national organization, Harriet Taylor Upton, told Harding explicitly that she understood "the

[36]Secretary to George H. Clark, Chairman, Republican State Advisory Committee, July 21, 1920, Warren G. Harding Papers, Reel 32, Frames 256–257; J. E. Johnson to Warren G. Harding, August 4, 1920, ibid., Reel 76, Frame 440; Secretary to George H. Clark, August 24, 1920, ibid., Reel 32, Frame 365; Mary Church Terrell to Warren G. Harding, October 30, 1920, ibid., Reel 57, Frame 1072.

[37]Warren G. Harding to Albert M. Sames, Chairman, Republican State Committee, Douglas, Arizona, August 25, 1920, ibid., Reel 33, Frame 646.

woman feeling," the "woman situation," and "the woman logic" much better than any man.[38] Ruth Hanna McCormick and Christine Bradley South, both prominent women active in the national Republican organization, also warned Harding that men oftentimes could not properly make effective appeals to women's norm of group identification, as they lacked good knowledge of "woman's psychology."[39] In responding to McCormick and South, Harding stated that, "I do not feel qualified to criticize your plans, which appear to me to be admirable. You know very much more about this matter than I do, and especially of the psychology involved."[40]

Party correspondence and campaign literature also reveal more about what party elites thought about the *content* of this norm of gender identification. While appeals made to men were targeted to appeal to various ethnic groups, occupations, sections, and so on, appeals to women were all couched in terms of women's domestic responsibilities. Home and children framed partisan appeals to women; this was not the case for men.[41]

Harding himself referred several times to the domestic responsibilities of women in his campaign correspondence. In response to a Republican editor's query about "just what kind of publicity matter is being prepared for circulation among women voters," Harding asked the RNC for some material for women elaborating what the party had done "for the home and the women and children of the country. Undoubtedly there can be some very good matter gotten out on the matter of child labor, and the child labor bureau established, and other matters along this line, which will appeal to the interest of women."[42] A few days later, upon the occasion of the ratification of the federal suffrage amendment, Harding proclaimed his respect for "the voice of womanhood," which ex-

---

[38]Harriet Taylor Upton to Warren G. Harding, June 23, 1920, ibid., Reel 66, Frame 870.

[39]Ruth Hanna McCormick and Christine Bradley South to Warren G. Harding, August 1920, ibid., Reel 39, Frames 500–501.

[40]Ruth Hanna McCormick to Warren G. Harding, August 1920, ibid., Frame 495; Warren G. Harding to Ruth Hanna McCormick, August 6, 1920, ibid., Frame 494; McCormick and South to Harding, ibid., Frames 501–502.

[41]Historians have documented in many different contexts the domestic or "private sphere" content of women's norm of gender identification in the late nineteenth and early to mid-twentieth centuries. However, that these norms could be appealed to by the male-controlled parties for strategic purposes has not been documented in the scholarly literature.

[42]Gus Karger, Washington bureau of the *Cincinnati Times-Star*, to Warren G. Harding, August 12, 1920, Warren G. Harding Papers, Reel 76, Frame 515; Warren G. Harding to Will Hays, RNC Chairman, August 16, 1920, ibid., Reel 32, Frame 1367.

pressed women's "primary concern for home and family and health and education."[43]

The most publicized single appeal to women's domestic sentiments was made on "Social Justice Day," one in a series of "front porch" events staged at Harding's home in Marion, Ohio. The speech made by Harding on that day before five thousand invited female guests was intended to be the campaign's major appeal to women voters, as disclosed by the following letter from a campaign worker in Marion to the RNC's chief publicity officer in Chicago: "Enclosed herewith you will find a copy of Senator Harding's speech on Social Justice, to be released for the afternoon papers of Oct. 1st. . . . I wish to present the idea that this speech will have a very great publicity among women. It will help to attach them to the Republican party. It will be something which they will readily understand and which they can use in political discussion one with another. . . . I respectfully suggest that it may be advisable to print it in considerable numbers and give it as rapid circulation as possible."[44]

The content of the speech ranged over several issue areas, but the centerpiece of the speech was how the various issues all related to women's concern "principally with the American home." The most prominent of the domestic references was to women's distinctive reproductive capacities. Proclaiming that the extension of women's sphere "must forever be taken, without peril to the fulfillment of that most precious of all American possessions – America's motherhood," Harding tied together laws regarding women's civil rights with policies concerning maternity:

Who can suggest one of these tasks [of social justice] which can supersede in our hearts, or in the rank which foresight and wisdom will give, that of the protection of our maternity? The protection of the motherhood of America can not be accomplished until the State and the nation have enacted and, by their example, have enforced customs, which protect womanhood itself. I know full well that there are women who insist that women shall be treated upon the same basis that men are treated. They would have a right to take this position in their own behalf, but I insist, that all true Americans must insist, that no woman speaks for herself alone. She is the possessor of our future, and though she becomes engaged in the tasks and services of civilization, we must preserve to her, the right of wholesome maternity.[45]

[43]"Harding Welcomes Women to His Party," *NYT*, August 20, 1920, p. 3; Harding press release, August 19, 1920, Warren G. Harding Papers, Reel 78, Frame 878.

[44]Marion secretary to Captain Victor Heintz, Republican National Committee, September 28, 1920, Warren G. Harding Papers, Reel 38, Frame 1065.

[45]Text of Harding's Social Welfare Speech, October 1, 1920, ibid., Reel 239, Frame 779.

Harding closed by touching on the League of Nations, which he also tied into women's domestic concerns: "I know that the mothers and wives of America do not wish to give their sons and husbands for sacrifice at the call of an extra-constitutional body like the Council of the Paris league. I know that the mothers and wives of America will give them only at the call of their own hearts, and honor, and conscience."[46]

Harding had spoken of the League of Nations before, and indeed had been alerted early in the campaign by a Republican editor to the idea that women's "unanimous opposition to militarism or war" could be useful; Harding replied that "The information contained [in your letter] tallies pretty closely with information which has come to me from other sources."[47] Another Republican operative was more specific, outlining a proposed appeal to women that used the League of Nations as a focus: "the women will be quick to respond to an appeal to them to trust you to protect their sons and husbands from the damnable, and UnAmerican conscription to send our Boys to fight other peoples battles."[48] This helpful tip was in fact forwarded to the RNC by Harding's campaign. And throughout the fall, Harding made several speeches to women's organizations that used such an appeal to women as mothers and wives.[49]

Similarly, an important element of the Democrats' 1920 presidential campaign was the mobilization of women as a group. Female campaign speakers were organized and special advertisements were placed in women's magazines.[50] The Democrats also coordinated with the American Federation of Labor in a campaign to attract working women to the Democratic Party, while in New York, the party worked with the Catholic Church to mobilize immigrant women.[51]

The content of the appeals made by Democrats and their allies in organized labor to potential female voters was essentially similar to that of Republican appeals. Evident throughout the campaign was these

[46]Ibid.

[47]J. W. Faulkner, *Columbus Enquirer*, to Warren G. Harding, January 26, 1920, ibid., Reel 29, Frame 50; Warren G. Harding to J. W. Faulkner, January 31, 1920, ibid., Frame 49.

[48]Lewis T. Ginger, Esq., to Warren G. Harding, July 28, 1920, ibid., Reel 34, Frames 318–319.

[49]"Harding Pleads for Women's Vote," *NYT*, September 16, 1920, p. 3; text of Harding speech to the Women's Harding and Coolidge Club, New York City, September 15, 1920, Warren G. Harding Papers, Reel 78, Frames 1210–1213; "Says Women Will Decide," *NYT*, September 16, 1920, p. 3.

[50]"Women to Speak for Cox," *NYT*, June 29, 1920, p. 3; *TWC*, October 30, 1920, p. 601.

[51]"Labor to Campaign for Women's Votes," *NYT*, September 2, 1920, p. 5; "Miss Marbury Asks Priests to Aid Cox," *NYT*, October 10, 1920, p. 6; the full text of the letter is reproduced in Warren G. Harding Papers, Reel 52, Frame 88.

elites' belief that women shared a distinctively domestic perspective on policy questions to which appeals could be made. Thus the American Federation of Labor asked its local unions to train female speakers in making appeals to "the better home, the well-fed and happy child, the elimination of exploitation of child labor for profit."[52] The nominee Cox also made several references to the domestic sphere in his speeches to women, for example by suggesting a national conference of women to discuss issues affecting maternal and infant health.[53] Even the Democrats' appeal to working women was likewise predicated upon the assumption that women in the work force possessed a set of concerns distinct from that of working men, which could be made the basis of a major campaign.[54]

The League of Nations was also seen by the Democrats as a crucial aspect of the party's appeal to women, again because of its tie-in to women's domestic concerns, although the Democrats were supportive of the league. In the speech regarded as opening the Democratic Party's campaign for women's votes, "Mrs. [Elizabeth] Bass left no doubt in the minds of her hearers that, so far as she and the women she represented were concerned, the League of Nations was the vital issue in the campaign. She regarded it as a movement to relieve the world of war and secure arbitration of international problems in place of an appeal to arms."[55] Candidate Cox went so far as to proclaim upon the ratification of the federal suffrage amendment that "The civilization of the world is saved. The mothers of America will stay the hands of war and repudiate those who traffic with a great principle."[56]

Cox went on to make the league the keystone of his speeches to women's groups. Speaking in Wheeling, West Virginia, for example, the governor proclaimed "that the League of Nations was the attempt of President Wilson to keep faith with American mothers, from whom he called their boys in 1917 and 1918, some never to return."[57] A Republican newspaper's assessment of this tactic reflects the presumed distinctiveness of "the woman feeling": "We imagine that Governor Cox has looked over the field and has made up his mind that the women of the country can be influenced more by the League of Nations appeals to their emotional hatred of war than they can be influenced by any other

---

[52]"Labor to Campaign for Women's Votes," *NYT*, September 2, 1920, p. 5.

[53]"Harding Now Cries 'Kamerad,' Says Cox," *NYT*, October 17, 1920, p. 3.

[54]"Women Democrats Seek Labor Votes," *NYT*, May 27, 1920, p. 7.

[55]"8,000 Hear Mrs. Bass Speaking for League," *NYT*, August 6, 1920, p. 3.

[56]"Cox and Harding Hail the Victory for Suffrage," *NYT*, August 19, 1920, p. 1.

[57]"Governor Cox Should Try to Explain to Women Voters Why League Fails to Stop Current Wars," *San Francisco Examiner*, August 21, 1920, from Warren G. Harding Papers, Reel 34, Frame 940.

considerations. Perhaps so."[58] A Republican informant wrote Harding that similar speeches were being made by women across the country: "I have heard in the last two weeks a half dozen magnetic vigorous speeches on the League of Nations delivered on Chatauqua circuits. I have found on investigation that the Democratic organization has women out all over the country making the same appeals without in any way giving the impression that they are being backed by the Democratic Party."[59] And at a mass meeting of women in Cleveland, "Governor Cox made a direct appeal to mothers to support the League as the only positive proposal to put an end to war. He said that he was convinced that the women would turn the scales and assure the defeat of the forces endeavoring, for selfish purpose and partisan victory, to destroy the League. . . . 'Theirs [women's] was the greater suffering in war and theirs the greater understanding of the lesson of the war.' "[60]

Partisan efforts to mobilize women as a distinctive electoral group continued after the 1920 national elections. In the months after the Republican victory in the presidential election, the eight states that made up the eastern region in the Republican Party's women's organization adopted plans for "the political education of women, which is expected to reach every election district";[61] the New York State women's division initiated the development of a national women's Republican club;[62] and permanent women's headquarters were established in the building housing the Republican National Committee organization.[63] As Harriet Taylor Upton reported to the National League of Women Voters in the spring of 1921, male Republican elites continued to see women as a distinct phenomenon in electoral politics: "The thing that astonishes me most is how little men understand women politically. Men know women, socially, domestically and in a business way, but they seem to think that there is something not understandable about them when it comes to politics."[64]

For the 1922 congressional elections, the Republican national women's division sent female organizers into key states and coordinated a national mobilization of women.[65] New publicity material was written

[58]Ibid.

[59]Sherman Rogers, Outlook Company, to Warren G. Harding, August 23, 1920, Warren G. Harding Papers, Reel 56, Frames 1264–1265.

[60]"Harding Now Cries 'Kamerad,' Says Cox," *NYT*, October 17, 1920, p. 3.

[61]"Republican Women to Educate Voters," *NYT*, December 17, 1920, p. 24.

[62]"Seeks Women's Aid in Primary Change," *NYT*, January 21, 1921, p. 5.

[63]"Hays Makes Report on Harding Victory," *NYT*, March 4, 1921, p. 4.

[64]"Will Press Harding for Anti-War Move," *NYT*, April 15, 1921, p. 16.

[65]Harriet Taylor Upton to Warren G. Harding, July 8, 1921, Warren G. Harding Papers, Reel 194, Frame 1290; Harriet Taylor Upton to Warren G. Harding, July 16, 1921, ibid., Frames 1294–1295; Harriet Taylor Upton to Warren G. Harding,

specifically for women, including pamphlets entitled "The Woman, the Child and the Republican Party" and "Why the Republican Party Appeals to Women,"[66] as well as special articles for the "woman's page" of the *National Republican.*[67]

The Democrats also acted in anticipation of the 1922 elections, announcing in the spring of 1922 a nationwide drive to establish women's Democratic clubs, which would provide the social context for women's mobilization and which would also train female speakers and campaign workers. These clubs were not to be independent of the regular precinct organizations, but would be organized by female Democratic leaders using party resources. As articulated by Democratic leaders, the rationale for creating women's Democratic clubs in addition to the regular Democratic women's organizations was to further distinguish women's mobilization activities from those of men, thereby facilitating appeals to gender identity. In order to ensure national implementation of the plan, national women's Democratic leader Emily Newell Blair convened a conference of Democratic national committeewomen in Washington to receive instructions on the club system.[68]

After the 1922 elections, Blair arranged for a "National School of Democracy" for women during the interelection years, to consist of a series of three-day meetings held across the country to train interested women as organizers for the party's women's division.[69] Between January 1923 and April 1924, the school held over forty meetings, and also initiated a "correspondence course."[70] Blair also held a series of meetings in each of the seven party regions for state organization workers, and reported that each was attended by approximately one thousand women.[71]

As the 1924 campaign approached, the Democratic women's division announced plans for six thousand "Victory Clubs" of women across the country, in which they hoped to enroll a hundred thousand women as

September 20, 1921, ibid., Frames 1340–1343; Harriet Taylor Upton to Warren G. Harding, March 29, 1922, ibid., Frames 1473–1477.

[66]Enclosure in John T. Adams, RNC Chairman, to Warren G. Harding, September 14, 1922, ibid., Reel 195, Frame 34; Enclosure in Florence Riddick Boys, Woman's Publicity Editor, Republican National Committee, to George Christian, October 12, 1922, ibid., Frames 63–64.

[67]Florence Riddick Boys to George Christian, October 12, 1922, ibid., Frame 64.

[68]"To Train Women Speakers," *NYT*, April 9, 1922, p. 2.

[69]"Women Will Open School of Democracy," *NYT*, January 1, 1923, p. 17; "Women Democrats Drop Party Barrier," *NYT*, February 2, 1924, p. 2.

[70]"Using Plattsburg Idea to Reach Women Voters," *NYT*, March 16, 1924, IX p. 18.

[71]Ibid.

campaign workers in 1924. The plan of operation for these clubs was to coordinate topics of discussion for members across the states on "issues which make an especially strong appeal to women, subjects dealing with the welfare of the family and the home."[72] Speakers from the regular party organizations were to be sent out on trips to visit the clubs with literature to distribute among club members, and were asked to plan these tours with an eye to attracting as much publicity as possible.[73] As justified by Democratic Party elites, these clubs could bring previously nonpolitical women into contact with already registered Democratic women, away from the potentially countervailing influence of male family members.[74]

The Republican women's division was pursuing similar campaign strategies between 1922 and 1924. For example, in 1923 Harriet Taylor Upton wrote President Harding that he should be speaking at female-only meetings on a proposed campaign trip:

I think it is very important, when you start on your western trip, for you to plan for three or four meetings for women. I am strongly of the opinion that these meetings should be arranged in this office so that we would be able to get the official women to manage them and no one knows the women who are at the head of the political machine in the states as well as I know them. *We want to emphasize that these meetings are for women and conducted by women.* . . . As I say every day, and several times a day, the result in 1924 is going to depend upon women.[75]

Upton also undertook her own tour of the midwestern states, telling Harding that "the woman's work must be done now and not a year from now."[76]

After Harding's unexpected death in August 1923, the Republican women's organization retooled its publicity to reflect the new incumbent, Calvin Coolidge. For example, the women's division issued a pamphlet entitled " 'The Hope of the Nation – A Message to Women' by Calvin

[72]"To Enroll Democratic Women," *NYT*, November 18, 1923, p. 21.

[73]See, e.g., the description of the "Singing Teapot" tour in New York State in "Women to Tour in Teapot," *NYT*, October 18, 1924, p. 2.

[74]"For Husband Who Keeps Politics in His Own Name," *NYT*, November 2, 1924, VIII p. 4.

[75]Harriet Taylor Upton to Warren G. Harding, April 4, 1923, Warren G. Harding Papers, Reel 195, Frame 162 (emphasis added); Harriet Taylor Upton to George Christian, June 1923, ibid., Frames 215–216; Harriet Taylor Upton to George Christian, July 20, 1923, ibid., Frame 236.

[76]Harriet Taylor Upton to Warren G. Harding, April 16, 1923, ibid., Frame 167; also Harriet Taylor Upton to George B. Christian Jr., June 13, 1923, ibid., Frame 227.

Coolidge."[77] And Republican women's leaders began advocating the formation of Republican women's clubs "as the best way of solidly enlisting the women in the fight for the Republican candidates and programs."[78] At a meeting of auxiliary Republican national committeewomen in December 1923, Republican women's clubs were further discussed, along with ongoing efforts to train female campaign speakers and launch women's newsletters.[79]

The Republican efforts to form women's clubs in anticipation of the 1924 campaign reflected the continuing belief of that party's elites that women were best mobilized quite separately from men. As Mary Livermore of New York was quoted during the committeewomen's conference, "We women understand the psychology of the women of today. The men trust us to tell them what women in the party desire and what women outside the party want." Pauline Morton Sabin, the auxiliary national committeewoman from New York, spoke of an ambitious national canvass of potential female voters: "There will be no such thing as an apathetic woman's vote in the 1924 campaign."[80]

As had occurred in the spring of 1920, in the spring of 1924 newspaper reports appeared predicting the significance of an independent "woman vote" in the impending elections. Prominent women in both parties were quoted as saying that women did not follow the partisan opinions of their husbands but rather paid careful attention to the material provided them by the parties' women's organizations.[81] And both parties again sought to cash in on this gender solidarity presumed to exist among women by making electoral appeals specifically targeted at women and communicated through female-specific channels.

The Republicans used the occasion of their national convention in June 1924 to feature a well-publicized campaign specifically directed at women.[82] Following the convention, two women's headquarters for the Coolidge-Dawes campaign were established, one in Chicago and one in

[77]George B. Lockwood to George Clark, September 25, 1923, ibid., Reel 121, Frame 395.

[78]"G.O.P. Must Back Tax Cut Now or in 1924," *NYT*, November 28, 1923, p. 4.

[79]"Republican Women Plan Active Work," *NYT*, December 5, 1923, p. 1; the report of Harriet Taylor Upton in "Using Plattsburg Idea to Reach Women Voters" contains details on club organizations in several states, as well as speakers' schools and women's Republican magazines in Massachusetts, New Jersey, Pennsylvania, New York, Illinois, and Missouri.

[80]"46 to 7 for Coolidge in Party Committee as Session Opens," *NYT*, December 12, 1923, p. 3.

[81]"Even the Children Follow Mother in Choice of Politics," *NYT*, March 9, 1924, IX p. 3.

[82]"Mondell Is Chosen by the Republicans as Convention Head," *NYT*, June 4, 1924, p. 1.

New York. The women's campaign was to be run entirely separately but on parallel lines to that of the men's campaign, with separate women's Coolidge-Dawes clubs established in every state as complements to the men's Coolidge-Dawes clubs and separate women's speakers' and contributors' committees.[83]

Throughout the summer, the new leader of the national Republican women's organization spoke of the importance of the "women's vote" to the Republican campaign.[84] And as in the 1920 campaign, Republican campaign appeals to the "women's vote" were couched largely in terms of motherhood and home. Republican female leader Sally Aley Hert declared that women would vote "to preserve home and country,"[85] while the Republican national committeewoman from North Carolina reported that women across the states were "rallying around the Constitution and the home."[86] Pauline Sabin in New York told the press that women were "naturally more conservative than men" and that Coolidge would "owe his re-election to the votes of the women of America."[87] And Maude Wetmore, the national organizer of the women's Coolidge-Dawes clubs, informed the press in September that "the average woman is a housekeeper," and that housekeepers would vote for the Coolidge-Dawes ticket.[88]

President Coolidge himself declared that American mothers would vote for the party that put America first over international entanglements: "Surely the womanhood of our country, who have lavished upon the sons and daughters of the land such a wealth of affection, who watch over them in every crisis, from the cradle to the grave, with immeasurable devotion, will not hesitate to make sufficient sacrifice to preserve for themselves and those they love 'the last best hope of the world' – American institutions."[89]

Similarly, in January of 1924 the Democrats issued female-specific campaign materials lauding "Morality in Government": "We knew this was a subject of strong appeal to women, because as mothers they are strongly opposed to the dissipation of their children's inheritance by

[83]"Women Lay Plans for G.O.P. Campaign," *NYT*, June 28, 1924, p. 14; "Republican Women Open Headquarters," *NYT*, August 6, 1924, p. 2.

[84]"Republican Women Predict a Victory," *NYT*, August 13, 1924, p. 2; see also "Coolidge Is Pleased by Praise of Speech," *NYT*, August 16, 1924, p. 2; "Republicans Plan Labor Bureau Here," *NYT*, September 1, 1924, p. 3.

[85]"Says Women of the West Will Back Coolidge," *NYT*, September 24, 1924, p. 14.

[86]"New England Safe, Says Senator Keyes," *NYT*, September 26, 1924, p. 6.

[87]"A Big Woman Vote Seen by Mrs. Sabin," *NYT*, August 27, 1924, p. 8.

[88]"Reports Women Favoring Coolidge," *NYT*, September 14, 1924, II p. 3.

[89]"Coolidge Appeals to Women to Vote to Protect Nation," *NYT*, April 15, 1924, p. 1.

anti-conservationists in such deals as the Teapot Dome and other oil reserve leases."[90] The effect of the tariff on women's cost of living was to be a major topic of discussion for women's clubs in the spring of 1924, with a pamphlet entitled "The Tariff as a Tax on Women" published by the DNC for use at club meetings, and women from the Democratic organization ready to "tour the country with exhibits of clothing and foodstuffs, placarded with the tariff tolls on each."[91]

By June 1924, the Democratic Party's women's division could report approximately two thousand Democratic women's clubs organized throughout the country "to spread the news among the women voters of what the party proposes to do for the things in which women are interested."[92] Democratic Party elites appeared hopeful that these clubs could start a bandwagon effect among unattached potential female voters: "The clubs, while of Democratic formation, have been operated on such a scale as to invite attendance of the great independent woman vote, which is expected to be of vital importance in the election."[93]

Also like their Republican counterparts in 1924, Democratic elites created a national campaign organization for women parallel to but clearly distinguished from that for the men's campaign,[94] and comprising separate organizations to propagandize among specific groups of women, for example, among female trade unionists[95] or reform-minded progressive women.[96] Parallel campaign organizations had been in evidence even in the Democratic presidential primary, as female campaign workers for the prospective presidential nominees had conducted their own politicking among female delegates to the Democratic National Convention. Because female delegates to the convention were seen as the proper responsibility of female party elites, prenomination campaigning had proceeded along strict gender lines.[97]

The director of the 1924 Democratic women's campaign organization

---

[90]Emily Newell Blair, "Using Plattsburg Idea to Reach Women Voters."

[91]"Democrats to Stir Women on Tariff," *NYT*, March 24, 1924, p. 26.

[92]"Women's Clubs Active," *NYT*, June 23, 1924, p. 8.

[93]Ibid. See also "A New Political Club," *NYT*, August 29, 1924, p. 3, for details on the New York State women's Democratic clubs, and "Third Party Lags in West Virginia," *NYT*, October 15, 1924, p. 6, for details on the West Virginia "victory" clubs.

[94]"Women Named to Aid Davis in New York," *NYT*, September 7, 1924, p. 28.

[95]"Berry Aiding Davis, Attacks Gompers," *NYT*, October 13, 1924, p. 8.

[96]"Appeals to Women to Vote for Davis," *NYT*, November 1, 1924, p. 6.

[97]"McAdoo Men Yield New York to Smith," *NYT*, January 23, 1924, p. 21; "Votes of Women Sought for Smith," *NYT*, May 25, 1924, II p. 2; "Convention Roll Includes 500 Women," *NYT*, June 22, 1924, VIII p. 5: "The feminine convention machinery precisely parallels the men's"; "Women Take Lead to Get 'Dark Horse,'" *NYT*, June 28, 1924, p. 2.

described her job as "directing women's attention to issues which we believe are predominantly interesting to them."[98] Those issues reflected the domestic themes familiar from 1920, as expressed by the Democratic presidential nominee John Davis in his speeches to women:

I realize the intense and proper interest which the women of the United States feel in the education and the upbringing of their young who are their primal care by the law of nature. And I recognize the proper interest they take in welfare legislation that has for its purpose to give the infant an opportunity to develop and to the adult to be a better man or woman tomorrow than he is today.[99]

In September 1924 the Democratic National Committee commissioned a "survey" of potential female voters across the country and concluded that "a majority of them will support the national Democratic ticket."[100] According to Democratic National Chairman Clem Shaver, the survey inquiring after a host of issues related to women and children revealed "that the Democratic Party, as the party of new ideas and progress, appeals to women. . . . we find women are for Davis because they know the reactionary leadership in control of the Republican Party does not want to and will not enact progressive, liberal measures."[101]

Again in the 1926 elections both parties pursued female-specific campaign initiatives. Republican elites continued to view women primarily in terms of their domestic responsibilities, and to use those responsibilities as a way to mobilize female voters. Shortly after declaring that "women can never escape the responsibility of home and children,"[102] President Coolidge urged female Republican supporters to work to get other women registered and voting.[103] The *Times* then reported that the mobilization of previously nonvoting women would be the centerpiece of the party's campaign strategy for the 1926 congressional elections: "The plan has been worked out carefully and its advisability has been impressed upon the Republican campaign managers by President Coolidge."[104] Likewise, the Democrats pursued a campaign to mobilize

---

[98]"Using Plattsburg Idea to Reach Women Voters."

[99]"Democratic Women Give Luncheon Here," *NYT*, October 26, 1924, p. 5; also "50,000 Hear Davis in Fighting Speech at Huge Barbecue," *NYT*, September 16, 1924, p. 2.

[100]"Women for Davis, in Shaver Survey," *NYT*, September 12, 1924, p. 3.

[101]Ibid.

[102]The speech was to the 1926 Women's Industrial Conference. "Coolidge Sees Duty to Women Workers," *NYT*, January 19, 1926, p. 1.

[103]Coolidge address to Daughters of the American Revolution, Calvin Coolidge Papers, Reel 132, Frame 473.

[104]"Republicans Seek Stay-At-Home Vote," *NYT*, April 26, 1926, p. 5; "Largest Woman Vote on Record Sought," *NYT*, October 27, 1926, p. 2.

women in the 1926 congressional elections, as a continuation of their ongoing efforts.[105]

In 1928, the mobilization of women appears to in fact have been the keystone of the Republicans' national campaign. Herbert Hoover, Coolidge's commerce secretary, had been working on building his own organization of women in California as an asset for a future presidential nomination campaign as early as 1924.[106] As the former food administrator for the United States during World War I, Hoover already had good name recognition among the members of women's organizations that had assisted his agency in the war conservation and relief efforts. His campaign managers moved quickly to take advantage of that name recognition, forming women's Hoover-for-President Committees throughout the states in early 1928.[107] (Hoover's campaign managers also organized more specialized national women's committees, such as a Professional Women's Committee and a Women's Hoover-for-President Engineer's National Committee.)[108]

Hoover did in fact win the Republican presidential nomination, at a national convention heralded by Republican elites as providing women with a visibility unprecedented in national politics.[109] Following Hoover's nomination, the *Times* reported that "Women are expected to play a more important part in the election this year than at any other time since they gained national suffrage. In several States it is believed [by Republican elites] they will hold the balance of power. The Republican managers plan a thorough canvass to register and vote the women in New York, New Jersey, and Massachusetts, States which are expected to be the battle ground in the East."[110] The campaign's emphasis on previously unmobilized women came from the party's highest authorities, with the chairman of the Republican National Committee, Dr. Hubert Work, declaring shortly after the national convention that "The Republican campaign, through different organizations, will be directed toward getting the women registered and voted."[111] The belief of campaign elites was that previously nonvoting women could be largely swung as a bloc behind Hoover.[112]

[105]"Largest Woman Vote on Record Sought," *NYT*, October 27, 1926, p. 2.

[106]Ralph Arnold to Lou Henry Hoover, May 16, 1925, Lou Henry Hoover Papers, Herbert Hoover Presidential Library, West Branch, Iowa.

[107]"Women to Help Hoover," *NYT*, February 29, 1928, p. 3.

[108]"Women Organize for Hoover," *NYT*, March 31, 1928, p. 3; "Mrs. Hoover to Join Drive for Husband," *NYT*, February 17, 1928, p. 3.

[109]"Many Women Delegates Expected," *NYT*, January 8, 1928, p. 9.

[110]"Woman Vote Plays Big Part This Year," *NYT*, July 9, 1928, p. 2.

[111]Ibid.

[112]"Women Organize New Hoover Drive," *NYT*, July 26, 1928, p. 3: "Hoover leaders appear to be convinced that women voters will determine the issue of the

This belief was reinforced by the private reports that national Republican elites received from their state informants. From Iowa the editor of the *Des Moines Register* wrote Hoover that "I believe the women will more than offset any liquor defections."[113] From New York, the editor of the Sunday magazine of the *New York Herald Tribune* wrote Hoover that "We are going to swing New York State, and Massachusetts too, if it lies in the power of the women."[114] From Washington State a leader in the Republican men's organization wrote a Hoover campaign advisor that

the Hoover pre-convention campaign in this State demonstrated to me that women can be induced to take a more active part in this campaign than in previous ones. A great many women who never before took any interest politically have evinced interest in Hoover's candidacy and can be induced to take an active part. This is probably the greatest reservoir we have for supplying new votes for the Republican ticket. . . . I think this source of increased votes should be worked far beyond what it has been in the past campaigns.[115]

The regional conferences held by the Republican Party in preparation for the presidential campaign were likewise a forum for national party elites to both give and receive information about the role that women's votes would play in Hoover's election. When the Republican organizations of the midwestern states met to plan their campaign, the two groups reportedly targeted for attention were farmers and women.[116] And when the southern and western states met in San Francisco, RNC Chairman Work took especial care to note the centrality of women's votes to Republican campaign strategy.[117] The kinds of appeals used by Republican elites to lure more women into the Republican fold were consistent with an apparent belief in a still-strong norm of gender identification among women. Women were asked to be "Hoover Hostesses" for women's campaign parties,[118] radio

campaign in the Eastern States. They intend to make special endeavors to get to the polls the 50 per cent group of women who have not voted at previous elections. Most of these women, they contend, can be swung into the Hoover column if the campaigning among them is effectively carried out."

[113]Harvey Ingham to Herbert Hoover, July 26, 1928, Campaign and Transition Papers, Box 38, Herbert Hoover Papers.

[114]Marie M. Meloney to Herbert Hoover, August 6, 1928, Campaign and Transition Papers, Box 48, ibid.

[115]Charles Hebberd to R. W. Condon, August 7, 1928, Campaign and Transition Papers, Box 33, ibid.

[116]"Hoover Campaigner Is Named for West," *NYT*, August 4, 1928, p. 3.

[117]"Hoover Chiefs Told of Break in South," *NYT*, August 14, 1928, p. 2.

[118]Report of Hoover Hostesses, Hoover-Curtis Organization Bureau, Margaret Strawn, Director, November 7, 1928, Lou Henry Hoover Papers, Box 25.

broadcasts included "housewives' hours,"[119] and publicity written for the campaign specifically stressed women's domestic responsibilities. For example, a Hoover speech prepared for distribution to women declared that homemaking and raising children were "not the sole responsibility of women, but in many phases they are the problems with which no one else is so competent to deal as are women."[120] These campaign releases specifically for women were distributed to women's magazines, as "an appeal to the stocking-darning, dish-washing, home-making woman to vote for Hoover. A Vote for Hoover is a vote for the home and a vote for peace."[121] And as noted previously, Republican elites believed they could enjoy even more success with this kind of strategy than previously, given Hoover's past history:

> One of the arguments for Hoover's nomination is that women throughout the country regard him as the champion of their domestic economies. They learned during the war to think of the Food Administrator as one who understood their kitchen problems and being women, were drawn to his leadership because of his humanitarian work among the starving non-combatants of Europe.[122]

The campaign planned by the Republicans among the women in fact took women's kitchens to be a focal point of action. The campaign's strategists planned a "kitchen" campaign among women, stressing their presidential nominee's history in food relief administration and aiming to put a picture of the nominee in "thousands of kitchens."[123] The campaign also sought to play up Hoover's support of listing "homemaking" as an occupation in the census: "For the past four years the General Federation of Women's Clubs has conducted a drive to have home making listed as a profession in the United States census report. Throughout this drive they have had the unfailing support of Mr. Hoover. The campaign and his election will give fresh impetus to their drive and bring them closer to the realization of this dream."[124]

The *Times* could report by August 12 that "both reformers and pol-

[119]"Republicans to Reach Housewives by Radio," *NYT*, September 14, 1928, p. 6.

[120]"Excerpts from Addresses and Writings of Herbert Hoover," 1928, Nathan William MacChesney Papers, Box 13.

[121]Marie M. Meloney to Herbert Hoover, July 24, 1928, Campaign and Transition Papers, Box 48, Herbert Hoover Papers; Marie M. Meloney to Herbert Hoover, August 2, 1928, ibid.; Marie M. Meloney to Herbert Hoover, August 6, 1928, ibid.

[122]"On the Distaff Side," *NYT*, July 13, 1928, p. 16.

[123]Ibid.

[124]Sallie A. Hert, in "Women Organize New Hoover Drive," *NYT*, July 26, 1928, p. 3.

iticians cherish a belief that on certain issues the hands that rock the cradle will mark their ballots alike. . . . they are not anticipating that [women's votes] will be governed by prejudice, but by definite considerations mainly connected with woman's particular business of children and the home. . . . Homemaking, both assume, is still the major interest and occupation of women in this country. And it is that vote that is chiefly sought."[125] A few days later, the RNC announced that it had appointed Mary Winter, president of the General Federation of Women's Clubs between 1920 and 1924, as director of the "Homemakers' Group" in the women's division of the national party organization. The slogan of the homemakers' group was to be "A picture of Hoover in every kitchen," and the group was also given the responsibility to oversee the distribution of campaign literature "especially prepared for family consumption." In announcing this new group, the Republican male leaders reiterated their belief in an overwhelming victory for Hoover if the women could be brought into the Republican coalition as a group: "Party leaders admit quite frankly that this hoped for majority is largely up to the women."[126] In the same vein, the RNC also oversaw an operation run by a former Democratic Party official that took as its theme "apron clubs": "Women put on their aprons for Hoover in the war, and they will do it again."[127]

The propaganda issued by the Republican National Committee for women is quite illustrative of its "home and family" strategy. One pamphlet, entitled "How to Win a Vote for Hoover" and issued by the women's division of the Republican National Committee, contained the following advice for those signing pledge cards to proselytize among women: "Ninety-nine women out of a hundred are interested first and foremost in home and family. Their usual reaction to a candidate is curiosity as to how the election will affect their homes."[128] The women's division also issued special pamphlets for women discussing the tariff, for example, and relating those issues to "the home": "Why do we women thrust tariff aside as something we cannot understand? . . . Our business is home-making. Ninety per cent of us, married or single, who have passed our twenty-first birthdays, are engaged in this great industry. . . . without our protective tariff we would have smaller incomes to

[125]Eunice Fuller Barnard, "The Woman Voter Gains Power," *NYT Magazine*, August 12, 1928, p. 1.

[126]Statement issued by the Republican National Committee, in "New Hoover Group Seeks Kitchen Vote," *NYT*, August 17, 1928, p. 2.

[127]Mrs. Atherton Dupuy, in " 'Apron Clubs' Formed to Work for Hoover," *NYT*, July 26, 1928, p. 5.

[128]Nathan William MacChesney Papers, Box 12.

budget, and less food and clothing to buy for the family."[129] Another pamphlet entitled "Hoover – the Man who took America's women into his confidence," reprinted the section of Hoover's acceptance speech where he referred to the situation facing farmers in terms presumably appealing to women: "The object of our policies is to establish for our farmers an income equal to those of other occupations; for the farmer's wife the same comforts in her home as women in other groups."[130] And the pamphlet written by Mary Winter, the head of the Republican National Committee's "Homemakers' Group," was rather unsubtly entitled "We Women Want Herbert Hoover," with subheadings including "Because of What He Is Doing for Homes and Children."[131] Finally, the women's division reissued the earlier address by Hoover to the International Council of Women in which he declared that the protection of home and children was an issue "with which no one else is so competent to deal as are women."[132]

The Republicans also used the homemaking angle in their radio appeals to housewives. The following excerpt, from a speech by Sally Hert, is a fairly typical example of this kind of broadcast to women: "In 1916 we women were sticking close to our own firesides. [Then the war came. . . .] We enlisted under Herbert Hoover for the conservation of food. He believed in our ability to help win the war and we did not fail him. When the war was over, we women had a new point of view, new ideals, a new place in the sun."[133] And a new item of campaign propaganda entered the repertoire of Republican tacticians: the campaign thimble, inscribed with the legend "Hoover, Home and Happiness." "I thought that would carry our message to the women," declared its creator.[134]

The Republican campaign among women as homemakers, despite earlier attempts in the same vein, nonetheless prompted media comment as being unusually segregated on gender lines: "[The Republicans] more than their rivals are making a special women's crusade. That is, they are taking the campaign into the kitchen – appealing to women on the lines of their special interests as home makers, rather than merely as human beings and citizens. Quite naturally, perhaps, their campaign seems more segregated than the Democratic women's from that of the men in their

[129]Anna Steese Richardson, *Woman's Home Companion*, in "What Every Woman Wants to Know about Tariff," ibid., Box 13.
[130]Nathan William MacChesney Papers, Box 13.
[131]Ibid.
[132]"Excerpts from Addresses and Writings of Herbert Hoover," ibid.
[133]"Mrs. Hert in Radio Appeal," *NYT*, October 3, 1928, p. 3.
[134]James Good, in "Enter Woman, the New Boss of Politics," *NYT Magazine*, October 21, 1928, p. 3; also Sally Hert in Press Release, Republican National Committee, October 25, 1928, Campaign and Transition Papers, Box 199, Herbert Hoover Papers.

own party. When the Republican men's eastern division was being organized in New York, the women were meeting in Washington, D.C."[135]

Although often thought to have been an important issue on which women voted in the 1928 election, prohibition (or "law enforcement," as it was commonly referred to) did not feature prominently in the Republican campaign.[136] There was mounting evidence by this point that many women, while sharing with other women sympathy for the goal of prohibition, nevertheless believed the total ban on liquor had led to the development of more offensive alcohol-related practices than had existed before the ban.[137] Moreover, Republican elites believed that they simply did not need prohibition as an issue to mobilize women, as evidenced by their other campaign efforts.

Although not documented as extensively as the Republican campaign, the Democrats' 1928 presidential campaign was also marked by a focus on mobilizing women, largely as a response to Republican efforts. The preconvention maneuverings of candidates for the Democratic presidential nomination revealed the importance those candidates placed on women as a voting group. As early as 1927, William Gibbs McAdoo had targeted "the women's vote" as a means to further his nomination, and was followed in this by New York Governor Albert Smith.[138] The Jackson Day Dinner of January 1928, the first gathering of the campaign for national Democratic elites, saw several speakers making reference to the potential force of mothers as a group at the polls.[139]

Upon receiving the Democratic presidential nomination, Al Smith held a private campaign meeting with male party elites in which he reportedly stressed the importance of capturing the "woman vote," noting that he did not believe that women voted as did their husbands. Likewise, his choice to lead the Democrats' women's organization declared upon her appointment that women as an electoral group would be a "powerful factor" in determining the result of the election.[140]

As in previous campaigns, the Democrats created a separate women's advisory committee as a parallel structure to a similar men's advisory

[135]Eunice Fuller Barnard, "Women Who Wield Political Power," *NYT Magazine*, September 2, 1928, p. 6.

[136]"Women to Be Active in the Middle West," *NYT*, August 12, 1928, II p. 8.

[137]A survey conducted by the Women's National Republican Club in 1927 of its members found that 89 percent of the 960 returned surveys demonstrated support for modification of the prohibition laws. Eunice Fuller Barnard, "The Woman Voter Gains Power," *NYT Magazine*, August 12, 1928, p. 1.

[138]"Political 'Plots,' " *NYT*, June 7, 1927, p. 28; "Governor Smith Enjoins Aides to 'Get Busy,' " *NYT*, July 13, 1928, p. 1.

[139]"Harmony Prevails as Democrats Dine," *NYT*, January 13, 1928, p. 1.

[140]"Mrs. Ross Bespeaks Support for Smith," *NYT*, July 12, 1928, p. 2; "Governor Smith Enjoins Aides to 'Get Busy,' " *NYT*, July 13, 1928, p. 1.

committee;[141] the women's campaign committee kept offices separate from those of the men's committee.[142] The party also operated a women's speakers bureau, appointed female vice-chairmen in each of the Democrats' regional campaign headquarters,[143] created a Committee on Women in Industry,[144] as well as an organization of business and professional women,[145] and implemented a series of half-hour radio broadcasts for women (a tactic apparently borrowed from the Republican campaign).[146] The speakers' campaign would assume the most importance in the Democrats' appeals to women, and constituted their primary response throughout the fall to evidence that the Republicans were succeeding remarkably with their club organization.[147]

Also as in previous campaigns, the Democrats' speaking campaign echoed the Republicans' appeals to women's domesticity. In his major appeal to women during the campaign, Governor Smith emphasized his support of "the future mothers of this country" as "one of our greatest national assets."[148] The leader of the party's women's division told her subordinates that Smith's support of protective legislation for working women in New York State could be sold to women as a record of support for "future mothers,"[149] while Eleanor Roosevelt gave a well-publicized speech to "women, the home-makers in both the city and the country."[150] The chairman of the DNC asked "the wives and mothers of the nation" to protect "the American home" at the polls by bringing "the woman's viewpoint" to the voting booth.[151] Even Franklin Delano Roosevelt was asked to write an appeal to female voters, which he did by proclaiming that "the feminine concern" with the protection of life could be a valuable counter to men's "hereditary warlike instincts."[152]

[141]"Smith Declares He Will Be Active in State Campaign," *NYT*, July 19, 1928, p. 1; "Prepares to Unite Democratic Women," *NYT*, August 4, 1928, p. 7; Marie M. Meloney to Herbert Hoover, July 23, 1928, Campaign and Transition Papers, Box 48, Herbert Hoover Papers; Marie M. Meloney to Herbert Hoover, July 24, 1928, ibid.

[142]"Prepares to Unite Democratic Women," *NYT*, August 4, 1928, p. 4.

[143]"Democrats in Drive for Women Wets," *NYT*, August 11, 1928, p. 2.

[144]"Agnes H. Wilson Chosen," *NYT*, August 12, 1928, p. 8.

[145]"Smith Commended by Leaders of Women," *NYT*, September 16, 1928, p. 4.

[146]"Lillian Wald for Smith," *NYT*, September 17, 1928, p. 3.

[147]"Lists 1,000 Women as Smith Speakers," *NYT*, September 4, 1928, p. 5; "Plans Drive to Win Women for Smith," *NYT*, September 21, 1928, p. 8.

[148]"Stenographic Report of Governor Smith's Address on Labor in Newark," *NYT*, November 1, 1928, p. 12.

[149]"Governor Smith Enjoins Aides to 'Get Busy,' " *NYT*, July 13, 1928, p. 1; also "On the Distaff Side," *NYT*, July 13, 1928, p. 16.

[150]"Prepares to Unite Democratic Women," *NYT*, August 4, 1928, p. 7; see also "Mrs. Ross Praises Smith as Reformer," *NYT*, October 2, 1928, p. 2.

[151]"Woman Votes Urged by Raskob as Duty," *NYT*, September 9, 1928, p. 4.

[152]"Roosevelt Praises Women in Politics," *NYT*, October 4, 1928, p. 2.

The Democratic vice-presidential nominee, Senator Robinson, also prepared several speeches directed to women voters, stressing the Democrats' concern with child welfare.[153]

The Democrats also used their focus on women's domestic roles to help them downplay the prohibition issue during the campaign.[154] Eleanor Roosevelt even made a speech in which she declared that the Democratic Party line was that women did not constitute an organized group because of prohibition, but rather because of an interest in any issue that touched on the home and children.[155]

Throughout the 1920s both NLWV and national major party elites continued to pursue actions and express opinions that indicated their shared belief that women constituted a distinct and mobilizable electoral group. The supposition of gender "sameness" would predict that at the very least such a belief would not have been maintained after 1923, after the league repealed its candidate endorsement policy. Yet as the foregoing makes clear, there is no marked change either in the organizational strategies pursued by these organizations after 1923, or in the opinions expressed by organizational leaders.

THE NLWV AND "NONPARTISANSHIP," 1920–1928

It appears relatively clear that both NLWV and national major party elites continued to believe throughout the 1920s that women constituted a distinct electoral group, sharing interests and norms of behavior easily distinguishable from those of men. The question of why the NLWV would choose not to participate in electoral politics thus remains open. Our second explanation for this decision rests on a hypothesized suffrage ideology of nonpartisanship. In the preceding chapter we reviewed both the presuffrage history of the NAWSA and its immediate postsuffrage history in order to ascertain its policy with respect to electoral politics. In those cases we found that neither NAWSA policy nor NAWSA elites' actions indicated an ideological prohibition on participation in partisan electoral politics. Here we can ask about the development of NLWV electoral policy throughout the 1920s. If the supposition of a suffrage ideology of nonpartisanship is correct, then we would expect to see a strong prohibition against candidate endorsements made by league elites as women entered the electorate. If any change occurred in this policy,

---

[153]"Robinson Prepares Western Speeches," *NYT*, September 26, 1928, p. 4; "Robinson Prepares for Dual Offensive," *NYT*, October 22, 1928, p. 7.

[154]"Woman Democrats Rule Out Dry Issue," *NYT*, July 13, 1928, p. 3.

[155]"Democratic Women Plan No Wet Drive," *NYT*, August 17, 1928, p. 3; also see Eleanor Roosevelt's remarks in Eunice Fuller Barnard, "Women Who Wield Political Power," *NYT Magazine*, September 2, 1928, IV p. 6.

we would expect that change to be in the direction of a weakening of the prohibition as women lost the ideological distinctiveness associated with disfranchisement. If change occurs in the opposite direction, for example, if the league began by sanctioning candidate endorsements and only gradually moved away from such a policy, then this account is undermined.

As reviewed in the preceding chapter, the national league's first action to proscribe league involvement in electoral politics did not occur until late 1920, *after* campaigning by both the NLWV and the New York State LWV to defeat Senator Wadsworth. Moreover, at that time the league governing board voted to refrain "for the present" from endorsing or opposing candidates; this decision was both subject to revision and was not announced to the press. It also did not necessarily apply to state leagues. There was in fact considerable support among some of the local and state leagues to take sides in electoral campaigns. In New York, for example, the New York City LWV announced in January of 1921 that it would endorse a candidate in the upcoming mayoral election, the selection of a candidate to be made by a three-quarters vote on the local league's board.[156] The Pennsylvania State LWV debated the endorsement issue at its 1921 convention and decided to allow local leagues to endorse candidates if two-thirds of the members in any given community were agreed upon a candidate.[157] On the other hand, the Virginia State LWV wrote into its constitution the provision that as an organization the league would neither endorse nor oppose candidates.[158]

In 1922, at the suggestion of an NLWV board interested in reevaluating its suspension of candidate endorsements in light of the experiences of state and local leagues with such endorsements, delegates to the NLWV convention in Baltimore openly debated the question, "Should the League indorse or oppose candidates?" Upon announcing the debate, league President Maud Wood Park stated that "The question [of candidate endorsements] is one of very great importance to the local and state leagues, as well as to the National League. It is a question that we want to make up our own minds upon with the utmost care and deliberation."[159] Park prefaced the actual convention debate by making clear that the league's constitution prohibited the endorsement of or opposition to candidates "in any way that would permit the League to support a political party," for example, by endorsing a full party slate of can-

---

[156]Mary Garrett Hay, in "Women's League Replies to Miller; Pushes Program," *NYT*, January 29, 1921, p. 1; Mary Garrett Hay in Papers of the National League of Women Voters, Pt. II, Reel 1, Frame 658.

[157]Papers of the National League of Women Voters, Pt. II, Reel 3, Frame 64.

[158]Ibid., Frame 68.

[159]Ibid., Frame 43.

didates. Speakers from New York and Texas both advocated at least allowing state and local leagues the freedom to engage in supporting or opposing candidates as electoral conditions permitted.[160] The discussion was reported in the press to have been inconclusive, with the subject matter bound over until the following year's national convention.[161]

By the 1923 NLWV board meeting immediately prior to that convention, however, the board had already privately decided to continue its previous policy without alteration: the national league would refrain from endorsing or opposing candidates, while the state leagues would be left free to act as they wished on this issue.[162] Later that year the board discussed and reaffirmed its prohibition on electoral activity when it voted to study the issue of how the league could encourage women to become candidates for office without actually endorsing them in electoral contests.[163] Neither of these board actions during 1923 was announced to the press.

In 1924 the national board's executive committee continued to take private action clarifying its candidate endorsement policy, voting in January that the policy prohibited league President Maud Wood Park from signing a letter of endorsement of a U.S. senator since it would be regarded as a league endorsement.[164] The 1924 convention saw debate on a recommendation from the NLWV board that the league work for the election and appointment of qualified women to government; in response to a delegate's confusion over how this recommendation related to the league's nonendorsement policy, Maud Wood Park replied that while the league was "ordinarily" in no position to campaign for women, league members as enrolled party members could work for the nomination and election of women within their parties. Park also noted that in several states the league had worked for the election of candidates in nonpartisan contests.[165] Finally, in July 1924 the NLWV board's executive committee voted that while the league could distribute the legislative records of congressmen, it could not supply the candidates themselves with letters that might be interpreted as campaign endorsements.[166]

In November 1925, the full NLWV board discussed and reaffirmed its policy on "political relations," including the prohibition on candidate

---

[160]Ibid., Frame 68.
[161]"Women Delay Decision on Entering Politics," *NYT*, April 27, 1922, p. 5.
[162]Minutes of NLWV Board Meeting, April 7, 1923, in Papers of the National League of Women Voters, Pt. I, Reel 1, Frame 612.
[163]Minutes of NLWV Board Meeting, October 28, 1923, ibid., Frame 730.
[164]Ibid., Reel 3, Frame 195.
[165]Ibid., Pt. II, Reel 6, Frame 10.
[166]Ibid., Pt. 1, Reel 3, Frame 195.

endorsements.[167] One year later, at a September 1926 meeting, the NLWV board again discussed its policy on political relations, including its candidate endorsement policy; "no suggestions were offered for correction of the policies as read."[168]

Although the national league continued to refrain from requiring its state and local affiliates to follow its nonendorsement policy, leaving it to the strategic discretion of state and local league boards whether they would participate in electoral contests,[169] on several occasions the board recommended to state and local leagues that they abstain from making those endorsements in the absence of unusually favorable circumstances. One state league that took that advice was the New York State LWV. In September 1926 the LWV announced that it would take no part in the campaign against Republican U.S. Senator Wadsworth, its former electoral target in 1920.[170] And in early 1928, when asked by a reporter if the New York State league would be participating in the Republican primary campaign, the chairman of the Manhattan Borough LWV demonstrated how the New York State league had, like the national league, altered its earlier policy. While from 1918 through 1922 New York league elites had been leading advocates of league participation in partisan electoral contests, now the New York league's electoral policy was the following: "The League of Voters is taking no part in any primary campaign. It is a strictly non-partisan organization and never recommends nor condemns candidates, nor takes any action in any campaign whatsoever. Nor are any of its local groups permitted to do so in the name of the League. If individual members wish to do so, they act as individuals and not as members of the league representing it."[171]

Throughout the 1920s league elites lobbied Congress and successive administrations for policies specifically designed to benefit women, and on several occasions expressed the belief that women had interests and norms distinct from those of men. Yet league elites refrained throughout this period from mobilizing women as an electoral group in support of those lobbying efforts. Reviewing the pattern of league decisions with respect to its electoral policy, it is difficult to ascribe those decisions to an ideology of nonpartisanship. The support for league involvement in electoral politics was strongest at the NLWV's creation, and in its first

[167]November 5, 1925, Board Meeting, ibid., Frame 22.

[168]September 17, 1926, Board Meeting, ibid., Frames 675, 676.

[169]In early 1927 the NLWV Board decided after discussion not to include a provision prohibiting the endorsement of candidates in a draft of suggested bylaws for state and local leagues. January 17, 1927, Board Meeting, ibid., Reel 4, Frame 7.

[170]"Keeps Out of Senate Fight," *NYT*, September 21, 1926, p. 19.

[171]Mrs. Edwin Chase Hoyt, in "Foes of Dr. Butler Turning to Hoover," *NYT*, February 25, 1928, p. 3.

year. For a period of approximately three years after the first action to suspend the league's electoral policy, that policy remained a viable option for league elites, who encouraged discussion on the policy at the 1922 NLWV convention. After 1923, however, despite the fact that the policy was discussed on several occasions by league elites, on no occasion was it a matter for convention debate. And even in league elites' meetings, the policy apparently ceased to be a matter for open discussion, and became rather standard operating procedure. The same pattern occurs with the New York State LWV, which moved from a public willingness to make candidate endorsements to a prohibition on such endorsements by the latter half of the 1920s. That the pattern in both cases was from sanctions of electoral activity to prohibitions on such activity mitigates against the notion of an inherited ideological tradition somehow constraining league elites. Rather, the constraints on league electoral activity appeared to become stronger over the course of the 1920s.

THE MAJOR PARTIES AND COMPETITIVE ADVANTAGES, 1917–1932

Our final theoretical account, that of competitive advantages for the major parties and competitive disadvantages for the NLWV, makes at least two predictions concerning the 1920s as part of an explanation for why the NLWV appeared to be increasingly, rather than decreasingly, constrained in its electoral policy over the course of that decade. First, the competitive advantages–disadvantages account predicts that the national major parties would have been able to initiate women's electoral mobilization before the NLWV, the latter having to adapt organizationally to the new institutional context of enfranchisement. Second, the competitive advantages–disadvantages account predicts that dominant parties would have had increasing success in coordinating female voters over the course of the 1920s, both with respect to subordinate parties and (particularly) with respect to independent women's organizations.

The evidence with respect to the timing of national major party efforts to initiate the electoral mobilization of women is simple and has already been reviewed in this chapter. In brief, the major party organizations had both created women's organizations at the national level and had directed state and local organizations to do the same by early 1919. These women's organizations immediately began planning campaigns of electoral mobilization in a substantial majority of states. In early 1919 the NLWV did not exist yet. By April 1919 the NLWV had been created, but only as an organization in the full suffrage states, and the nascent organization was not ready to begin campaigns of electoral mobilization in even those states. Not until the fall of 1920 was the NLWV ready to begin electoral campaigning, and then only in one state.

The evidence with respect to whether the parties were experiencing increasing returns from coordinating women's votes can be found in two different sources. The first consists of major party elites' evaluations of the return on their investments in mobilizing potential female voters. Though only a crude measure of whether increasing returns from coordination existed, such evaluations at least reveal to us whether party elites believed that their investments in specifically female electoral mobilization were justified.

This evidence is much more extensive for the Republican Party during the 1920s, given the problems of documentation discussed earlier. The first estimates that Republican elites made of women's votes came in the Maine state elections of the fall of 1920:

> But something that is worrying the politicians even more than the French vote or the Irish vote is the woman vote. . . . Just what the women will decide to do with their ballots is keeping the politicians in both quarters worried. They fear to make predictions of results, having no previous experience with the woman vote. Both sides would be pleased to be able to discount their strength; both sides would be pleased to let them remain in the state of indifference and apathy under which the large majority of them seem to be resting, but each is afraid that the other will steal a march, so both are going out for the women.[172]

The Republican Party won resounding victories in the Maine elections, and both state and national Republican elites attributed their electoral success to their early and strong organization of women.[173]

The next sign that the Republicans' interelection mobilization efforts among women were paying off was given in the state Republican primaries held in the spring of 1922. In both Pennsylvania and Indiana, "organization" candidates for gubernatorial and U.S. senatorial nominations were defeated by insurgents who attributed their victories to their endorsement by the leaders of the women's party organizations.[174]

---

[172]"Republicans Count on Maine Victory," *NYT*, September 9, 1920, p. 3; also see "Women Hold Key to Maine Result," *NYT*, September 12, 1920, II p. 1.

[173]"Republicans Sweep Maine by 65,000, with Women Casting a Heavy Vote," *NYT*, September 14, 1920, p. 1; Warren G. Harding to Anne M. Gannett, Augusta, Maine, September 13, 1920, Warren G. Harding Papers, Reel 44, Frame 513; Anne M. Gannett to Warren G. Harding, September 14, 1920, Warren G. Harding Papers, Reel 44, Frames 511–512; Simon Wolf to Warren G. Harding, September 14, 1920, Warren G. Harding Papers, Reel 44, Frame 520.

[174]"Pinchot by 15,000, Machine Hard Hit in Pennsylvania," *NYT*, May 18, 1922,

The National Race to Mobilize Women

National party elites took careful note of the results in the Indiana and Pennsylvania primaries. President Harding corresponded with Harriet Taylor Upton on how to interpret the primary results; their consensus was that the mobilization of women had played a large role in the elections.[175] National male Republican elites then called a special meeting in Washington to discuss the "revolts" against these state machines; the meeting reportedly concluded that one of the principal causes for the primary results lay in the voting behavior of returned soldiers and women (the two groups targeted by party elites for mobilization in the spring of 1920), who had been induced as groups to vote against the organization candidates.[176]

After this conference, national Republican elites specifically urged greater investments in women's votes in the 1922 fall elections.[177] For example, the former director of the RNC's Bureau of Publicity for Women Voters said in an interview that the interelection mobilization work had resulted in the creation of local party followings of women, which, however, required constant maintenance: "In 1920 the Woman Vote was too new to be known of men; by the elections of November, 1922, it should become more or less determined. . . . it behooves both of the great parties carefully to preserve the enthusiasms that they have created; Democrats and Republicans must alike labor to keep the woman members that they have acquired."[178] Upton herself told the *Times* that "Women will be a deciding factor in the congressional elections in some States more than others. I think women will decide the outcome in Ohio, my native State."[179]

By 1924 the RNC had begun to use crude analyses of election returns to try to predict the voting behavior of various electoral groups, and women as a group figured prominently in these analyses. In the fall of 1924 Washington statistician Simon Michelet used a variety of sources

p. 1; Esther Everett Lape, "Women's Vote Revolt," *NYT*, May 28, 1922, VII p. 2; "Progressives Seek to Reform Party," *NYT*, May 19, 1922, p. 19.
[175]Harriet Taylor Upton to Warren G. Harding, May 6, 1922, Warren G. Harding Papers, Reel 197, Frames 254–257; Harriet Taylor Upton to George Christian, May 17, 1922, ibid., Reel 236, Frames 853–854; Warren G. Harding to Harriet Taylor Upton, May 18, 1922, ibid., Frame 855.
[176]"Republicans Find Young Men in Revolt," *NYT*, June 9, 1922, p. 2.
[177]Warren G. Harding to Harriet Taylor Upton, September 30, 1922, Warren G. Harding Papers, Reel 232, Frame 685.
[178]Reginald Wright Kauffman, "Her Whims as Voter," *NYT*, October 1, 1922, VIII p. 3.
[179]"Sees Woman Vote Vital," *NYT*, September 19, 1922, p. 4; Harriet Taylor Upton to George Christian, August 7, 1922, Warren G. Harding Papers, Reel 195, Frame 17; Harriet Taylor Upton to Warren G. Harding October 3, 1922, Warren G. Harding Papers, Reel 195, Frames 54–55; Harriet Taylor Upton to Warren G. Harding, October 30, 1922, Warren G. Harding Papers, Reel 195, Frame 78.

across the states to estimate the percentage of women who had voted in the 1920 election (his estimate being 43 percent nationally of native and naturalized white women of voting age), and hypothesized to Republican elites that mobilization efforts on the remaining large pool of potential female voters could be significant in the 1924 presidential election: "The nation-wide movement of the women in getting out the stay-at-homes, which is now going on in most of the States, indicates that on November next the women of America will make a far more impressive showing than in their first general ballot in 1920."[180] In fact, Michelet went so far as to say that "women will be the controlling factor in the 1924 election."[181]

Republican elites turned again to Michelet for an analysis of the results of the 1924 election, which he performed for them in the spring of 1926.[182] Once again he noted the importance of women as an electoral group. Michelet claimed that turnout in the 1924 election had increased from 49.5 percent of the voting-eligible population in 1920 to 52.5 percent, and that, as the largest unmobilized group, women were potentially primarily responsible for the increase.[183] A senior Coolidge advisor acknowledged receipt of Michelet's analyses by writing that they were "even more interesting and useful than I supposed."[184]

Following Republican losses in the 1926 congressional elections, national party elites concluded that they needed more rather than fewer resources devoted to mobilizing women as a group. As President Coolidge told a 1927 conference of Republican women, "You are representing particularly the women of the country who have lately had placed upon them the privilege and duty of voting. I think their response has been particularly encouraging."[185]

In 1928, a focus on the potential influence of women's votes was even more pronounced in the correspondence of male Republican elites. The first Republican primary of that year was held in Ohio, and it was predicted by none other than Republican statistician Simon Michelet that

---

[180]Simon Michelet, "American Women at the Ballot," October 5, 1924, Warren G. Harding Papers, Reel 132, Frame 473; "Says Women's Votes Could Decide the Issue," *NYT*, October 5, 1924, p. 8. See "To Bring Out Stay-At-Home-Vote," *NYT*, May 11, 1924, I pt. 2 p. 5, for an earlier analysis done by Michelet that was commissioned by the Republican National Committee.

[181]Michelet, "American Women at the Ballot."

[182]Edward T. Clark to Simon Michelet, April 3, 1926, Calvin Coolidge Papers, Reel 132, Frame 473; Simon Michelet to Edward T. Clark, April 5, 1926, ibid.

[183]"Republicans Seek Stay-At-Home Vote," *NYT*, April 26, 1926, p. 5.

[184]Edward T. Clark to Simon Michelet, April 6, 1926, Calvin Coolidge Papers, Reel 132, File 473.

[185]"Coolidge Praises Women in Politics," *NYT*, January 13, 1927, p. 3.

women could very likely control the result.[186] The Indiana primary was likewise closely watched by Hoover's campaign managers, with the women's organizer sent into that state from California claiming that "I believe the Indiana women will be the deciding factor in swinging the state into the Hoover column."[187] The effort to mobilize women in these early primaries appeared to pay off, according to Hoover's managers: "From the viewpoint of the student of politics, the most illuminating thing about the Indiana voting was the large part played in it by the *women* voters. They went to the polls by thousands and registered their conviction that Hoover was the right man for the Presidency."[188]

By the end of the 1928 campaign, Republican elites felt confident that their focus on women would pay big dividends on election day. Republican statistician Simon Michelet reported to these elites in late October that women would in all likelihood turn out as a group more than they ever had before: "of this increase [over 1924] all the signs are that the biggest increase will come from the women. . . . This time it looks as if by hundreds of thousands they will vote regardless of the views held by their male kinsmen. . . . Watch for a record-breaking vote by the women."[189] And the *Times* reported that

This year the President of the United States will probably be chosen by women. . . . American women for the first time in eight years since their enfranchisement are about to vote in numbers strong and decisive enough to determine the result. The one constant factor in the heavy registration reported in every township in the land is the unusual outpouring of women.[190]

Boosted by these analyses, Republican national leader Sally Hert proclaimed in the closing days of the campaign that the "woman vote" would be the chief factor in electing Hoover: "women are taking an interest in the election of Herbert Hoover as they have never before shown in a candidacy. . . . The fervor of women in behalf of the Hoover

---

[186]"Women Voters in Ohio," *NYT*, February 25, 1928, p. 16.

[187]Clara Burdette, President, California Federation of Women's Clubs, quoted in Press Release, Hoover-for-President New York State Committee, May 1, 1928, Campaign and Transition Papers, Box 210, Herbert Hoover Papers; "Says Women Are Backing Hoover," *NYT*, May 2, 1928, p. 17.

[188]William H. Hill, President, New York State Hoover-for-President Committee, in Press Release, New York State Hoover-for-President Committee, May 9, 1928, Campaign and Transition Papers, Box 210, Herbert Hoover Papers.

[189]"This Year's Woman Vote to Set a High Record," *NYT*, October 21, 1928, X p. 8.

[190]"Enter Woman, the New Boss of Politics," *NYT Magazine*, October 21, 1928, p. 3.

cause has taken on the aspect of a crusade. . . . these words, I believe will be on every lip: 'More than all, the women did it.' "[191]

True to Hert's prediction, Republican male elites largely attributed the election's favorable outcome to the mobilization of women. The postelection report of the women's Hoover clubs noted this fact with some pride: "For the first time in the history of the Republican Party, it has been unhesitatingly acknowledged that women were a telling factor in the last election."[192] For example, RNC Chairman Hubert Work declared that Hoover would not have won the election if it had not been for the part played by women.[193] Earle Kinsley, Republican national committeeman from Vermont and Chairman Work's personal aide, proclaimed that "the women were to a large extent responsible for the results,"[194] while the male director of the western Hoover clubs described the mobilization of women through these clubs as spreading "like wildfire."[195] Hoover himself, in letters to Republican national committeewomen thanking them for their efforts on his behalf, wrote that "Particularly are we indebted to the women who have shown such devotion to our cause";[196] his letter to Republican state committeewomen declared that the election results were due to "particularly the women who have played so large a part in our success."[197]

While "unhesitatingly" attributing to women an important electoral role in the 1928 presidential election, national Republican elites desired a more systematic analysis of the precise dimensions of that role. A few statistical analyses were performed immediately after the election, but these mostly concerned turnout. Simon Michelet estimated that approximately 60 percent of the roughly ten million more votes cast in 1928 over 1924 were cast by previously unmobilized women.[198] Irving Fisher, an economist at Yale University, also performed some rudimentary sta-

---

[191]"Predicts Women Will Elect Hoover," *NYT*, November 1, 1928, p. 5.

[192]Estelle MacChesney Northam, Assistant Director, Hoover-Curtis Organization Bureau, Western Headquarters, Republican National Committee, 1928, Lou Henry Hoover Papers, Box 25.

[193]Minerva Allen, President, Kentucky Women's Republican League, to Herbert Hoover, January 2, 1929, Campaign and Transition Papers, Box 87, Herbert Hoover Papers.

[194]"Gains in Congress Will Help Hoover," *NYT*, November 8, 1928, p. 9.

[195]Nathan William MacChesney, Director, Hoover-Curtis Organization Bureau, to Herbert Hoover, November 7, 1928, Campaign and Transition Papers, Box 163, Herbert Hoover Papers.

[196]Herbert Hoover form letter to Republican National Committeewomen, November 13, 1928, Campaign and Transition Papers, Box 75, Herbert Hoover Papers.

[197]Herbert Hoover form letter to Republican State Committeewomen, November 12, 1928, Campaign and Transition Papers, Box 75, Herbert Hoover Papers.

[198]"Figures 39,000,000 Voted on Tuesday," *NYT*, November 11, 1928, p. 11.

tistical analyses of the election returns and listed as the primary factor determining the outcome "the women's vote." However, Fisher also noted that "It is impossible to demonstrate from the statistics what effect, if any, the women's vote had on the results."[199]

To further clarify the factors contributing to Hoover's election, the RNC's Research Bureau, "as requested by the President-elect," conducted an extensive survey of local Republican elites in the hope that they might be able to shed light on questions that remained murky in national analyses of election returns.[200] This appears to have been the first such survey on the part of national Republican elites, who inquired after specific voting groups, including women:

Finally, but very important, let us have your estimate of the alignment of women. How much of an increase was there in the total women's vote over 1924? Did we obtain for our Presidential ticket women who are normally Democratic and, if so, what percentage, in your opinion, of normally Democratic women did we obtain? What was the reason of their stepping outside of their party and voting for our Presidential candidate? By this question we mean, was it because of a positive support of our candidate and his policies, or was it a combination of both, or was it for other reasons?[201]

Significantly, the survey was for the private consumption of party elites, thereby lessening the probability that the resultant reports were inflated for publicity reasons.[202]

The questionnaire was sent to twenty-three state and local Republican elites. One woman was asked to respond, namely Ruth Hanna McCormick, but as she replied that she did not have the time, all the reports eventually received by Hoover were written by men.[203] The summary of the collected reports, written by J. Bennett Gordon for Herbert Hoover, was striking in its conclusions:

[199]"Fisher Analyzes Hoover's Victory," *NYT*, November 25, 1928, II p. 1.

[200]J. Bennett Gordon to Lawrence Richey, January 3, 1929, Campaign and Transition Papers, Box 157, Herbert Hoover Papers.

[201]J. Bennett Gordon, Research Bureau, Republican National Committee, form letter to Miss Mary B. Sleeth, November 12, 1928, Campaign and Transition Papers, Box 157, Herbert Hoover Papers. Versions of this cover letter were also sent out over at least one other name, that of Lawrence Richey, assistant to Hoover. Lawrence Richey form letter, n.d., ibid.

[202]J. Bennett Gordon to Miss Mary B. Sleeth, November 12, 1928, ibid.

[203]J. Bennett Gordon to Lawrence Richey, January 3, 1929, ibid. This memo presenting the collected reports to Hoover contains the list of all those to whom the questionnaire was sent and also all those who responded. The states that returned reports were California, Connecticut, Florida, Illinois, Indiana, Maryland, Massachusetts, Mississippi, Missouri, New Hampshire, New Jersey, Ohio, Oregon, Rhode Island, Texas, and Wisconsin.

Most conspicuous and important was the tremendous support given President-elect Hoover by the women. No matter how variant were other influences, or how the support from other groups of voters fluctuated, according to local conditions and political cross-currents, the militant support of Mr. Hoover by America's womanhood was constant in every state. Indifference or aversion to political activity which had characterized a large percentage of women ever since equal suffrage became a fact was overcome, and hundreds of thousands of women who never had participated in politics and never voted were brought into the campaign as zealous workers in behalf of Mr. Hoover. The enthusiasm of women for him cut across party lines, broke down sectional barriers and prejudices of 50 years duration and survived the blight of religious intolerance. Hoover's support by women was the one constant, dominating factor in every state making a report – in many states women offsetting all losses of normal Republican votes due to variously assigned causes. Without this support, Hoover undoubtedly would have lost some states he carried, his margin of safety would have been dangerously narrowed in others, and his defeat in those few states he did not carry would have been overwhelming.[204]

The indirect evidence as to whether the parties were experiencing increasing returns from investments in mobilization is at least consistent with the account presented in Chapter 2. But it is still indirect, requiring inferences to be made as to the likely behavior of female voters during this period. Direct evidence as to the latter would be, to say the least, helpful. But it is impossible to ascertain how women voted during the 1920s, as ballots were not kept separately for men and women, nor were voter surveys or even reliable public opinion polls performed during this period. Moreover, as women and men are relatively evenly distributed across voting districts, we cannot use aggregate electoral data to ascertain the voting behavior of women.

In a very limited number of areas, however, partisan registration data were kept separately by sex. By combining these records with census data, we can ask some questions about men's and women's partisan registration behavior as a surrogate for their voting behavior.

What does the theoretical account discussed in Chapter 2 predict? Recall that the theory predicts that if an organization gets a significant head start in coordinating the mobilization of a particular group, that organization will benefit from increasing returns to coordination, making it more difficult for other organizations to compete in the mobilization of that group. One way to operationalize this prediction would be to hypothesize that a party would be more likely to have an advantage in mobilizing women in areas dominated by that party than in areas that were more competitive or were dominated by another party. The Re-

[204]Ibid.

publican Party in an area strongly Republican *before* the enfranchisement of women should show more of an advantage in the mobilization of female Republican registrants than the Republican Party in an area strongly Democratic before female enfranchisement.

But this also should have been true for mobilizing male voters in the 1920s. Dominant local parties should have an advantage in mobilizing men as well as women: because men as well receive solidary benefits from affiliating with a particular party, they also receive increasing returns from electoral coordination. In a disproportionately Republican area, the dominant Republican Party should have a competitive advantage in the mobilization of men, an advantage it may lose if the parties are of equal strength or if the Democratic Party can claim more adherents. Finding that a dominant party had an advantage in the mobilization of new female voters thus does not tell us that anything particularly unique was occurring in the mobilization of women.

The hypotheses discussed in Chapter 2, however, also imply a prediction with respect to the postsuffrage partisan registration of women that should distinguish it from that of men. Not only should the competitive advantage of a party in mobilizing women increase with an already existing advantage in the mobilization of men, but that party should also have more of an advantage in the mobilization of women in any given area than in the mobilization of men.

If the league's withdrawal from electoral politics can in fact be traced to the earlier constraints posed on suffrage organizations by the institutional context of disfranchisement, then the organizational context of female registration behavior in the 1920s should have been different from that of men. Women's organizations would have been at a *unique* disadvantage with respect to the parties in the mobilization of women's electoral loyalties during the 1920s. The same would not have been true for any organizations seeking to compete with the parties in the coordination of male electoral loyalties, however. As discussed in Chapter 2, men's organizations might very well have been able to compete quite well with the parties in the mobilization of men around various occupational, ethnic, or other identities. And, in fact, unions, ethnic nationality associations, and veterans' and farmers' organizations were all competing with the parties for men's electoral loyalties during this period. This competition with the parties should logically be reflected in men's registration and voting behavior: male registration and voting behavior during the 1920s should reflect not only the mobilization efforts of the two parties, but also the efforts of independent benefit-seeking organizations attempting to mobilize male votes for their own purposes. Conversely, women's registration and voting behavior would reflect only the efforts of the parties to mobilize their loyalties.

Operationally, this difference in the organizational context of men's and women's voting behavior implies that, holding the partisan strength of any area constant, we should see women registering and voting disproportionately with the locally dominant party, relative to registering and voting men. Men were being mobilized by the parties *and* by benefit-seeking organizations, while women were being mobilized solely by the parties. This difference should be reflected in men's and women's registration behavior.

How can we test for the existence of this predicted difference in the registration behavior of men and women? We want to control for the historical patterns of registration in any given area, and compare only the registration behavior of those men and women being newly mobilized into the electoral arena. This is, unfortunately, impossible to test directly. Simply comparing the percentages of men and women registered with the parties in any given year will not tell us anything about the partisan biases of newly registered voters as opposed to those already on the rolls. Similarly, even comparing rates of change in the partisanship of men and women over time does not distinguish between those entering the rolls, those leaving the rolls, and those switching between the parties.

We can, however, discern the partisan predispositions of newly registering voters indirectly by calculating partisan elasticities. That is, we can measure the responsiveness of a group's partisan bias (defined as the Democratic share of the group's two-party registration) to changes in the group's level of mobilization (defined as the percentage of the group's total adult population registered to vote with a major party). A significant positive elasticity for the group would indicate that as a group's population registered, the group's Democratic share of the two-party registration increased; a significant negative elasticity would indicate that the Republicans were making net gains from the group's mobilization. We can compare male and female partisan elasticities to see whether proportionate increases in male and female registration levels produced similar changes in male and female partisan biases.[205]

[205] The elasticities calculated here take the form of expression

$$\beta = \frac{d\ln Y_i}{d\ln X_i},$$

where Y_i = group i's partisan bias (group i's Democratic registration)/(group i's two-party registration) and where X_i = group i's registered population (group i's two-party registration/group i's total adult population). The beta values can be estimated by running OLS regressions on the equation

$$\ln Y_i = a_i + \beta_i \ln X_i + \varepsilon,$$

where the coefficient on group i's logged mobilization level (β_i) may be interpreted as group i's partisan elasticity for that time interval. Negative elasticities indicate a

Furthermore, we can control for the level of mobilization already attained by the group. It is harder to budge the Democratic bias of a large group than that of a small group by mobilizing new registrants. But by using changes in the percentage of the group registered as our independent variable, we require larger changes in the mobilization of already mobilized groups (e.g., men) as a comparison with changes in the mobilization levels of less registered groups (e.g., women).

Finally, in Boston we have the luxury of possessing detailed information on the ethnic and class composition of election precincts. This information was carefully compiled by Gerald Gamm, who isolated precincts that were ethnically homogeneous (defined as a threshold of 85 percent) with respect to one of five ethnic groups: Irish, Italians, blacks, Jews, and wealthy white Protestants (Yankees).[206] Comparing male–female registration patterns *within* these ethnic groups gives us a further means to test whether men and women were registering similarly during this period.

Boston, 1922–1928.   Prior to female enfranchisement, Boston was an overwhelmingly Democratic city: 68 percent of all male registrants were registered with the Democratic Party. Only 42 percent of potential male voters were registered to vote with one of the major parties, leaving room for partisan mobilization activity during the 1920s. Mobilization did occur for both men and women between 1922 and 1928; men increased their overall registration by 7 percent, while 35 percent of eligible women were registered by 1928.

The partisan elasticities for Boston as a whole and for these five ethnic groups, calculated separately by sex, are given in Table 1. They reflect the movement in a group's partisan bias, given a 1 percent change in the group's level of registration. For example, a 1 percent change in the overall registration of Yankee women produced a statistically significant net gain for the Democrats equivalent to a .51 percentage point increase in the Democratic share of the group's two-party registration. A similar percentage increase in the registration of Yankee men, however, produced approximately a 1 percentage point increase for the Republicans, slightly below the level of statistical significance.

For Boston as a whole, and for four out of five ethnic groups, women exhibit a greater Democratic bias than do men. Neither men nor women show a significant bias for the remaining ethnic group. And since so many more women were registering than men during this period, this

Republican bias in partisan registration. These regressions were run separately for men and women in the various geographical areas. Year dummies were included to control for time trends in registration patterns.

[206]Gerald H. Gamm, *The Making of New Deal Democrats: Voting Behavior and Realignment in Boston, 1920–1940* (Chicago: University of Chicago Press, 1989).

Votes without Leverage

Table 1. *Partisan elasticities by gender and ethnicity*

	N	Women	Men
Boston total	1,220	.391**	.363**
		(.041)	(.044)
Irish	137	.043*	.011
		(.025)	(.035)
Italians	16	.016	.027
		(.018)	(.047)
Blacks	10	.654	.111
		(.389)	(.656)
Jews	44	-.695**	-1.182**
		(.116)	(.148)
Yankees	14	.510*	-1.037
		(.254)	(.604)
Philadelphia/	14	1.183*	2.204**
Pittsburgh		(.622)	(.945)
Native white	33	-1.015**	-.203
Pennsylvania		(.323)	(.453)

Notes: N = number of precincts analyzed for Boston, 1922-1928, and number of counties analyzed for Philadelphia and Pittsburgh from 1925-1936, and native white Pennsylvania from 1925-1928. Standard errors are in parentheses. * indicates coefficient is significant at α = .10; **, coefficient is significant at α = .05.
Sources: Annual Report of the Board of Election Commissioners, Boston Public Library, Boston, Massachusetts; *Pennsylvania State Manual.*

Democratic bias added up for the Democratic Party; women accounted for 78 percent of the Democrats' net gains in registration over the Republicans during this period.

Pennsylvania, 1925–1936. Table 1 also reports the partisan elasticities for men and women registering in the Republican strongholds of Philadelphia, Pittsburgh, and rural white Pennsylvania counties during approximately the same period. The registration data here are from the counties composing the urban areas, and the eleven counties whose population was composed of more than 90 percent whites of native parentage in 1930. The population in the latter counties was also, predictably, overwhelmingly rural; only 21 percent of the population in these counties lived in towns of twenty-five hundred or more. Prior to female enfranchisement, the male population was registered as follows: in Philadelphia 48 percent of the eligible population was registered with a major party, with 94 percent enrolled with the Republicans; in Pitts-

150

burgh 62 percent of the eligible male population was registered to vote, with 89 percent of registrants enrolled with the Republicans; in rural white Pennsylvania counties 84 percent of the eligible population was registered to vote, with 60 percent of registrants enrolled with the Republican Party.

All of these areas experienced registration increases among both men and women during the 1920s: in Philadelphia, men increased their two-party registration by 37 percent, while 48 percent of women were registered by 1928; in Pittsburgh, men increased their registration by only 2 percent while 51.2 percent of women were registered by 1928; and in rural white Pennsylvania counties, men increased their registration by 4 percent while 77 percent of women were registered with a major party by 1928.

Again, the elasticities support our hypothesis concerning the potential for female electoral bandwagons in dominant party areas. Newly registering women are clearly more Republican than newly registering men in these heavily Republican areas. And the magnitude of the contributions of registering women to net Republican gains is again striking: in Philadelphia women accounted for 70 percent of net Republican registration gains; in Pittsburgh women accounted for 100 percent of net Republican gains and even offset net Democratic gains among men; and in rural white Pennsylvania counties women accounted for exactly half of the small net Republican gains during this period.

These elasticities thus support our hypothesis that registering women were more susceptible to the mobilization efforts of dominant parties during the 1920s than were registering men. The absence of any benefit-seeking organizations competing with the dominant parties for the electoral loyalties of women, an absence *unique* to women as a result of their previous disfranchisement, is the likely cause of such differences in the registration behavior of men and women.[207]

CONCLUSION

It would seem that of our three stories as to why the NLWV after 1923 might have refrained from competing in the electoral mobilization of

---

[207]Intriguingly similar results were obtained by Philip J. Ethington in his study of men's and women's voting behavior in Chicago between 1914 and 1919 (Illinois is the only state that ever recorded ballots separately by sex, and did so only during that period). Ethington found that within every geographically based group that had a significant partisan bias, women were *more* biased toward that party than were men. "Women Voters and Politicians in American Cities during the Progressive Era: A Report on Mass and Elite Participation," paper presented to the Annual Meeting of the Social Science History Association, Baltimore, November 5, 1993.

women, only one is supported by the available evidence. The supposition of gender "sameness," a supposition that has both ideological and simple strategic versions, makes predictions that are not consistent with the historical record. Specifically, throughout the 1920s, including after 1923, the NLWV continued to develop a legislative program its leaders believed to be representative of women's policy preferences, and to present legislative demands to the parties in the form of a "Woman's Platform" during presidential election years. In between presidential election years, the league lobbied the current administration and members of Congress to pass bills of interest to the league, mounting a particularly intense drive to save the Sheppard-Towner maternal and infant health act from extinction in 1929. Presumably, league elites would have had no incentive to engage in these activities if they did not somehow hope to anchor their status as women's leaders by securing policy concessions desired by the distinctive group they claimed to represent.

Moreover, these elites' apparent belief in the existence of women as a distinct group, and their apparent willingness to treat women as a distinct group, was shared by other electoral elites. Specifically, in the late months of 1917 and into early 1918 elites in both national parties began to develop plans for the electoral organization of women in all states. Just as in New York State, the formation by party elites of organizations that appeared to be exclusively women's organizations reflects these elites' desire to capitalize on a norm of gender identification by creating the impression that other women were enrolling with their party or voting for their candidate. If male elites had not believed that norm to exist, they would neither have constituted the women's divisions as they did nor have given those divisions valuable party resources. Yet throughout the 1920s, including after 1923, male party elites continued to rely on the distinct women's divisions to mobilize women as a distinct electoral group.

Our second supposition to account for the withdrawal of the NLWV from electoral mobilization, a supposition that hypothesizes an inherited suffrage norm prohibiting participation in partisan electoral politics, is similarly unsupported. This account predicts that to the extent this prohibition existed, it should have been strongest as women entered the electorate, and have either remained strong or gradually weakened as women lost the distinctiveness associated with disfranchisement. But in fact, the direction of change appears to be directly the inverse of this prediction. As we saw in the preceding chapter, as women entered the electorate the NLWV strongly sanctioned electoral mobilization as a strategy to attain its legislative goals. Such mobilization was provisionally suspended at the close of 1920. Between 1920 and 1923 this suspension remained in effect, with league elites still considering electoral mobilization as a strategy but not actually implementing that strategy. Finally, in 1923 the suspension was made more permanent. Despite several reconsiderations of that prohibition on electoral mobilization, the prohibition remained in effect throughout the 1920s.

The evidence for the third theoretical account, however, is more supportive of the latter's predictions. First, the supposition of competitive advantages predicts that as in New York State, the major party organizations would have been able to begin the electoral mobilization of women before the NLWV. And this was in fact the case. Partisan women's divisions were already in place at the national level and, indeed, in a majority of the states before the NLWV even existed as a national organization. As in the case of New York State, the national party organizations and most other state organizations were able to begin mobilizing women to register and vote while the league was still in a transitional state.

The supposition of the parties' competitive advantages in the electoral mobilization of women also predicts that the parties would have realized increasing returns from their mobilization efforts among women. And certainly in the case of national Republican elites, women were seen as increasingly important electorally over the course of the 1920s. By 1928, postelection analysis by the Republican Party appeared to demonstrate not just that women were a significant electoral group, but that they were the electoral group *primarily* responsible for Hoover's election to the presidency.

Moreover, by looking at previously unanalyzed partisan registration data, we indirectly tested our hypothesis that the parties were able to build local followings of women that forced the NLWV from the market for women's electoral loyalties. By comparing women's partisan registration with that of men in the same election precincts or counties, we were able to ask whether women's registration behavior was influenced by the unique circumstances of their entry into the electorate of the 1920s. Women were uniquely subject only to the mobilization efforts of the parties during this period, after the NLWV left the market in women's mobilization in late 1920. Male voters, on the other hand, were subject to the mobilization efforts of the parties *and* of various benefit-seeking groups competing with the parties for male voters' electoral loyalties. These latter groups, such as ethnic associations, unions, veterans' groups, and farmers' organizations, would have presumably weakened somewhat the ability of the parties to capture newly registering male voters. The partisan registration data supported this hypothesis.

In short, throughout the 1920s the leaders of the NLWV had no reason to doubt the continued existence of a norm of gender identification among the vast majority of women still primarily responsible for care of the household and family. Nor were NLWV leaders apparently ideologically averse to using that norm in campaigns of electoral mobilization. The fact that the league's leaders did not seek to tap that norm to support their lobbying efforts, particularly in their campaign to save their most publicized legislative victory from extinction between 1929 and 1932, is explicable only if league leaders had reason to believe that they, unlike the parties' women's organizations, would be unsuccessful in drawing upon that norm to mobilize women's votes. Our argument is that league elites would have had such reason.

The next chapter turns to the question of the lobbying successes and failures of the league and its allies in the WJCC. Did the repeal of the NLWV's policy of electoral mobilization account for the diminished success rate of those organizations after 1924?

5

One Step Forward, Two Steps Back: Women in the Parties, 1917–1932

As the previous chapters have suggested, the decision of the National League of Women Voters not to engage in endorsing or opposing candidates for office is perhaps best understood in the context of the competition between the league and the political parties' women's divisions for the loyalties of women during electoral campaigns. In the early 1920s, both the league and the parties' women's divisions sought to tap the apparent desire of many women, evident during the suffrage drive, to follow the cues of other women in matters affecting primarily women and children.

In order to be able to compete effectively with the league for women's group loyalties, elites in both major parties sought to give their women's divisions all the trappings of independent women's organizations. The parties' women's divisions were set up to be organizationally distinct from the men's party committees, they were staffed entirely by women, they were given a task different from that of the men's committees, and the appeals they made to potential voters were clearly distinguishable from those made by the men's committees. At times, the women's divisions took on the appearance of women's clubs to mirror more closely the most predominant form of women's organization. In addition, male party elites often sought to give these divisions even more of an "authentic" appeal to potential female voters by staffing them with prominent women drawn from independent women's organizations, who would be recognizable to at least some female voters as trustworthy spokespersons for women's group sentiments.

Given the foregoing, it is not surprising that the parties' women's divisions were able to attract large followings of women to the parties' ranks in the years before the NLWV was organizationally ready to seek the electoral mobilization of women in support of a legislative agenda, forcing league elites to reconsider their initial attempt in 1920 to compete with the women's divisions in that mobilization. Nor should it be surprising, given the parties' continued reliance on the women's divisions to mobilize women by appeal to gender solidarity, that NLWV elites apparently were deterred from such competition throughout the 1920s.

VOTES AND POLICY OUTCOMES

Now we may turn to our other question of interest. Why was it that the NLWV was successful between 1920 and 1925 in lobbying policy concessions for women as a group, but rather dramatically ceased winning such concessions after 1925, and even saw earlier victories rolled back by the end of the 1920s? Three kinds of explanation purport to account for that puzzle. We reviewed the theoretical merits of these arguments in Chapter 2 and found them unsatisfactory on those grounds alone. It turns out, perhaps not coincidentally, that the empirical merits of these arguments are weak as well.

One answer to the question of what accounted for these policy victories in the first half of the 1920s is that women's elites built a "policy network" in Washington even before the passage of female suffrage. This network, documented by several scholars, was institutionalized primarily through the Children's Bureau in the Department of Labor and later also in the Women's Bureau in that same department. Linking feminists in government with feminist lobbyists, this network was able to facilitate the transmission of policy proposals from women's organizations to governmental and legislative elites. If policy victories for women's organizations ceased in the bottom half of the 1920s, then this policy network must have weakened dramatically in the mid-1920s.[1]

As discussed in Chapter 2, the notion of "policy networks" is theoretically unsatisfying, given the absence of any role for strategic electoral considerations in the policy network account. Moreover, the argument simply does not fit the facts of this case particularly well. A policy network linking women's organizations and key governmental elites in the Women's and Children's Bureaus had definitely developed by the 1920s, but by all accounts it continued into the New Deal years.[2] Regardless of the difficulties inherent in measuring the existence and strength of such networks, it is at least relatively easy to argue that no sharp break

---

[1]See, e.g., Robyn Muncy, *Creating a Female Dominion in American Reform, 1890–1935* (New York: Oxford University Press, 1991); and Theda Skocpol, *Protecting Soldiers and Mothers: The Political Origins of Social Policy in the United States* (Cambridge, Mass.: Belknap Press of Harvard University Press, 1992).

[2]See Susan Ware, *Beyond Suffrage: Women in the New Deal* (Cambridge, Mass.: Harvard University Press, 1981), for a discussion of the women's New Deal policy network. Also see Ware, *Holding Their Own: American Women in the 1930s* (Boston: Twayne, 1982).

in such a network occurred that corresponds with the relatively sharp break in the political influence of organized women. Indeed, students of this period who have placed explanatory weight on the concept of a policy network confess some bewilderment at the abrupt nature of the cessation of policy benefits to the constituents of that network.[3]

A second nonelectoral argument is that the "climate" of the 1920s grew increasingly hostile to progressive or reform legislation of any kind, including that sponsored by women's organizations. Women's elites were simply lucky that they were able to get a few progressive measures passed in the early 1920s before the legislative climate turned against them.[4]

Again, as discussed in Chapter 2, the idea that "moods" or climates independently affect the passage of legislation is dubious without some underlying assumption of strategic action on the part of legislators. And empirically, the notion of alternating moods or ideological cycles does not neatly fit the facts of this case. The most thorough study of "waves" of legislation concludes that the Progressive legislative "surge" at the national level may be dated from 1906 to 1916.[5] The legislative victories of women's organizations between 1920 and 1925 are thus not well explained by the ideology of Progressivism. And this same study documents that the New Deal legislative "surge" actually began in the second half of Herbert Hoover's tenure in office.[6] Yet as discussed in Chapter 1, women's organizations did not fare any better under the resumption of a more progressive ideological "mood" in 1931 than they had in the supposedly conservative 1920s.

Finally, there is the simple strategic explanation for the absence of legislation benefiting women in the second half of the 1920s: whereas legislators feared that women would vote as a bloc immediately after the passage of suffrage, by the mid-1920s legislative elites had realized that they need fear no punishment at the polls by not responding to women's policy preferences.[7]

[3]Skocpol, *Protecting Soldiers and Mothers*, pp. 520–521.
[4]See, e.g., William H. Chafe, *The American Woman: Her Changing Social, Economic, and Political Roles, 1920–1970* (London: Oxford University Press, 1972), p. 29; Clarke A. Chambers, *Seedtime of Reform: American Social Service and Social Action, 1918–1933* (Minneapolis: University of Minnesota Press, 1963); Muncy, *Creating a Female Dominion*, pp. 129–135; Skocpol, *Protecting Soldiers and Mothers*, p. 521.
[5]David R. Mayhew, *Divided We Govern: Party Control, Lawmaking, and Investigations, 1946–1990* (New Haven: Yale University Press, 1991), p. 157.
[6]Ibid., p. 154.
[7]See Chafe, *The American Woman*, pp. 29–30; J. Stanley Lemons, *The Woman Citizen: Social Feminism in the 1920s* (Chicago: University of Chicago Press, 1975), pp. 157, 174; Michael McGerr, "Political Style and Women's Power, 1830–1930,"

Once more, as discussed in Chapter 2, this simple strategic model is suspect because of its internal inconsistencies. If legislators are assumed to be strategic, then why should not voters be assumed to be strategic as well? And if voters are assumed to be strategic, then we must conclude that voters will logically have an impact on policy only if they are organized independently of office-seeking elites. The simple strategic account omits any discussion of the role of electoral organizations in converting mere votes into electoral leverage. Empirically, the simple strategic account also performs poorly. As documented in the previous chapter, if anything can be inferred from the writings and actions of electoral elites from this period, it is that these elites believed women to constitute an *increasingly* important electoral group over the course of the 1920s, not a *decreasingly* important electoral group. And yet policy concessions moved in a directly inverse trend.

This, then, leads us to the argument made in Chapter 2. As long as NLWV elites were willing to threaten the independent mobilization of women in electoral contests, legislative elites had incentives at least to consider the potential electoral consequences of ignoring the lobbying efforts of the coalition of women's organizations formed at the behest of the NLWV. After all, legislative elites had every reason to believe that the former suffrage machine would be able to muster women by appeal to some form of gender solidarity, much as the parties' own women's divisions were seeking to accomplish.

We can reasonably surmise that legislative elites would have possessed such incentives through the 1924 national elections. The absence of any mobilization activity by the NLWV in 1922 would have given legislative elites reason to hope that the league would no longer be a factor in electoral contests, but many women were still not part of a partisan female network and the league was still publicly considering continuing its previous policy of targeted electoral intervention. But after the 1924 elections, with again no activity by the league in any electoral contests, and no public discussion of the league's electoral role, legislative elites must have felt much safer in ignoring the lobbying efforts of women's organizations.

Our revised strategic explanation thus appears to fit the facts of the case better than do existing explanations. And it connects the presuffrage history of the NAWSA with the postsuffrage history of the NLWV in a chronological chain of causally linked events. The organizational in-

Journal of American History 77, no. 3 (December 1990): 882; Muncy, *Creating a Female Dominion*, p. 126; Eleanor Flexner, *Century of Struggle: The Woman's Rights Movement in the United States* (Cambridge, Mass.: Harvard University Press, 1975), p. 338; Skocpol, *Protecting Soldiers and Mothers*, p. 521.

vestments made by NAWSA elites in the presuffrage era appear to have had downstream consequences for the ability of NAWSA's postsuffrage incarnation to affect the course of public policy.

But although we appear to have explained the policy outcomes of the 1920s with our set of causally linked arguments, we have thus far tested those arguments on only one dependent variable, namely policies for which the NLWV lobbied during the 1920s. We would be able to have much more confidence in the strength of our arguments if they predicted outcomes in other dependent variables we could investigate.[8] Indeed, theoretical arguments that did not make predictions beyond the original case they were developed to explain would not be particularly powerful theoretical arguments.

Fortunately, our arguments do make predictions for another set of dependent variables with which we can test the proposition that it was the potential electoral threat posed by the NLWV that produced policy concessions for women in the first half of the 1920s. Women in the parties throughout the 1920s lobbied male partisan elites for *organizational* concessions within the parties themselves. The fact that both parties' elites set up "women's" divisions at the national level and in most states upon female enfranchisement implied that existing party committees became exclusively "men's" committees unless explicit provisions were made for designated women's seats on those committees. Believing (correctly) that the "real" party decisions were being made by the men's committees, female party leaders in both parties throughout the 1920s sought access to the men's committees.

What would we predict would be the response of male party elites to the women's demands for organizational concessions? As discussed in Chapter 2, we reasonably assume that electoral elites, both legislative and party, are reluctant to make policy concessions, given the constraints on their strategic options which such concessions necessitate. For the same reason, we can as reasonably assume that party elites would be unwilling to make any organizational concessions that would restrict their flexibility to make strategic electoral decisions. Allowing women both new to party politics and clearly possessing a benefit-seeking agenda rather than an office-seeking agenda to have an influence on party strategy would constitute just such a restriction on the strategic freedom of male party elites.[9]

---

[8]Gary King, Robert O. Keohane, and Sidney Verba, *Designing Social Inquiry: Scientific Inference in Qualitative Research* (Princeton: Princeton University Press, 1994), pp. 223–224.

[9]Throughout the 1920s, women in both major party organizations, New York State and nationally, lobbied party elites for a women's policy agenda. For details on this lobbying, see chapters 6 and 7 of Anna L. Harvey, "The Legacy of Disfranchise-

But if the women responsible for mobilizing potential female voters under the organizational auspices of the parties were successful in that mobilization, and could credibly claim to be able to withhold turnout, for example, if their demands were not met, would not party elites be forced into responding to their demands? The answer is simple: not if male party elites continued to *control* the women's divisions through their power to appoint female personnel and to provide budgets for those divisions. As long as male party elites continued to control the women's divisions in either or both of these ways, then any threats emanating from the leaders of the women's divisions could be effectively countered by removing these troublemakers from the party organization or by withdrawing funds for the committee in question. If women could be removed from their party positions at the discretion of male party leaders, then they would think at least twice before threatening the latter with the very votes they were supposed to be mobilizing.

Given the incentives of male party elites, and given that it was in fact male party elites who created the women's divisions in the first place, it is likely that those elites would in fact have organized the women's divisions so as to allow male elites to maintain control of the women's party organizations. Only through such organizational control could male party elites ensure that the women's organizations could not be used to threaten party leaders and candidates with women's votes (or the lack thereof) if organizational concessions were not forthcoming.

If male party elites ensured that they retained control of the women's divisions, then they would have had no internal incentives to respond to any demands originating from within those organizations. Only an external threat somehow linked to those demands could have given them any incentives to respond favorably. That is, if male party elites had reason to believe that failing to respond to the demands of women from within the parties could have electoral repercussions from women's organizations that were independent of the parties, then they would have had incentives to respond to those demands, which would have varied depending on the cost to the parties of fulfilling those demands, and the likelihood and severity of the potential electoral retaliation.

That this threat could in fact exist is quite plausible if women in the parties' women's divisions maintained ties with and/or membership in independent women's organizations. Those women's organizations, in particular the NLWV, would then have been aware of the demands of women within the parties and perhaps even lobbied the parties to be receptive to the women's demands. If female party leaders with connec-

ment: Women in Electoral Politics, 1917–1932" (Ph.D. dissertation, Princeton University, 1995).

160

tions to independent women's organizations sought costly organizational concessions from male party elites, the response of those elites to these demands should have followed a pattern identical to their response to the NLWV's congressional lobbying activity. As long as the league was perceived by male party elites to be a potential electoral threat, the latter should have made at least some concessions to the demands from women in the parties who were members in or sympathetic to the aims of the league, albeit reluctantly and in all likelihood with much protest. Once the league came to be seen as harmless, however, that stream of concessions to women in the party organizations should have ceased. Some of those concessions might even have been rescinded, as certain early policy victories of the league were later rescinded.

If the foregoing conditions hold, then the response of male party elites to the female leaders' organizational demands constitutes a new dependent variable on which to test the hypothesis that the NLWV's electoral mobilization policy produced incentives for electoral elites to respond to organized women's demands. Moreover, because we can examine the pattern of organizational concessions in both national parties and also in parties at the state level, we can further multiply the number of dependent variables with which to test our argument. If a pattern like that found with respect to the league's lobbying for policy concessions can also be found with respect to the demands of women from within the parties for greater access to party committees, then the hypothesized causal link between the league's electoral involvement or lack thereof and its efficacy in congressional lobbying is lent additional support.

In addition to simply looking at the timing of grants of access to women in the parties, we can also look for documentary evidence that may (or may not) support our causal account. That is, did female party elites reference independent women's organizations in their negotiations with male party leaders? Were the latter aware of the existence of those organizations? Did they voice any opinions as to the potential electoral threat posed by those organizations?

This chapter documents for the major parties' New York State organizations and for their national organizations the evidence that speaks to these questions, considering first whether the three conditions necessary to use the grants of access to women in the parties as a test for our independent variable are satisfied. Did women in all party organizations seek greater access to the parties' men's committees? Were the parties' women's divisions controlled by male party leaders? Did the National League of Women Voters lobby male party elites to accede to the demands of women within the parties' women's divisions?

If these conditions are satisfied, then we can look at the pattern in the grants of access made to women in each of the four party organizations. If the pattern found is similar to the pattern of the success rate of the NLWV in congressional policy victories, then we may have greater confidence in the existence of a causal link between the threat of electoral mobilization by independent women's organizations and the policy concessions made to the latter. We may also investigate the historical record to see whether any documentary evidence supports the existence of the causal link in the case of the parties' internal politics. If partisan women made reference to the NLWV in their internal lobbying efforts, and/or if male party elites appear to have considered the NLWV an electoral threat, then this hypothesized causal link is further supported.

FEMALE PARTISAN DEMANDS, MALE PARTISAN CONTROL, AND THE NLWV, 1917–1932

The first condition necessary to use the grants of access to the parties' women's divisions as a new dependent variable appears to be well satisfied for all four party organizations. In the New York State Republican Party, for example, female party leaders throughout the 1920s sought access to the male county, state, and national party committees and executive committees, and representation at the party's state conventions and on the state's delegations to the Republican national conventions.[10] Like their Republican counterparts, New York State Democratic women also asked for more access to previously all-male party committees, seeking "fifty-fifty" representation on all party committees throughout this period.[11] In the absence of such equality of representation, they referred to Democratic state conventions as men's meetings.[12]

---

[10]See, e.g., "Republican Women Want Equal Status – Mrs. Livermore Tells Committee Every Unit Should Have Double Representation," *NYT*, January 11, 1920, p. 16; "Chairman Morris Asks Women to Aid," *NYT*, May 24, 1923, p. 19; Charles D. Hilles to Warren G. Harding, May 31, 1923, Warren G. Harding Papers, microfilm edition, Ohio Historical Society, Columbus, Ohio, Reel 195, Frame 182; Charles D. Hilles to Mary Livermore, May 31, 1923, Warren G. Harding Papers, Frames 183–186; "Women Seek Places in State Committee," *NYT*, June 10, 1923, II p. 1; "Republican Women to Press Demands," *NYT*, June 14, 1923, p. 10; "State Republicans Dodge Dry Question," *NYT*, June 15, 1923, p. 1; "Women Will Get Political Wish," *NYT*, January 10, 1925, p. 15; "Hay Fight Is Only Convention Cloud," *NYT*, February 17, 1920, p. 17; "Mrs. Livermore as Big 4 Alternate," *NYT*, February 19, 1920, p. 1.
[11]"Women Democrats Form Organization," *NYT*, February 5, 1920, p. 8; "Two Women Urged on 'Big Four' Slate," *NYT*, February 24, 1920, p. 1; "Lehman Is Named for Appeals Court," *NYT*, September 29, 1923, p. 3; "Says Women Will Cast Record Vote This Fall," *NYT*, September 21, 1924, VIII p. 9; "More Smith Bills Offered at Albany," *NYT*, February 18, 1925, p. 7.
[12]"Expect Smith to Be Conference Choice as against Hearst," *NYT*, July 7, 1922, p. 1.

Women in the national Republican organization also asked for more access within the party organization. At various times throughout this period, they asked for "fifty–fifty" representation on the Republican National Executive Committee, the Republican National Committee, and on all state and local party committees, an increased number of female national convention delegates, representation on all convention committees, especially the important platform and rules committees, and equal membership on all national campaign committees.[13] And like their Republican counterparts, Democratic women also asked for equal access to the men's party committees, including half the seats on the Democratic National Committee, half of state delegations to the national conventions, half of the membership and chairmanships of all convention committees, and representation on any temporary convention committees held to resolve deadlocked ballots.[14]

The second condition specified here also appears to be well satisfied. That is, women were unlikely to see concessions to their demands from party leaders given continuing male control of the women's division within both parties, state and national. In New York State, state election laws stipulate the process by which county and state party committees and delegates to state and national party conventions are selected. In 1918, these laws required that the state committees consist of one representative from each district of the lower house of the state legislature (the 150–member State Assembly), and that the county committees consist of at least one representative from each election district or precinct. The election laws also stipulated that state and county committeemen were to be elected by registered party members in the fall primaries (with the exception of presidential election years, in which special spring pri-

---

[13]"G.O.P. Women Ask Equality with Men – Demand Representation in Equal Number on National Committee," *NYT*, January 6, 1920, p. 1; "Women Announce Demands at Chicago," *NYT*, June 4, 1920, p. 2; "Militant Suffragists Open Drive at Chicago," *NYT*, June 5, 1920, p. 2; "Women Plan Rush on Convention Hall," *NYT*, June 6, 1920, p. 5; "Women Organize to Press Demands," *NYT*, June 7, 1920, p. 6; "Women Not Content but Remain Loyal," *NYT*, June 10, 1920, p. 6; "Harding's Day Long and Busy," *NYT*, March 8, 1921, p. 3; Charles D. Hilles to Warren G. Harding, May 31, 1923, Warren G. Harding Papers, Reel 195, Frame 182; "Women Seek Places in State Committee," *NYT*, June 10, 1923, II p. 1; "Mrs. Martin Heads Organization Body," *NYT*, June 8, 1924, p. 3; "Republican Women Plan Model Campaign," *NYT*, November 30, 1927, p. 6; "Women Are Active among the Boomers," *NYT*, June 11, 1928, p. 2; "Women Plan Fight to Elect Hoover," *NYT*, July 25, 1928, p. 2.

[14]"Women Confident at San Francisco," *NYT*, June 19, 1920, p. 2; "Mrs. Blair's Allies Foresee a Contest," *NYT*, June 24, 1924, p. 6; "Women Plan Fight on Any Wet Plank," *NYT*, June 25, 1924, p. 15; "Declares Conferees Flouted the Women," *NYT*, July 8, 1924, p. 3; "Miss Marbury Denies Slighting of Women," *NYT*, July 9, 1924, p. 3; "Democratic Women Move for Harmony," *NYT*, July 11, 1924, p. 3.

maries were held). County committeemen served one-year terms, while state committeemen served two-year terms. The parties' county and state executive committees, however, being creatures of the parties themselves, were not covered by state law. These committees were elected by the county and state committees, respectively.[15]

Sitting party committee members, then, controlled the membership of their own executive committees. But even the elections regulated by state election law were heavily if not entirely determined by the sitting party committees. Before the primaries the county chairmen would present election board officials with a list of all offices to be filled, including party offices, then would circulate petitions for their chosen nominees for those offices. After they obtained the requisite number of signatures, the parties' nominees' names would appear on the party's official primary ballot. Rarely did candidates other than organization nominees gather enough signatures to appear on the primary ballot; in this eventuality, the parties' county organizations would print sample "organization ballots" and distribute them. If voters did not approve of the organization candidates on the ballot, they could also write in their own choice (again, rarely resulting in the election of candidates other than organization nominees).

An identical process took place for the parties' nomination of delegates to state and national party conventions, when the former were official (during the years when New York State made statewide nominations under a primary system, both parties held "unofficial" state conventions for the purpose of "designating," not nominating, candidates). That is, the parties would circulate petitions for their state and national delegate choices so that those names would appear on primary ballots; rarely, if ever, were petitions circulated for any delegates other than those nominated by the parties' committees. When state conventions were unofficial, the delegate selection process continued as before but without the step of voters ratifying the choices of party elites.[16]

State election laws thus guaranteed that those who sat on the party committees at any given point in time controlled the selection of future party committee members. And when the women's party committees were created, they were subject to these same rules. In the Republican Party, auxiliary women's county and state executive committees were

---

[15]This paragraph and the next two are taken from "Priming the Feminine Voter for the Primary," *NYT*, April 4, 1920, p. 2.

[16]"Democrats Are for Women Delegates," *NYT*, June 20, 1918, p. 13; "Kings Delegation Chosen," *NYT*, July 17, 1918, p. 11; "Want Roosevelt to Lead in State," *NYT*, July 18, 1918, p. 9; "Four State Leaders Houston Delegates," *NYT*, February 5, 1928, p. 3.

first formed as creatures of the male party committees, and these appointed female leaders were then given the responsibility of appointing female subleaders and election district workers.[17] Later, as women were added to the male party committees, male Republican elites selected the female nominees for whom the party would circulate petitions.[18] New York State's Democrats likewise formed auxiliary committees of women at the state and county levels and, in addition, created new positions specifically for women on their existing state and county executive committees. These latter were filled by appointments made by sitting male committees.[19]

The national party organizations, when they created their women's organizations shortly after the creation of those in New York, followed similar procedures. Because the national party organizations were to some degree creatures of the state and local organizations, the selection of their personnel was somewhat dependent upon the prior decisions of state and local party elites. National committees in both parties were composed of one member from each state, the members typically being elected by the state delegations to each party's national convention. (In most states these delegations were selected by the county and state committees.) National executive committees were elected from this national committee after each party's national convention, although this meant in practice that the presidential nominee designated a national chairman who in turn selected his executive committee. The national chairmen also had the de facto authority to compose the important convention and preconvention committees that wrote the party platforms.[20]

When women's committees were added to the national parties, just as in the state parties, these committees were filled by appointments made by national male party elites. Later, when women were given des-

[17]For the Republicans in New York State, see "Office for Mrs. Yawger," *NYT*, November 15, 1917, p. 6; "Republicans Admit Women as Partners," *NYT*, December 21, 1917, p. 11; "Republican Women Keen," *NYT*, April 18, 1918, p. 12.

[18]For an early example from New York County, see "Hays Urges Party to Forget Politics," *NYT*, June 21, 1918, p. 8. Also see "Lehman Named by Republicans, Too; Smith Is Assailed," *NYT*, September 30, 1923, p. 2.

[19]"Will Put Women on State Committee," *NYT*, December 12, 1917, p. 10; "Hunt for Candidate to Oppose Hearst," *NYT*, April 8, 1918, p. 8; "Democrats Discuss Women," *NYT*, April 14, 1918, p. 18; "Tammany Women on Par with Men," *NYT*, February 22, 1918, p. 1; "Women Now Eligible for Tammany Ranks," *NYT*, March 1, 1918, p. 20; "Tammany Welcomes Women in Council," *NYT*, May 8, 1918, p. 7; "Women Sachems in Tammany Wigwam," *NYT*, June 8, 1919, VII p. 9; "Widen Vote for Women," *NYT*, January 28, 1918, p. 14; "Women Leaders in Bronx," *NYT*, March 13, 1918, p. 7.

[20]"Hays Announces Republican Aids on Party Policy," *NYT*, January 29, 1920, p. 1.

ignated seats on the men's national committees, these seats were filled as were the men's seats.[21] Even the women's national partisan clubs, nominally independent of the party organizations, were under the official thumb of male party elites. For both parties the women's clubs were allowed use of the parties' names only if the clubs were officially approved by state central committees.[22] Organizers of specific campaign clubs – for instance, the women's Hoover clubs created during the 1928 campaign – would be appointed by the regular women's committees.[23] At no time were women in either national party organization allowed to choose their own representatives or leaders.

In theory, then, male party leaders could use their control of appointments within the party's women's division to remove female party leaders who showed a disposition to make trouble. A female party leader who pursued costly concessions for women too vigorously, or who perhaps threatened to withhold female turnout if such concessions were not forthcoming, could easily be removed from the party organization by male party leaders. But is there any evidence that this kind of control took place? In short, the answer is yes. A comprehensive search of the *New York Times* between 1917 and 1932 revealed several instances of male party leaders using their power of appointment to quell female activism within the party organizations.

In the New York State Republican Party, as early as 1920 male leaders were strategically selecting the female delegates to the unofficial 1920 Republican state convention: "There will be no trouble worth mentioning from the women who will sit as delegates in the convention, and there will be about 200 women delegates – more than have ever sat in

[21]"Republicans Plan to Enlist Women," *NYT*, January 23, 1918, p. 10; "Democrats Choose Mrs. J. S. Crosby," *NYT*, February 28, 1918, p. 5; "Adams Drops Out, Hays Elected," *NYT*, February 14, 1918, p. 3; "Report of Republican Women's National Executive Committee, September 3, 1918–June 8, 1920," Warren G. Harding Papers, Reel 54, Frames 978–983; "Republicans Urge Woman's Suffrage," *NYT*, January 11, 1919, p. 3; "Elects Cummings Party Chairman," *NYT*, February 27, 1919, p. 8; "Democrats Plan for Women's Vote," *NYT*, September 28, 1919, p. 7; "G.O.P. Cmte to Meet on December 10," *NYT*, November 11, 1919, p. 4; "Lesson Women Learned at Chicago," *NYT*, June 20, 1920, VIII p. 2.

[22]"Republican Women Settle Working Plans," *NYT*, May 24, 1919, p. 3; "To Unite Women Democrats," *NYT*, December 13, 1919, p. 6; "Women's Party Delayed," *NYT*, December 27, 1919, p. 3; "Oppose Their Party Plan," *NYT*, December 28, 1919, p. 20; "Women Democrats Form Organization," *NYT*, February 5, 1920, p. 8; "Mrs. Crosby Takes Office," *NYT*, February 7, 1920, p. 6.

[23]Nathan William MacChesney, Director, Hoover-Curtis Organization Bureau, to Herbert Hoover, November 7, 1928, Campaign and Transition Papers, Box 163, Herbert Hoover Papers, Herbert Hoover Presidential Library, West Branch, Iowa; Press Release, Women's National Committee for Hoover, September 29, 1928, Campaign and Transition Papers, Box 187, ibid.

a convention. But they will all be good organization women."[24] At the convention itself, male leaders reportedly selected the female delegates to the 1920 Republican National Convention so as not to allow Mary Garrett Hay, the former suffrage leader and vocal female Republican activist, to attend the national convention in an official capacity:

> In an effort to head off any trouble that might be started in the Republican unofficial State Convention . . . by Miss Mary Garrett Hay, . . . the Republican State Committee yesterday selected Mrs. Arthur L. [Mary] Livermore as one of the four alternates at large [to the National Convention]. . . . Fearing that certain women in the organization might seize the opportunity [of a potentially open spot for delegate at large] to demand that one of their number be chosen in his place, pressure was brought to bear upon Mr. Root by Republican leaders to have him submit to the demands of the convention, and when he decided to do so the leaders turned their attention to arranging a "trouble-proof" slate of alternates. Expecting that with the Big Four opportunity closed to Miss Hay she might want to carry her fight against Senator Wadsworth to the floor of the convention, the leaders decided to fill up the four vacancies for alternates and forestall any criticism by the women by naming one of their sex for the latter position. The leaders considered they had made a happy selection in Mrs. Livermore, for she is acceptable to the suffragists, being a believer in the cause, and yet not offensive to the anti-suffragists, as she has not been an active suffragist worker.[25]

The rest of the state's delegation to the national convention was selected from the congressional districts by the male county committees; Hay was also not selected as a district delegate from her Manhattan congressional district.[26]

Again in 1922, male party elites were apparently able to eliminate any women who were likely to cause trouble from the delegations to the Republican State Convention:

> If disposition arises among the 1,000-odd delegates to the Republican convention to oppose Governor Miller's wishes as regards platform or ticket it is not likely to be among the 285 women delegates who are attending their first official party assembly.[27]

[24]Republican State Chairman George Glynn, in "Leaders Prepare to 'Steamroller' Saratoga Meeting," *NYT*, July 25, 1920, p. 1.
[25]"Mrs. Livermore as Big 4 Alternate," *NYT*, February 19, 1920, p. 1.
[26]"But One Woman Delegate," *NYT*, March 2, 1920, p. 17; "Republicans Finish Up-State Slates – Only One Woman Chosen by the Organization for National Convention Delegate," *NYT*, March 5, 1920, p. 17; "Republicans Slate Only Two Women," *NYT*, March 8, 1920, p. 15.
[27]"Women Stand by Miller," *NYT*, September 27, 1922, p. 3.

167

Nominations for office were also an occasion that male party leaders could use to reward female obedience to male party leaders over female activism. Just as in 1920 state party leaders chose to reward a nonsuffragist with a trip to the national convention, so was former antisuffragist Ruth Pratt the recipient of several plum positions from male Republican leaders. In 1925 Pratt was the first woman nominated by a district committee in New York to serve on the Board of Aldermen; Pratt won handily in her overwhelmingly Republican district.[28] The *Times* reported, however, that many women in the district and in the district organization were unhappy with the choice, given Pratt's antisuffrage history.[29] Pratt later secured the Republican congressional nomination in her district and became the first woman from New York State to serve in Congress. In 1929 Pratt was appointed by male state Republican leaders to serve as New York's Republican national committeewoman, despite well-reported protests by female state leaders that Pratt was not the women's choice to represent them on the national committee.[30]

Republican male state leaders were also selecting the women who would receive any state patronage jobs, and were reportedly using these jobs as a way to advance the party fortunes of the female leaders more willing to follow the lead of male Republican elites. As the director of the national Republican women's organization wrote to President Coolidge in February of 1925: "I understand that some of these ['Regular Republican women of New York'] have served notice on political men that they wanted a voice in the appointment of women. To quote them literally, 'We do not propose to stand for any further choice of "pansies." ' "[31]

---

[28]"Mrs. J. T. Pratt to Be First Woman Alderman; 'Silk Stocking District' to Support Her," *NYT*, June 5, 1925, p. 1.

[29]*NYT*, June 8, 1925, p. 3.

[30]"Up-State Woman in Sabin Post Urged," *NYT*, March 12, 1929, p. 12; "Miss Butler Not in Race," *NYT*, March 13, 1929, p. 27; Florence Wardwell to Herbert Hoover, August 17, 1929, Presidential Personal Files, Box 214, Herbert Hoover Papers; "Works for Mrs. Schindler," *NYT*, July 17, 1929, p. 52; "Will Back Mrs. Schindler," *NYT*, July 23, 1929, p. 29; "Mrs. Livermore Seeks to Succeed Mrs. Sabin," *NYT*, August 19, 1929, p. 21; "Calls Parley to Fill Mrs. Sabin's Place," *NYT*, August 28, 1929, p. 27; "Agree on Mrs. Pratt to Succeed Mrs. Sabin," *NYT*, August 29, 1929, p. 4; Florence Wardwell to Herbert Hoover, August 30, 1929, Presidential Subject Files, Box 265, Herbert Hoover Papers; "See Move to Force Vote for Mrs. Pratt," *NYT*, August 31, 1929, p. 17; "See Mrs. Pratt Elected," *NYT*, September 4, 1929, p. 22; "Mrs. Pratt Slated to Get Party Post," *NYT*, September 5, 1929, p. 2; "Demand Mrs. Schindler Get Mrs. Sabin's Place," *NYT*, September 5, 1929, p. 2; "Mrs. Pratt Elected for Committee Post," *NYT*, September 7, 1929, p. 1; "Huston Is Chosen Mid Party Harmony," *NYT*, September 10, 1929, p. 3.

[31]Harriet Taylor Upton to Calvin Coolidge, February 16, 1925, Calvin Coolidge Papers, microfilm edition, U.S. Library of Congress, Washington, D.C., Reel 121, File 395. For more on the structure of patronage distribution in New York State, see

Women in the Parties

In the New York State Democratic Party as well, on several occasions were outspoken Democratic female leaders displaced in favor of more pliant women. In 1920, the choice of male party elites for New York's female representative on the Democratic National Executive Committee and for one of the two female delegates-at-large to the Democratic National Convention was made over the vociferous protests of women in the state party organization. The women were unhappy over the selection of Elizabeth Marbury to receive these leadership positions, as Marbury was well identified as one of Tammany boss Charles F. Murphy's personal loyalists and was, moreover, a former antisuffragist with no current or previous ties to any women's organizations.[32]

After the 1920 Democratic National Convention, the leader of the state Democratic women's organization was actually removed from office by male leaders, and Elizabeth Marbury was installed in her place.[33] By this time, Marbury also held the post of New York's female representative on the Democratic National Committee. The deposed female leader took the occasion to comment on the more general issue of male selection of female party leaders:

Most of the women's organizations among Democrats, I have found, are dominated by men holding political office by grace of Tammany Hall. . . . We found at [the national convention in] San Francisco that a number of delegates to the Democratic national convention were related to the district leaders by marriage. Thus, a leader would send his wife as a delegate on the theory that this would be recognition of women voters.[34]

Women in the state party organization continued to protest the selection of Marbury to head the state party through 1922. In that year male party leaders named a new female state party leader, again of their own choosing.[35] Marbury continued to retain her other party posts, however, and was again selected by the New York State delegation to the 1924

Memorandum for Mr. Hoover from Mr. Huston, January 4, 1929, Campaign and Transition Papers, Box 37, Herbert Hoover Papers; "Maier Becomes Job Dispenser for His Party," *New York Sun*, May 22, 1930, Presidential Subject Files, Box 265, Herbert Hoover Papers.

[32]"Women Democrats Divided," *NYT*, February 6, 1920, p. 3; "Miss Marbury Opposed," *NYT*, February 9, 1920, p. 15; "Mrs. Crosby Halts Her Big 4 Backers," *NYT*, February 17, 1920, p. 17; "Two Women Urged on 'Big Four' Slate," *NYT*, February 24, 1920, p. 1.

[33]"W. B. W." to Harry Daugherty [forwarded to Warren G. Harding], September 1, 1920, Warren G. Harding Papers, Reel 94, Frames 188–191.

[34]Nellie Fassett Crosby, in "Mrs. Crosby Will Sue to Rescind Expulsion," *NYT*, October 25, 1920, p. 2.

[35]"Democrats Appoint Harriet May Mills," *NYT*, January 22, 1922, p. 16.

Democratic National Convention to serve a four-year term as national committeewoman.[36]

Marbury was not the only former antisuffragist or nonsuffragist that Tammany leaders appointed to the women's division of the state party, as instanced by the female leader of the 1st Assembly District of New York County: "When Mr. Foley asked me to be his co-leader . . . I had not even been a suffragist. . . . The subject had simply never appealed to me. . . . always I have consulted with the men and have counted on their advice. It is not the kind of work for a woman to do alone. . . . I think men are best fitted for the big jobs. And I think that women can be of the greatest service by cooperating with the men."[37] At no time during the latter half of the 1920s were party procedures changed to allow the members of the women's division the authority to choose their own leaders.

Similar incidents occurred within the national Republican Party. Most broadly, male Republican elites were clearly concerned about quashing any tendencies toward political "independence" exhibited by women within the party organization.[38] More specifically, party elites used their control of appointments to undermine any efforts by women to control the women's division. For example, when the women present at the 1920 Republican National Convention selected Ruth Hanna McCormick to be the party's national women's leader as vice-chairman of the Republican National Executive Committee, the *Times* erroneously reported that the women's action "practically assured" McCormick's selection by the national committee for this position.[39] However, this was not to be; McCormick did not even receive a place on the executive committee, much less its vice-chairmanship.[40] Instead, presidential nominee Harding and his advisors made their own choice for this position, giving the leadership of the national women's organization to Harriet Taylor Upton.

In 1924, Harriet Taylor Upton resigned her post as leader of the national women's division, and the "associate" national committee-

---

[36]"New York Delegates Elect a Woman as Chairman," *NYT*, June 22, 1924, p. 1.

[37]Mrs. Thomas Nolan, in "Woman Tammany Leader Thinks Men More Capable," *NYT*, February 22, 1925, VIII p. 10; "Woman Politician Depends on Men," *NYT*, February 5, 1925, p. 7.

[38]Secretary to George H. Clark, Chairman, Republican State Advisory Committee, July 21, 1920, Warren G. Harding Papers, Reel 32, Frames 256–257, relating Harding campaign's receipt of a report of a prominent Republican woman in Ohio who "shows a disposition to be independent."

[39]"Suffragists Show Fight at Chicago," *NYT*, June 12, 1920, p. 3; "Name Mrs. McCormick," *NYT*, June 13, 1920, p. 3.

[40]"Picks Women to Aid Harding Campaign," *NYT*, June 23, 1920, p. 1.

women sought to make their own selection of her successor.[41] But this was also not to be; to the associate committeewomen's dismay, male Republican leaders selected Harriet Taylor Upton's successor without consulting any of the women present at the 1924 national convention, choosing moreover the widow of a former Republican national committeeman who had no ties to women's organizations whatsoever.[42] Sally Aley Hert was again selected in 1928 by male party elites to lead the women's organization of the party.[43]

After the 1928 election, the Republican national chairman rather casually suggested Hert for a cabinet position, given the important role Republican elites believed women to have played in the election.[44] At once women within the Republican organization began protesting, both publicly and privately, that Hert should not receive such an honor as a "man's woman."[45] Hert did not get a cabinet post, but neither did any other woman.

Perhaps offended by the uproar surrounding the question of whether she was in fact merely a puppet for male party elites, Hert submitted her resignation from the vice-chairmanship of the Republican National Committee in February 1929.[46] The dispute over the control of the party's women's organization then focused on Hert's successor. Hert and several men floated the name of the Pennsylvania national committeewoman in the press, and this angered many of the women who had

[41]"Mrs. Upton Resigns Post," *NYT*, June 6, 1924, p. 3.

[42]"Mrs. Martin Heads Organization Body," *NYT*, June 8, 1924, p. 3; "Primary System Attacked," *NYT*, June 10, 1924, p. 3.

[43]"Dr. Work Ratified as Hoover Leader; Opens the Campaign," *NYT*, June 22, 1928, p. 1.

[44]Minerva Allen, President, Kentucky Woman's Republican League, to Herbert Hoover, January 2, 1929, Campaign and Transition Papers, Box 87, Herbert Hoover Papers.

[45]Stella Beck, Secretary, Kentucky Woman's Republican League, to Herbert Hoover, November 12, 1928, ibid.: "[Hert] is a representative of the men *and not of the women*. . . . if such an appointment is being considered to please the men that is a different matter, *but kindly do not do so to please the women*, for it *does not please us* in any sense of the word, of this you can be sure" (emphasis in original); Minerva Allen to Herbert Hoover, January 2, 1929, ibid.; Ruth Hanna McCormick to Herbert Hoover, September 4/5, 1928, Campaign and Transition Papers, Box 45, ibid.; William Hard to Herbert Hoover, January 1, 1929, Campaign and Transition Papers, Box 87, ibid.; "Women Protest Place in Cabinet for Mrs. Hert," *New York Herald Tribune*, January 4, 1929, ibid.: "Republican Senators and leaders generally have been deluged with protests from women leaders in the organization throughout the country insisting that Mrs. Hert is not the choice of the Republican women workers, but of a few male leaders."

[46]"Work to Call Meeting to Elect Successor," *NYT*, August 3, 1929, p. 2; "Mrs. Hert Retains Kentucky Post," *NYT*, August 4, 1929, p. 14.

protested Hert's potential cabinet appointment, on the basis that Marjorie Scranton had been no less a selection of the men than Hert. (The *Washington Post* reported that "Mrs. Scranton would make the ideal vice chairman, it is said. She is attractive and has plenty of money, and would not try to nose about too much.")[47] Ruth Baker Pratt, the former antisuffragist from New York, was also a candidate for the post but, somewhat ironically, she was reportedly rejected by male elites on the basis that she was not enough of a "rubber stamp." This conflict continued until August 1929, when Hoover asked Hert to stay on for another year until a successor could be agreed upon without the further airing of internal party disputes.[48]

In January 1930, however, Hert resigned as director of the women's division anyway and left Washington for Louisville.[49] The new head of the women's organization, Hert's former assistant Louise Dodson, was by her own admission "a young, green creature who had been nothing but housewife and teacher"; her first official act was to announce a plan to procure a tea service for every county committeewoman (an announcement derided by Democratic National Vice-Chairwoman Nellie Tayloe Ross).[50] Dodson did not last long in the post; by August 1930 she had submitted her resignation, reportedly at the request of the new chairman of the Republican National Committee, who immediately announced that the new head of the women's division would be a former student of his from Antioch College.[51] Lenna Yost, Republican national committeewoman from West Virginia and member of the Republican National Executive Committee, was reportedly opposed by the other women on the committee.

Women in the national Republican organization also did not control the distribution of patronage to any female supporters. This issue was raised by the women on the Republican National Executive Committee with Harding in the spring of 1921, and continued to be a source of tension between men and women in the national party organization.[52]

[47]"Work Sets Sept. 9 to Name Successor," *NYT*, August 6, 1929, p. 3; "Mrs. A. T. Hert Changes Plan to Quit Post," *Washington Post*, September 4, 1929, Presidential Subject Papers, Box 254, Herbert Hoover Papers.

[48]Herbert Hoover to Mrs. Alvin T. Hert, Presidential Personal Files, Box 147, Herbert Hoover Papers; "President Takes Up Politics with Work," *NYT*, September 4, 1929, p. 4.

[49]"Mrs. Hert Quits Republican Post," *NYT*, January 19, 1930, p. 24.

[50]"Republicans Plan 'Tea Cup' Campaign," *NYT*, January 20, 1930, p. 3; "Spurns Teacup Politics," *NYT*, January 24, 1930, p. 48.

[51]"Mrs. Dodson to Quit Post," *NYT*, August 5, 1930, p. 3; "Mrs. Yost Selected for Dodson Place," *NYT*, August 14, 1930, p. 2.

[52]"Harding's Day Long and Busy," *NYT*, March 8, 1921, p. 3.

Ruth McCormick in particular pressed the argument that the women on the Republican National Executive Committee should be consulted before the appointment of any woman to a federal post.[53] Upton also conveyed the appointment preferences of women in the state organizations to national Republican elites, but had no authority to act on those preferences.[54]

The norm was for either Republican senators or, in the absence of the latter, national committeemen to control all federal patronage in the states.[55] In the late 1920s the national committeewoman in Texas wrote several letters to President Hoover, protesting that, as the women's organization in the party was supposed to be responsible for all matters pertaining to women, she should have control over female appointments either within or from Texas.[56] Florence Griswold also wrote the secretary of commerce concerning the appointment of workers for the 1930 census, noting: "It might prove helpful if you suggest to [Hoover's secretary] that consideration be given women of the States through the National Committeewoman. This will strengthen the National Committeewoman's position with the men's organization for many feel that we are splendid to work for them but not with them."[57] Griswold's letters were not answered to her satisfaction during Hoover's Administration.

Republican women in Wisconsin took a different approach to this question. Amid press reports that the national committeeman had been relieved of his patronage function because of severe illness, and had been replaced in those duties by a nationally appointed triumvirate of male party elites, state organization women mounted a campaign to have the Republican national committeewoman recognized as at least second in line to dispense patronage: "The Republican women of Wisconsin resent the attitude of self styled Republican men leaders toward Mrs. Thomas and we frankly want to know whether women are only to be used for

[53]Harriet Taylor Upton to George Christian, October 1921, Warren G. Harding Papers, Reel 194, Frame 1453; Harriet Taylor Upton to George Christian, October 7, 1921, ibid., Frame 1371.

[54]Harriet Taylor Upton to George Christian, October 7, 1921, ibid.; Harriet Taylor Upton to George Christian, November 28, 1921, ibid., Frame 1400; Harriet Taylor Upton to Warren G. Harding, July 11, 1922, ibid., Reel 203, Frame 1158.

[55]Charles D. Hilles to Herbert Hoover, January 19, 1929, Campaign and Transition Papers, Box 34, Herbert Hoover Papers, referring to the "custom" and "traditional procedure" in the dispensation of patronage.

[56]Florence Griswold to Herbert Hoover, March 12, 1929, Presidential Subject Files, Box 267, ibid.; Florence Griswold to Walter H. Newton, April 2, 1929, ibid.; Florence Griswold to Walter H. Newton, November 20, 1929, Presidential Subject Files, Box 97, ibid.

[57]Florence Griswold to R. T. Lamont, Secretary of Commerce, April 2, 1929, Presidential Subject Files, Box 267, ibid.

vote getting purpose, and their representative on the National Committee is without the authority that the male members enjoy."[58] When Hoover's secretary denied the existence of the reported patronage committee and claimed that the committeeman was perfectly able to perform his patronage duties (although no one appeared to know where he was), Thomas then argued that patronage assignments should require the signatures of both national committee members.[59] Thomas's letters were also not answered to her satisfaction, and her protests continued throughout Hoover's administration.[60]

Male elites in the national Democratic organization also behaved predictably in acting to quell the desire of female party elites to control their own committees. As we already saw in the case of New York State, the control of the appointment of Democratic national committeewomen by the largely male state delegations to the Democratic national conventions could be a strong weapon in the hands of male party elites. In 1920, the "strong opposition" to Elizabeth Marbury's appointment to such a position from the women on New York's "Associate" (women's) Democratic State Committee, many of whom were attending the 1920 Democratic National Convention as observers, was not enough to prevent Marbury's selection.[61]

The head of the Democratic Party's national women's organization, Emily Newell Blair, had also been selected by male leaders at the 1920 Democratic National Convention. (Blair's official title was vice-chairman of the Democratic National Committee, but, in her words, "As Vice Chairman of the committee I am directly in charge of many matters pertaining to women.")[62] In 1924, the Democratic bosses of Chicago and New York, George R. Brennan and Charles Murphy, sought to replace Blair as vice-chairman with the national committeewoman from Illinois, a Brennan loyalist. Blair was able to keep her seat, however, because she had the support of many male leaders at the convention, one of whom expressed his support by saying, "She has never been uppish with the men and never patronizing with the women."[63]

[58]Adele Willis, Treasurer, Wisconsin Organization of Republican Women, to Walter Newton, January 15, 1930, Presidential Subject Files, Box 268, ibid.; also Mrs. R. W. Bowen to Walter Newton, January 20, 1930, ibid.; Mrs. E. M. Fairbank to Walter Newton, January 24, 1930, ibid.

[59]Walter H. Newton to Adele Willis, January 25, 1930, ibid.; Jennie E. Thomas to Walter H. Newton, Secretary, March 15, 1930, enclosing letter from Claude R. Sowle to Jennie Thomas, March 13, 1930, ibid.

[60]Jennie Thomas to Walter H. Newton, September 29, 1930, ibid.; memo of letter from Jennie Thomas to Lenna Yost, forwarded to Herbert Hoover, September 14, 1931, ibid.; M. H. Levenick to Walter Newton, October 18, 1932, ibid.

[61]"Democratic Women Divide over Leader," *NYT*, January 22, 1921, p. 4.

[62]"Convention Roll Includes 500 Women," *NYT*, June 22, 1924, VIII p. 5.

[63]"Mrs. Blair's Allies Foresee a Contest," *NYT*, June 24, 1924, p. 6; "Women Plan

The 1928 convention, however, saw Emily Newell Blair ousted from her position as vice-chairwoman of the Democratic National Committee by her state delegation, which elected another as Missouri's national committeewoman.[64] With the departure of Blair, the women present at the convention interested themselves with her probable successor, but played no role in selecting the new head of the party's women's organization.[65] The woman eventually selected by the male elites to run the party's women's division had been a homemaker before being thrust into Wyoming politics by the death of her husband, the governor, whereas the candidates favored by the women present at the convention had histories in independent women's organizations and in advocacy within the party's own women's organization.[66]

Although the new vice-chairwoman, Nellie Tayloe Ross, does not appear to have been as pliant as her Republican counterpart Sally Hert, she was much less confrontational than Blair had been, announcing during the campaign that the purpose of all the women's committees of the Democratic Party was "cooperation to the utmost with the men of the party. There will be no suggestion of an effort to assert themselves as women."[67] It is not surprising that the displaced Emily Newell Blair commented bitterly a short time after this announcement that memberships on partisan committees for women too often rendered their holders "mere stage furniture, belittling to one's reputation and insulting to one's self-respect. . . . The doors to political success are guarded by men."[68]

In short, to be a woman in the party organizations was to know that one's tenure and advancement in the party critically depended upon whether one kept favor with male party leaders. To be a male party elite, on the other hand, was to possess the means to control the potentially unruly women's divisions.

What of the third condition for using the grants of access to women in the parties as a test for the effect of a threatened independent electoral mobilization of women: were NLWV leaders aware of the struggle of women within the parties, and did they seek to assist those women? Again, this condition appears to be satisfied. One of the issues lobbied for by NLWV elites during the 1920s was the equal status of women

Fight on Any Wet Plank," *NYT*, June 25, 1924, p. 15; "Mrs. Blair Seeks Party Post Again," *NYT*, June 29, 1924, p. 9; "Women Worn Out by Long Debates," *NYT*, June 30, 1924, p. 8.

[64]"Women Join Trend to Smith Standard," *NYT*, June 29, 1928, p. 7.

[65]"Women of Note Share Opening Day," *NYT*, June 27, 1928, p. 3.

[66]"Raskob Elected Chairman, Stresses Dry Law Change as Big Democratic Issue," *NYT*, July 12, 1928, p. 1.

[67]"Women Who Wield Political Power," *NYT Magazine*, September 2, 1928, p. 6.

[68]Emily Newell Blair, "Many Roads Lead Women into Politics," *NYT Magazine*, October 28, 1928, p. 7.

within political party organizations.[69] Even in the latter half of the 1920s, after the repeal of their electoral policy, league officials continued to make known their dissatisfaction with the parties' efforts. Thus in September 1925 the executive committee of the NLWV board discussed "the policy of the dominant political parties towards women's organizations within the party[ies]," with members expressing their unhappiness with those policies.[70] Similarly, the following year the league board castigated the "insufficient" representation of women on party committees, and agreed that "even where 50–50 representation is provided for by law they [women] are not permitted to function and are practically powerless."[71]

VICTORIES AND DEFEATS FOR WOMEN IN THE PARTY ORGANIZATIONS, 1917–1932

Now we may look at the pattern in the grants of access to men's committees that were made to women in each of the four party organizations. Does that pattern match the pattern in the league's electoral policy? The answer again appears to be yes: despite ongoing male control of the women's divisions throughout the 1920s, between 1920 and 1925 male leaders in all four party organizations did in fact respond favorably to the demands of female party leaders for greater access to male party committees.

In the New York State parties, winning access to the men's committees meant changing the electoral laws that governed those committees. Yet in the Republican Party, for example, between 1920 and 1925 women won support from state party leaders for changing those laws. In 1920 the Republican state leadership announced its support of legislation that would have made women eligible for election to new seats on the state committees, if the parties so desired; this bill did not make it through the state legislature.[72] In early 1922 the Republican governor again endorsed the general principle of granting women more access to party committees. Also in 1922, a bill passed by the Republican-controlled state legislature called for the election of at least two county

[69]"Women's Progress in Year Applauded," *NYT*, August 26, 1921, p. 3; "Still Human Beings," *NYT*, August 27, 1921, p. 8.

[70]September 16, 1925, Executive Committee Meeting, in Papers of the National League of Women Voters, 1918–1974, microfilm edition (Frederick, Md.: University Publications of America, 1985), Pt. I, Reel 2, Frame 728.

[71]September 17, 1926, Board Meeting, ibid., Reel 3, Frames 676, 675.

[72]"Mack Senate Boom Started by Women," *NYT*, February 8, 1920, p. 12; "Puts Women on Committees," *NYT*, February 23, 1920, p. 15; "Two Women Urged on 'Big Four' Slate," *NYT*, February 24, 1920, p. 1.

committee members from election districts previously represented by only one seat on these committees.[73] And in August 1922, in response to yet more prodding from the women in the party, the Republican State Committee voted to change the party rules governing county committee elections so that the doubling of county committee representation would result in one woman being elected for every man.[74] Later that same year, the Republican State Convention endorsed the representation of women on the state committee.[75]

The following year, the Republican State Executive Committee adopted resolutions calling for an equal number of men and women on this body, asking the legislature to amend the election law to provide for two members of the state committees from the larger senatorial districts instead of the Assembly districts, and endorsing the principle of equal representation by sex from those districts.[76] Meeting in September, the Republican State Committee also adopted the recommendations of its executive committee.[77]

In 1924, after several weeks of conferences, the Republican legislative leadership agreed on a bill to change the basis of representation on the state committees from the 150 Assembly to the 51 Senate districts, with two members elected from each Senate district.[78] However, this bill was killed in the Democratically controlled Senate.[79] That year's Republican State Convention reaffirmed the endorsement by male party elites of the principle of female representation on the state committees.[80]

From 1925 to the end of the decade, the Republican State Committee and Republican state conventions made no new promises as to female representation on party committees. Republican legislators did act in 1925 to fulfill the many promises made by the party in earlier years to provide for women on the state committees; in that year the Republican-controlled legislature enacted legislation permitting the parties to change

[73]"Legislature Opens Session with Rush," *NYT*, January 5, 1922, p. 4; "Get Bill for Party Committee Women," *NYT*, January 26, 1922, p. 19; "Report Will Favor Women," *NYT*, February 8, 1922, p. 19.

[74]"County Committees to Be Half Women," *NYT*, August 6, 1922, p. 10.

[75]"Platform Pleases Republican Women," *NYT*, September 29, 1922, p. 2.

[76]"Women Seek Places in State Committee," *NYT*, June 10, 1923, II p. 1; "Republican Women to Press Demands," *NYT*, June 14, 1923, p. 10; "State Republicans Dodge Dry Question," *NYT*, June 15, 1923, p. 1.

[77]"Lehman Named by Republicans, Too; Smith Is Assailed," *NYT*, September 30, 1923, p. 2.

[78]"Equality Planned on State Committees," *NYT*, February 14, 1924, p. 19.

[79]"Stand by Film Censorship," *NYT*, February 29, 1924, p. 19; "Mrs. Sabin Replies to Mrs. Blair's Charge," *NYT*, June 22, 1924, p. 24.

[80]"Women Play a Big Part," *NYT*, September 24, 1924, p. 2; "Anti-Klan Forces Win by One Vote," *NYT*, September 25, 1924, p. 1; "Roosevelt Nominated for Governor," *NYT*, September 26, 1924, p. 1.

the basis of representation for their state committees, and allowing for sex-based representation if the parties so desired.[81] Early in the following year the Republican State Committee acted on its own prior promises, moving to amend its internal rules so that of two representatives elected from each Assembly district in the fall primaries to the state committee, one was required to be a woman.[82]

The combination of the new law, silent on sex-based balloting, and the party's sex-based rules, proved susceptible to legal challenge.[83] Not until 1929 did the legislature pass a constitutionally permissible amendment to the state election law that empowered the state committees to "provide for equal representation of sexes from each unit," with the addition, "When any rule provides for the equal representation of sexes from each unit, the designating petitions and primary ballots shall carry party positions separately by sexes."[84] During this period women served for only a brief time on the Republican State Committee, although the time was apparently long enough to generate resentment among many of the male state committee members, several of whom called at the close of 1927 for the county chairmen to run the affairs of the party.[85]

By 1930, then, Republican organization women could finally sit on the Republican State Committee, as had been promised to them as early as 1920 by male state party elites. But also by 1930, male Republican elites had found a way to, in effect, revoke that earlier grant of access. Male party leaders in Erie County had never acceded to the state committee's directives that county state committee delegations be evenly split between men and women, and had kept these groups all male. When state party women attempted to rectify this situation in 1930, they invoked the state committee's rule, passed in 1926, that required all county committees to send one woman and one man from each Assembly district to sit on the state committee. The secretary of the Republican State Committee, however, flatly denied the existence of such a rule, forcing the women to contest the county organization's nominations in the fall

---

[81]"Lowman to Control Party in Senate," *NYT*, January 25, 1925, p. 17; "Finds Leaders Friendly," *NYT*, January 26, 1925, p. 2; "Women Press Leaders for Equality Bill," *NYT*, February 10, 1925, p. 25; "Assembly Passes Measure Affecting Women Politicians," *NYT*, March 26, 1925, p. 2.

[82]"Smith Sticks to Retirement Plan; Says 'It Must Be,'" *NYT*, January 16, 1926, p. 1; "State Republicans Meet Here in Fall; Wet Victory Seen," *NYT*, May 22, 1926, p. 1.

[83]"Test on Women Members," *NYT*, September 26, 1926, p. 18; "Legislature Delays Adjourning a Week," *NYT*, March 8, 1928, p. 3.

[84]*NYT*, April 13, 1929, p. 6; "Up-State Women in Fight for Place," *NYT*, August 24, 1930, III p. 5.

[85]"Republican Chiefs in Up-State Revolt," *NYT*, December 18, 1927, p. 26.

primaries.[86] Moreover, the backtracking by male state elites now left the door open for other counties to again send only male representatives to the state committee.

But after another party reorganization at the close of 1930, this issue was essentially rendered moot. Amid growing complaints from male state committeemen that the newly doubled state committee (now 316 members) was too large to transact party business, the Republican state chairman announced the creation of an even newer committee to manage the affairs of the party. This new state executive committee was intended, said the chairman, to function much as had the old state committee during the years prior to the enfranchisement of women. The new committee was appointed by the state chairman and consisted of nineteen men and only five women.[87] The long struggle of Republican organization women to gain access to the elected state committee appeared now to be irrelevant.

A similar pattern may be seen with respect to the New York Republicans' selection of delegates to the national and state party conventions. In 1920, the state party sent four male delegates at large to the Republican National Convention, and only one woman out of four alternates at large.[88] In 1924, women received two out of seven delegates at large, and three out of seven alternates at large.[89] In 1928 women received no further gains, receiving again two out of seven state delegates at large and three out of seven alternates at large.[90] At their own state conventions, the percentages of women who were delegates and alternates grew from a combined total of 20 percent in 1918 to 29 percent in 1924, but then fell to 24 percent in 1932.[91]

In the New York State Democratic Party, a similar pattern in grants

---

[86]"Up-State Women in Fight for Place," *NYT*, August 24, 1930, III p. 5; "Women Take Active Part," *NYT*, September 14, 1930, III p. 5.

[87]"24 Named by Macy to Lead State Party," *NYT*, December 21, 1930, p. 1.

[88]"But One Woman Delegate," *NYT*, March 2, 1920, p. 17; "Republicans Finish Up-State Slates – Only One Woman Chosen by the Organization for National Convention Delegate," *NYT*, March 5, 1920, p. 17; "Republicans Slate Only Two Women," *NYT*, March 8, 1920, p. 15.

[89]"State Republicans Commend Coolidge and Attack Smith," *NYT*, April 17, 1924, p. 1.

[90]"Republican Chiefs in Up-State Revolt," *NYT*, December 18, 1927, p. 26; "Plan Republican Meeting," *NYT*, January 9, 1928, p. 2; "Republican Women Meet," *NYT*, January 13, 1928, p. 12; "Republican Women Want 3 Delegates," *NYT*, January 14, 1928, p. 2; "Republican Women Gain a Delegate," *NYT*, May 23, 1928, p. 2.

[91]"Want Roosevelt to Lead in State," *NYT*, July 18, 1918, p. 9; Marguerite Fisher, "Women in the Political Parties," *Annals of the American Academy* 151 (May 1947): 92–93.

of access occurred. In 1920 male Democratic leaders announced their support of legislation permitting women to serve on the party state committees.[92] And after the passage of the 1922 bill doubling county committees, the Democratic State Committee enacted a rule making compulsory the selection of a woman for every man serving on the county committees, and calling for the appointment of vice-chairwomen of those committees.[93]

The following year the Democratic State Committee adopted a resolution asking the legislature to provide for the election of two rather than one state committee member from each Assembly district, "in order that if the electorate so desire the representative from each district may consist of one man and one woman."[94] In 1924 the Democratic State Committee again endorsed legislation doubling the number of seats from each Assembly district on the parties' state committees, with the expressed intent that the new seats would be filled by women.[95] After a bill permitting such representation became law in 1925, the Democratic State Committee voted to double itself by electing two members from each of the state's 150 Assembly districts, with a statement that it was "the sense of the committee" that a man and a woman should be elected from each district.[96]

As discussed previously, the representation of women on the Democratic State Committee would not be legal until 1930. In the meantime, Democratic women saw no other grants of representation by male state party elites. In fact, at the 1926 Democratic State Convention, where women sat for the first time on the state committee, the Democratic state chairman sought to remove the leader of the state party's women's organization as the first vice-chairman of the state committee in favor of a man, Caroline O'Day holding that post by "courtesy" only.[97]

Male state Democratic elites also displayed a willingness to grant women partial access to national convention delegations during the early 1920s, but had backed away from those grants by the early 1930s. In 1920 party leaders named two women out of a possible four as delegates at large to the Democratic National Convention.[98] In 1924, in response

[92]"Mack Senate Boom Started by Women," *NYT*, February 8, 1920, p. 12.
[93]"Anti-Hearst Women Will Organize City," *NYT*, June 28, 1922, p. 19.
[94]"Lehman Is Named for Appeals Court," *NYT*, September 29, 1923, p. 3.
[95]"Women Democrats Lose Equality Point," *NYT*, September 26, 1924, p. 3.
[96]"Smith Sticks to Retirement Plan; Says 'It Must Be,' " *NYT*, January 16, 1926, p. 1.
[97]"Women Fight for Mrs. O'Day," *NYT*, September 27, 1926, p. 3; "Democrats Re-Elect Committee Officers," *NYT*, September 28, 1926, p. 14.
[98]"Democratic Women Win Two Places on Party 'Big Four,' " *NYT*, February 26, 1920, p. 1; "State Democrats Declare Boldly for Dry Repeal," *NYT*, February 27, 1920, p. 1.

to a nationwide request from the Democratic National Committee, state party elites made a fifty–fifty male–female split in their at-large delegation to the Democratic National Convention a matter of party policy.[99]

However, by 1932 the Democratic State Committee was prepared to renege on the fifty–fifty male–female split in the at-large delegation to the Democratic National Convention. In March 1932, male Democratic state leaders decided to nominate only four women out of sixteen delegates-at-large to the impending national convention. This action was taken despite the repetition by the Democratic National Committee in its convention call that it advised the equal division of delegates at large between men and women.[100]

Nearly identical patterns can be found for both parties' national committees. In 1920, the Republican National Convention increased the membership of the Republican National Executive Committee from ten to fifteen members, with seven of the newly enlarged committee to be female appointees.[101] In June 1923, President Harding asked the Republican national committeemen to each appoint an "associate" Republican national committeewoman, who would not possess any voting powers. Harding also promised to request the 1924 National Convention to grant women full voting status on the national committee.[102]

At this convention, Republican women had greater representation than they had had in 1920, with 120 female delegates attending the convention compared to 26 in 1920.[103] Also in 1924, male Republican elites gave women in the national party organization a specific policy role for the first time in the party's history. The female members on the Republican National Committee's Subcommittee on Policies and Platform were charged with "making suggestions for planks of especial concern to women."[104]

---

[99]"Democratic Women Win," *NYT*, April 16, 1924, p. 2.

[100]"Democrats to Pick 16 for Convention," *NYT*, March 5, 1932, p. 2.

[101]"Recommend Putting Women on the Executive Committee," *NYT*, June 9, 1920, p. 2.

[102]Charles D. Hilles to Warren G. Harding, May 31, 1923, Warren G. Harding Papers, Reel 195, Frame 182; Charles D. Hilles to Mary Livermore, May 31, 1923, ibid., Frames 183–186; Warren G. Harding to Charles D. Hilles, June 2, 1923, ibid., Frame 181; "Republican Women Gain Recognition," *NYT*, June 9, 1923, p. 1; "Republican Leaders Want Women's Advice," *NYT*, June 13, 1923 p. 21; "Republican Committeewomen," *NYT*, June 29, 1923, p. 16; "G.O.P. Women to Enter National Committee," *NYT*, June 26, 1923, p. 14. This action was approved by the full Republican National Committee in December 1923; "South Wins Back Delegates Dropped by 1920 Convention," *NYT*, December 13, 1923, p. 3.

[103]"Few Women Named by Republicans," *NYT*, June 3, 1928, p. 4. Sophonisba Breckenridge counted twenty-seven female delegates in 1920; see *Women in the Twentieth Century* (New York: McGraw-Hill, 1933), p. 289.

[104]Harriet Taylor Upton, in "Women Offer Planks for G.O.P. Platform," *NYT*,

The 1924 convention delegates did in fact vote favorably on a rec-ommendation from the rules committee to have one man and one woman elected by each state or territorial delegation to sit on the party's national committee; the active membership of the latter was thus in-creased from 53 to 106, and the number of vice-chairmen was increased from one to three, with the provision that one of those posts would go to the female leader of the national women's organization.[105] Male Republican leaders also named a woman to head the committee on per-manent organization of the convention, one of the four major conven-tion committees.

By 1928, however, such advances had ceased. The delegate selection process leading up to the 1928 Republican National Convention resulted in approximately half the number of female delegates as had attended the national convention in 1924, namely seventy female delegates.[106] Assistant Attorney General Mabel Willebrandt was given the chairman-ship of the committee on credentials; this did not constitute an improve-ment over the chairmanships of convention committees held by women in 1924.[107] After the convention, the national advisory committee named by Hoover to run his campaign for the party contained no women. When it met to plan Hoover's campaign in the East, the Republican national committeewomen were directed to meet in a separate city to plan the women's campaign.[108]

After Hoover's election, the controversy over Sally Hert, the leader of the Republican national women's organization, revealed the demotion of the women's organization in the party hierarchy. In both the Demo-cratic and the Republican national organizations, the national leaders of the parties' women's divisions had since 1920 held the position of vice-chairmen of the national committees. This mirrored the organizational plan in most states, where women served as vice-chairmen of county and state committees. In at least the Republican Party, the award of an RNC vice-chairmanship to the director of the party's women's division had been a rule enacted by the 1924 Republican National Convention. But when Sally Hert resigned her post as national director of the Republican

April 7, 1924, p. 3. Women held twenty-nine out of fifty-eight spots on this subcom-mittee.

[105]"Butler Is Beaten in Rules Committee," *NYT*, June 11, 1924, p. 1; "Platform Wins amid Cheers," *NYT*, June 12, 1924, p. 2.

[106]Out of 1,089 voting delegates, 64 were women, compared to 120 female voting delegates present at the 1924 national convention. "Few Women Named by Repub-licans," *NYT*, June 3, 1928, p. 4. Breckenridge counted 70 female delegates. Breck-enridge, *Women in the Twentieth Century*, p. 289.

[107]"Women Win Plums at the Convention," *NYT*, June 12, 1928, p. 4.

[108]"Women Plan Fight to Elect Hoover," *NYT*, July 25, 1928, p. 2.

women's organization in early 1930, she was allowed to keep her vice-chairmanship of the national committee. Hert's assistant was named the new director of the party's women's division, thereby severing the tie (however nominal) between leadership in the party and leadership of the women's division.[109] A new leader of the national women's organization was subsequently named in August 1930; she also was not given a vice-chairmanship of the national committee, further indicating that these offices had been disassociated.[110] In fact, the director of the women's division would in the future be referred to as merely an assistant to the RNC chairman, and would not have a designated seat on the RNC's executive committee.[111]

National male Democratic elites also responded favorably to the women's demands for greater access between 1920 and 1925, but not afterward. Women had already been given seventeen out of thirty-four places on the Democratic National Executive Committee before the 1920 national convention. The convention itself then voted to change the composition of the national committee by adding one woman from each state.[112] The national Women's Bureau remained in existence to operate as the organizational arm of the national committeewomen and national executive committeewomen.[113]

Prior to the 1924 Democratic National Convention, women's division leader Emily Newell Blair was able to win even more access for Democratic women to the national party's deliberations when she convinced the Democratic National Committee to "suggest" to the state parties that they split their at-large national convention delegations evenly between men and women. In order that men would not be displaced from their former positions of honor, where a state had previously had four at-large delegates, it would now have eight, each with a one-half vote (a state could also send more at-large delegates, further reducing the voting power of each).[114] Women wound up with 184 votes at the convention, compared with 104 in 1920.[115]

[109]"Mrs. Hert Quits Republican Post," *NYT*, January 19, 1930, p. 24.

[110]"Mrs. Yost Selected for Dodson Place," *NYT*, August 14, 1930, p. 2.

[111]Josephine Good, *Republican Womanpower: The History of Women in Republican National Conventions and Women in the Republican National Committee* (Washington, D.C.: Republican National Committee, 1963), pp. 24, 27, 33, 37.

[112]"Committee Votes for Full Hearing," *NYT*, June 26, 1920, p. 2; "Women Prominent in Day's Session," *NYT*, June 30, 1920, p. 2.

[113]"To Keep Women's Bureau," *NYT*, July 5, 1920, p. 2.

[114]"Smith Boom Grows, State Leaders Say," *NYT*, February 8, 1924, p. 1.

[115]"Women to Muster 308 at Convention," *NYT*, June 27, 1920, p. 2. Sophonisba Breckenridge counted 93 female delegate votes at the 1920 convention. See *Women in the Twentieth Century*, p. 289.

Also prior to the 1924 national convention, the Democratic national chairman appointed a special women's "advisory" subcommittee on the national platform, to be chaired by Eleanor Roosevelt, and asked the subcommittee to craft a "woman's platform of legislation":[116] "The Democratic National Committee has turned over to women that part of the platform dealing with women and children in industry, in education, in economic and social life. . . . [Women's organizations] have been invited to work on planks of especial interest to them. These will be turned into our committee and worked over. The planks on child welfare . . . will be studied and condensed by a committee best fitted for that work. The same is true of planks on women in industry, on minimum wage bills, on education, on international laws affecting women and society."[117] This women's platform committee, appointed before the announcement of the similar Republican women's platform group, was pathbreaking in the party's explicit recognition of the distinctive legislative agenda of women's organizations.

However, such gains in access were not to continue beyond the 1924 Democratic National Convention. And female Democratic leaders in fact became increasingly pessimistic about the likelihood that they would see more such victories. Harriet Taylor Upton noted their changing attitude in a letter to Coolidge as early as 1925:

The Democratic women have assumed an entirely different air than they had during my four years of service. Then they were boasting about the future, about what their party had done for them, how wonderful their women were and now their speakers are most pessimistic, particularly on the woman question.[118]

In 1927, Emily Newell Blair complained to *Harper's* magazine: "There has never been a time when if I asked any one of these men to do a personal favor for me, to give me patronage or tickets, or help me put something across, he would not have done it. But when I asked for a place on the firing line, that was another matter."[119]

In 1928 Blair was joined in her public criticism of male Democratic elites by Eleanor Roosevelt, who in a series of interviews given that spring both attacked male leaders' exclusionary practices and identified their control of the women's organizations as the source of their power to continue to deny access to female party leaders.

[116]"Democratic Women to Help on Platform," *NYT*, March 31, 1924, p. 2.

[117]Eleanor Roosevelt, in "Women Are Slow to Use the Ballot," *NYT*, April 20, 1924, IX p. 1.

[118]Harriet Taylor Upton to Calvin Coolidge, February 16, 1925, Calvin Coolidge Papers, Reel 121, File 395.

[119]"When New York Gave Woman the Vote," *NYT*, November 6 1927, V p. 4.

Women have been voting for ten years. But have they achieved actual political equality with men? No . . . their votes are solicited by politicians and they possess the external aspect of equal rights. But it is mostly a gesture without real power. With some outstanding exceptions, women who have gone into politics are refused serious consideration by the men leaders. Generally, they are treated most courteously, to be sure, but what they want, what they have to say, is regarded as of little weight. In fact, they have no actual influence or say at all in the consequential councils of their parties. In those circles which decide the affairs of national politics women have no voice or power whatever. . . . Before national elections they will be told to organize the women throughout the United States . . . but when it comes to those grave councils at which possible candidates are discussed, as well as party policies, they are rarely invited in. At the national conventions no woman has ever been asked to serve on the Platform Committee. Beneath the veneer of courtesy and outward show of consideration universally accorded women there is a widespread male hostility – age-old, perhaps – against sharing with them any actual control. There is a method by which, I believe, the end of a fair representation and share in control may be attained. . . . Our means is to elect, accept and back women political bosses; to organize the women, but within the parties. . . . With the power of unified women voters behind them, such women bosses would be in a position to talk in terms of "business" with the men leaders.[120]

The 1928 Democratic National Convention provided an empirical demonstration of Roosevelt's analysis. Despite the continuation of the Democrats' affirmative action plan for delegates-at-large, whereby the DNC suggested to state committees that they double their delegations-at-large to include women,[121] the Democrats wound up with many fewer female delegate votes than in 1924 (78.75 female votes, compared with 184 in 1924).[122] And despite the pressure of Democratic women at the convention, no women were appointed to the resolutions committee by the state delegations; only one woman each was appointed to the credentials and rules committees; and no women received convention committee chairmanships.[123]

After the 1928 convention, Democratic women were shut out of the planning for presidential nominee Al Smith's campaign, as Republican women had been excluded from planning Hoover's campaign; several national committeemen remaining in New York met to plan Smith's campaign while the national committeewomen remaining in New York were not invited and indeed met separately. (When the women found out that Smith and the national committeemen were strategizing over

---

[120]"A Woman Speaks Her Political Mind," *NYT Magazine*, April 8, 1928, V p. 3.
[121]"Democrats Issue Convention Call," *NYT*, January 28, 1928, p. 6.
[122]"Mrs. Blair Urges a Short Platform," *NYT*, June 24, 1928, p. 3.
[123]"Few Committeewomen," *NYT*, June 27, 1928, p. 2.

the "woman vote," they crashed the men's meeting.)[124] The men's meeting created an all-male national advisory committee, consisting of ten to fifteen regional representatives who would manage the campaign; only at the insistence of Nellie Tayloe Ross was a woman's advisory committee also named, chaired by Eleanor Roosevelt.[125]

After their defeat in the 1928 election, national Democratic elites sought once again to reorganize and strengthen their party organization. Conferences were held between the Democratic national chairman, the male members of the Democratic National Executive Committee, the male advisory committee from the past campaign, and selected senators.[126] One outcome of these all-male conferences was that it was decided that the policy commitments of the party would come from the Democratic senators' speeches and sponsored bills.[127] This was not good news for women within the party organization who were seeking to further their policy preferences by securing more access to previously all-male party committees. Now women would have to be elected to the United States Senate in order to have a voice on the party's policy commitments.

The unhappy situation of women within the national Democratic Party, although no worse than the situation of women in either the national Republican Party or the state party organizations, was the subject of public addresses by female Democratic elites in 1931. Former DNC Vice-Chairwoman Emily Newell Blair declared in a radio address that "politics is still a male monopoly,"[128] while the current holder of that title, Nellie Tayloe Ross, spoke of the "subordination" of Democratic women in an address to the Democratic women's clubs of Maryland: "[I have] a deep conviction that, generally speaking, all over the country men have failed to give due cognizance to the fact that we have entered upon a new era when women in politics, as in most other fields of endeavor, constitute an incalculable source of strength. . . . There is a disposition in too many units, State, county and precinct, to regard the efforts of women as something auxiliary to those of masculine party leaders rather than an essential integral part of party projects."[129]

Given the continuing male control of the women's division, what explains the grants of access which *were* made to women in the party organizations up to 1925? As argued in Chapter 2, the most plausible

[124]"Governor Smith Enjoins Aides to 'Get Busy,' " *NYT*, July 13, 1928, p. 1.
[125]"Smith Declares He Will Be Active in State Campaign," *NYT*, July 19, 1928, p. 1.
[126]"Democrats Confer on National Policy," *NYT*, April 20, 1929, p. 2.
[127]"Senators to Guide Democratic Party," *NYT*, April 21, 1929, p. 13.
[128]"Lauds Women Politicians," *NYT*, March 4, 1931, p. 25.
[129]"Cites 'Subordination' of Women in Politics," *NYT*, May 22, 1931, p. 13.

answer is the same as that given for the analogous pattern in policy concessions to women by national party leaders: the electoral threat posed by independent women's organizations that supported the demands of female party leaders. But is there any documentary evidence that female party leaders made male party elites aware of their support in independent women's organizations, and/or that male party elites in fact perceived the latter to pose an electoral threat? Again, the answer is yes.

For their part, women appointed to the women's divisions of the various party organizations often maintained ties with independent women's organizations, particularly the National League of Women Voters.[130] In New York State, female Republican leaders throughout the 1920s contacted independent women's organizations for consultation on their legislative agenda. In the early 1930s the state female Republican leader even stated that such consultations were a primary component of her job: "One of the chief functions of Republican women is to act as liaison officers between the party and various organized non-partisan groups which are interested in particular legislative measures. Some of these measures can often be incorporated into the party program, some cannot, but it is our constant effort to bring new ideas and new points of view to the party leaders."[131]

Moreover, on several occasions throughout this period female Republican workers publicly gave notice to male party elites that they would be unwilling to work for the party if their demands for access were not met. At the same time, these women shrewdly raised the specter of independent female electoral organization. As early as November 1917 the president of the Women's Republican Club of the City of New York was declaring that "We certainly shall decline, politely but firmly, to become mere auxiliaries of the men's political organizations, although, of course, we shall cooperate with them along party lines in every possible way. The Republican women will undoubtedly establish organizations of their own in every county of the State."[132] A few years later, the chairman of the Republican Women's State Executive Committee, Mary Livermore, told the *Times* that "Half a million women in

---

[130]Other studies documenting this point include Elizabeth Perry, *Belle Moskowitz: Feminine Politics and the Exercise of Power in the Age of Alfred E. Smith* (New York: Oxford University Press, 1987), p. 75; Melanie Gustafson, "Partisan Women: Gender, Politics, and the Progressive Party of 1912" (Ph.D. dissertation, New York University, 1993), p. 195.

[131]Sarah Butler, in "Republican Women Seek 10,000 in State," *NYT*, January 7, 1932, p. 12.

[132]Mrs. James Griswold Wentz, in "Glynn Ordered G.O.P. Bosses to Aid Suffrage," *NYT*, November 13, 1917, p. 1.

the State have not enrolled with any party. At present, they are party shy, but to us as Republicans they present an opportunity. We can get them into our party if we offer them the proper inducement. Women will not have the devotion nor will they give their time to the work, unless they are made part and parcel of the Republican party. For that reason I urge that there be a double representation from every political unit on the party committees."[133]

When their demands were not met immediately, Republican Party women sought to convey the impression that there would be electoral consequences. In the spring of 1920, an anonymous Republican female leader told the *Times* that female resentment at male Republican unresponsiveness was widespread throughout the state, and that there existed "a drift of women away from the Republican party in this State."[134] An open letter the following year to the Republican governor of New York indicated continuing female Republican dissatisfaction with their status in the party:

Our experience within the organization of the parties, however, is a humiliating one. It has taught us that there is as yet no real equality in the management of party affairs, nor in the choice of delegates or candidates. We are forbidden to exercise independence or judgement, and are openly advised that there is no place in the party except for those who take orders.[135]

As a result of this continuing dissatisfaction, Republican women in 1923 held a conference to publicize both their discontent and also their continuing intention to withold work from the party if their demands were not met. At the conference, a Mrs. Ernest Thompson Seton of Westchester declared that "Women have done a great deal for the party since they got the vote and it is not likely that they will be content to continue to occupy a subordinate position. I have no plan, but I am of the opinion that the women should agitate and protest until they obtain their rights." Mrs. James Griswold Wentz, a member of the New York County Republican Committee, agreed: "Women have been working right along, but the men don't seem to know it. We are not satisfied with the calibre of men who go up to Albany, and we shall demand something better. . . . If we cannot get high-class men, then we should have women." Sev-

---

[133]"Republican Women Want Equal Status – Mrs. Livermore Tells Committee Every Unit Should Have Double Representation," *NYT*, January 11, 1920, p. 16.

[134]"Republicans Issue 'Model' Platform; Women Resentful," *NYT*, February 21, 1920, p. 1; "Equality," *NYT*, March 4, 1920, p. 10.

[135]"Women's League Replies to Miller; Pushes Program," *NYT*, January 29, 1921, p. 1.

eral other speakers confirmed that the women were growing "more and more disgusted" with their lack of influence over candidate and policy selection, and threatened the male elites with electoral consequences: "The women are complaining on all sides more than ever, and I doubt if they will jump at the crack of the party whip for the Fall campaign."[136]

These threats continued throughout the 1920s, although growing less frequent. As late as 1931, Helen Varick Boswell, still the vice-chairwoman of the New York County Republican Committee after fourteen years, told the Women's National Republican Club that female leaders were now simply ignored by the male leaders. In order to get their demands heard by the latter, they needed to be able to threaten male leaders with women's votes.[137]

For their part, Republican state male leaders in the first half of the 1920s clearly viewed independent women's political organizations as a threat. In numerous speeches given and publicized after the passage of female suffrage, male state Republican elites sought to discourage such independently organized women from using electoral politics as a means to advance their policy goals. For example, in a speech to Republican women made immediately after the passage of female suffrage in 1917, the man charged with setting up the New York County Republican women's organization told his audience that, "I believe that women's interests, broadly speaking, are identical with those of men, and they will do more effective and constructive work inside of parties, because they will have fully one-half the votes. There is no more reason why there should be a woman's party in politics than that there should be a woman's Red Cross or a woman's church party. I hope the women will not attempt to organize along sex lines."[138] Another Republican speaker at the same gathering echoed these sentiments: "There is no essential difference between men and women. . . . There is no need of a woman's party, and I do not think it is the duty of women to divide."[139]

Male Republican elites were also reportedly fearful in 1918 of the potential for electoral trouble from an independently organized women's Republican club in the 15th Assembly District of Manhattan, led by a woman active in the League of Women Voters: "The growth of the Republican Neighborhood Association was not looked upon with entire favor by the party leaders in the district. . . . The party leaders much preferred to have women enrolling as Republicans join the regular dis-

[136]"Republican Women Threaten Revolt," *NYT*, June 5, 1923, p. 3.
[137]"Asserts Men Ignore Women in Politics," *NYT*, March 31, 1931, p. 22.
[138]"Tanner Appeals to Women," *NYT*, December 12, 1917, p. 10.
[139]Ezra D. Prentice, in ibid.

trict club. . . . It is a fair statement to say that they did not care greatly about the Neighborhood Association because they could not control it."[140]

In January 1921 the newly elected Republican governor of New York delivered two scathing speeches on the subject of independent women's organizations, first to the state Republican women and then to the New York State League of Women Voters. In the first, Nathan L. Miller warned the assembled Republican women against belonging to "groups" other than parties: "I believe in partisanship, and this is going to be a partisan administration. . . . We have too much group government."[141] In the second, the governor told the league that it had no excuse for existence, making particular reference to the league's 1920 campaign against Senator Wadsworth:

I do think that there is no proper place for a league of women voters. . . . if you are to exert the influence that your ability and your standing in the community entitles you to exercise, you must do it through the medium of a political party. . . . when, without being organized as a political party, any organization seeks to exert political influence, to coerce officials, either in the legislative or administrative positions to their particular views by intimidation or otherwise, by promise of support at the elections, or by threats, open or covert, of opposition at an election, such an organization in my judgment is a menace to our free institutions and to representative government. . . . you cannot be nonpartisan and seek to exert political power. You were not nonpartisan in the last election when you sought to exert political power, and, in my judgment, the signal failure of your effort to punish an official because he had stood for what he thought was right was one of the most hopeful signs that I have seen of the enduring nature of our institutions.[142]

Miller's speech got widespread publicity, and he continued on the attack. The next month he wrote the league that what he particularly objected to in its case was the threat of women's votes being used for or against the election of candidates, and he reiterated his defense of parties versus independent electoral groups: "I deplore the continuance of sex distinctions in the discharge of political obligations, and I consider that women will accomplish more by exerting their influence within the party organization of their choice than by acting independently."[143]

Miller's attack on the league and its electoral involvement in the pre-

---

[140]"Women Take Lead in Political Fight," *NYT*, March 9, 1924, II p. 3.

[141]"Miller Warns Women of Rule by Groups," *NYT*, January 20, 1921, p. 2.

[142]"Miller Tells League of Women Voters It Is a Menace to Our Institutions; Attacks Its Social Welfare Program," *NYT*, January 28, 1921, p. 1.

[143]"Miller Says Women Misunderstood Him," *NYT*, February 10, 1921, p. 3.

vious election was followed up by the Republican state chairman, who was even more blunt in his denunciation of the league:

If a group of men got together and said they wanted to elevate the teamsters or any other class of men, they would be laughed out of court. . . . I don't deny that these women are in earnest. They have no flag and they fight between the lines. . . . Many of them are actuated by front-page vanity. Thank goodness, we have come back into power with a man-elected Governor and a man-elected President who believe in fixed stars and not meteors.[144]

These attacks on the league did not let up; at the inauguration of the Women's National Republican Club in New York some weeks later, Miller sent a telegram endorsing the club as a welcome alternative to the league: "Allow me to praise the wisdom which leads you to avoid the semblance of non-partisanship and to ally yourselves openly with one of the two great political organizations."[145] A year later, Miller was again on the attack, recalling to a conference of Republican women his January speech of the previous year:

The two propositions that I advanced, as I recall it, were that we ought not to have any sex divisions in politics and that non-political groups that undertook to exert political pressure so as to exercise political power were a menace to our institutions, and my observations of the last year, in a position to note the influences that operate on those charged with the discharge of public functions, have convinced me that those views were sound.[146]

Similar stories of ties between female party leaders and independent women's organizations can be told about New York State's Democratic party. For example, immediately after Elizabeth Marbury's appointment to the Democratic National Executive Committee in 1920, the soon-to-be deposed female Democratic state leader publicly joined the independent Women Democrats of America, and announced that she would arrange to have the officially sanctioned Women's Democratic Club, which she chaired as the women's Democratic state leader, merged with the independent organization.[147] Nellie Crosby also joined the state League of Women Voters at this time and urged other Democratic women to do the same.[148] Another prominent state Democratic woman also active in the state League of Women Voters threatened in March

[144]George A. Glynn, in "Glynn Hits Friends of Welfare Bills," *NYT*, February 13, 1921, p. 12.
[145]"Republican Heads Back Women's Club," *NYT*, February 18, 1921, p. 11.
[146]"Miller Still Firm against Sex Groups," *NYT*, February 9, 1922, p. 17.
[147]"Mrs. Crosby Takes Office," *NYT*, February 7, 1920, p. 6.
[148]"Joins Voters' League," *NYT*, February 22, 1920, II p. 6.

1920 that women would act as a bloc within the party to see their preferences realized if male party leaders were not more forthcoming:

Women must have responsibility if the parties expect their confidence and wholehearted allegiance. . . . The women will soon grow impatient if they continue to be left out of the management of the parties. Unless they are made members of the important committees which shape the platform and nominate the candidates they will be urged by their own women leaders to organize within the party. To their way of thinking it would be for the party's welfare. Here they can work for the insertion of desired planks and the nomination of more desirable candidates. Women do not choose to have their votes divorced from men's; they do not believe in a separate party, but if they are barred from membership on vital committees they will have to use their united votes to force their way into places of power and responsibility.[149]

After being removed as the head of the state Democratic women's organization in late 1920, Nellie Crosby formed an independent "Harding and Wadsworth Democratic League of Women Voters" to mobilize Democratic women behind the Republican ticket. In announcing her new loyalties, Crosby declared that "I am, as I have always been, a Democrat, but I intend to support Harding . . . if only as a protest against conditions on the Cox side, which are intolerable to women voters of independence, intelligence, and I may say, self respect."[150]

In 1924, the then leader of the state Democratic women's division told a reporter that, "Women are no longer lulled by a slogan. Those who are interested enough to vote, and even those who are not want to know the facts. You can't feed them up with sentiment. When in doubt they go to the League of Women Voters or to some other authority on political questions."[151] A few days later, Eleanor Roosevelt, an officer in the state party organization, announced that she would be appearing before the state convention in a dual capacity as both a party official and a representative of women's organizations: "I will appear before the Platform Committee officially representing the united women's organizations, which include over 30 influential women's societies, to urge a plank in the platform calling for the ratification by New York State of the Child Labor Amendment. At the same time, as representing the Women's Trade Union League, I will present planks calling for the eight hour day and minimum wage law."[152]

[149]Mrs. Charles L. Tiffany, in "Shall Women Practice Party Regularity?," *NYT*, March 7, 1920, VI p. 3.
[150]"Mrs. Crosby for Harding," *NYT*, October 9, 1920, p. 3.
[151]Caroline O'Day, in "Says Women Will Cast Record Vote This Fall," *NYT*, September 21, 1924, VIII p. 9.
[152]"Women Drop Fight on Smith's Appeal," *NYT*, September 25, 1924, p. 4.

Women in the Parties

Male state Democratic leaders appeared to be wary of the potential electoral power of independently organized women. In 1917 the Democratic mayor-elect of New York City proclaimed his willingness in the aftermath of the suffrage victory to give women patronage in equal proportion to the men. The account of the incoming administration's political calculations in the *New York Times* is instructive:

The Mayor elect reiterated his determination to give women representation on the new Board of Education that he will appoint. As to whether women would be represented in other departments and to what extent Judge Hylan was not prepared to say, but it is understood that the whole question will be taken up at a conference of all the newly elected city officials in the near future. The political leaders of "the other sex" are looking with some alarm at the tendency of the newly elected to "coddle" the newly enfranchised, as one of them put it. There are enough male applicants to fill ten times over every job that the incoming administration will have to give and many of the candidates have political claims. The advent of women could not have come at a more inconvenient time in the view of male patronage hunters. This phase of the situation is supposed to have had much to do with the determination to call the conference to discuss woman patronage. There is no doubt that the politicians would like to see all the women turned down, and all the good salary jobs filled with men. But since women are voters, the politicians must be cautious and not offend them, for if they should combine they could outvote the men of either party. So the patronage conference will seek some equitable basis of job distribution between men and women.[153]

However, after 1924 it would have been clear to male party elites that they had nothing to fear either from the women's division of their own party, which could easily be controlled, or from independently organized women's groups like the National League of Women Voters.

For their part, national female Republican leaders on occasion would broadly warn male party elites that the "female vote" could be swayed by independent female leaders, as in this 1920 statement by a prominent female Republican official:

As political leaders try to engage women on the side of any political party they must keep in mind that women are not swayed by party tradition to the extent that men are and will often be found unwilling blindly to follow party dictation. I myself am a strong party woman, but I know from the contacts of my work that the women generally who are entering the electorate this year are not as yet solidified in party molds.[154]

---

[153]"Many State Jobs to Go to Women," *NYT*, November 15, 1917, p. 1.
[154]Mary Garrett Hay, in "Recognize Women, Miss Hay Demands," *NYT*, June 2, 1920, p. 3.

The leader of the Republican Party's national women's organization after the 1920 national convention reiterated this theme to candidate Harding: "Women are not as attached to party as are men, women care less for the regulars, the machine than do men."[155] After the 1920 election Upton publicly declared that women as a distinct voting group had "contributed more than their share to the final great victory," and asserted that "the force of women in American politics is to be a persistent, continuing force," led by "the leading women of the country. . . . it rather looks to some of us as though the entry of women into municipal politics means the smashing of political machines nation-wide."[156] After the 1922 Republican primaries Upton noted the "restiveness" of Republican women, both as voters and as leaders: "Women are restive every where because men do not take them into the machine. . . . the result in Indiana – the stir up in Pa. – the condition in many states goes to show that we have got to do more for women than we have done."[157]

National female Republican leaders also continually referred to and defended the existence of specific independent women's organizations, in particular the National League of Women Voters, in their correspondence with male party elites. Throughout her term as leader of the Republican Party's women's organization, Harriet Taylor Upton maintained membership in and ties with independent women's organizations, including the NLWV. Early in 1920 Upton was already discussing the NLWV with President Harding, writing him that the league would seek "to strengthen old laws and make new ones which would appeal particularly to the home, to women and to children. . . . You will see as we proceed that it works out that way."[158] In 1921 Upton told Harding that she was still "loyal" to the league's leaders, whom she called "a fine lot."[159] When asked by Republican Party elites to denounce the League of Women Voters, she refused.[160] In 1922 Upton even joined a so-called Little Cabinet, a group composed of the leaders of women's organizations (including the NLWV) and party organization women, who would meet weekly to discuss "questions of moment to

[155]Harriet Taylor Upton to Warren G. Harding, June 27, 1920, Warren G. Harding Papers, Reel 66, Frames 864–867.
[156]"Expects Municipal Clean-up by Women," *NYT*, November 29, 1920, p. 21.
[157]Harriet Taylor Upton to Warren G. Harding, May 6, 1922, Warren G. Harding Papers, Reel 197, Frames 254–256.
[158]Harriet Taylor Upton to Warren G. Harding, February 26, 1920, ibid., Reel 30, Frames 815–817.
[159]Harriet Taylor Upton to George Christian, August 15, 1921, ibid., Reel 194, Frame 1317.
[160]Harriet Taylor Upton to Warren G. Harding, January 4, 1922, ibid., Frames 1153–1154.

women all over the country."[161] Upton's affiliation with the NLWV was in fact explicitly recognized by that organization, whose executive committee in February 1923 voted to thank Upton for her work on behalf of the league.[162]

Upton also made sure to hint of the potential electoral power of women's organizations, again particularly the NLWV, when she was engaged in asking male party leaders for specific policy or organizational concessions. For example, when lobbying Harding on suffrage ratification, Upton referred to the NLWV's campaign against Wadsworth in New York State: "I believe that the ratification of Vermont will help New York. Suffragists there are furious towards Senator Wadsworth, and I believe that will mollify them some if you can get ratification. They have the vote but I believe they will lose some of the fight that is in them if they feel the Party has really gotten the last state."[163] Upton also sought to entice Harding to do more for suffrage ratification by promising public gratitude from the NAWSA/NLWV if a Republican state legislature secured that ratification.[164]

Upton's efforts on behalf of the Sheppard-Towner maternal and infant health bill were similar in tone. In May 1921, Upton wrote Harding that the chairman of the House Interstate Commerce Committee was not sympathetic to Sheppard-Towner, and that this could cause problems for Harding with women's organizations if he did not intervene:

This slowness will aggravate the legislative committee of women from a dozen or more women's organizations, which is working for the passage of the bill. These women will want a hearing with the President to ask him to hurry Mr. Winslow along. . . . I want always to save the President as much as I can and at the same time hold the confidence of these women who are a fine lot.[165]

---

[161]"Women's Political Success No Longer Seems Unusual," *NYT*, February 25, 1923, VII p. 7. The group's members also included Julia Stimson, chief of the Army nurses; Dr. Valeria H. Parker, executive secretary of the U.S. Interdepartmental Social Hygiene Board; Anita E. Phipps, director of the Women's Relations Department of the Army; Emily Newell Blair, vice-chairman of the Democratic National Committee, Helen Gardiner, the only female National Civil Service commissioner; Bessie Parker Brueggeman, chairman of the Civil Service Employee's Compensation Committee; Mina Van Winkle, head of the Woman's Bureau of the District Police Department; Clara Taylor, rent commissioner of the District of Columbia; and Mabel Willebrandt, assistant U.S. attorney general.

[162]NLWV Executive Committee Meeting, February 8, 1923, Papers of the National League of Women Voters, Pt. I, Reel 1, Frame 566.

[163]Harriet Taylor Upton to Warren G. Harding, July 11, 1920, Warren G. Harding Papers, Reel 66, Frames 879–880.

[164]Harriet Taylor Upton to Warren G. Harding, July 2, 1920, ibid., Frames 874–875.

[165]Harriet Taylor Upton to George B. Christian, May 31, 1921, ibid., Reel 179, Frames 381–382.

A few days later Upton wrote Harding that "some women are now getting so anxious about the passage of this bill and I am so fearful that the delay will hurt our political condition. It will be hard to hold Republican women if we haven't something to show for what we said we would do."[166]

The following month saw hearings in the House of Representatives on Sheppard-Towner; Upton attended them all and again asked Harding to help the bill's passage, referencing the electoral support of women: "I do not know as you could start anything which will make them hurry, but since there has been more interest manifested in this Bill than any other, unless it was the Packers' Bill, and since women voted largely our ticket; have not pressed for offices, and are depending on us to get this thing through, I think somebody ought to try to do it."[167]

When Sheppard-Towner did pass the House in November 1921, after Harding specifically mentioned it in his message to the special session of Congress, Upton wrote Harding of the electoral consequences: "In some States the Senators' election is going to depend upon women and it has been impossible to organize until we could know whether a Republican Congress was going to grant their only request." Upton also told Harding that the leaders of women's organizations were quite happy with her work, and attached a note from such a woman who wrote, "I do not know how well you suit the President and his staff, but you are giving great and gleeful satisfaction to the women. I hear it from all sides."[168]

Upton continued to follow up on the question of adequate appropriations for Sheppard-Towner, fighting the efforts of those within Harding's administration to cut the bill's appropriations in the federal budget. Upton argued for at least the bill's congressionally authorized appropriations in December 1922 in order to "strengthen us politically with women." When Harding was less than helpful, Upton proclaimed the political importance of "keeping faith with the women" and told Harding that she was going to intervene with the House Appropriations Committee: "I am going to the assistance of the women who are interested in this. . . . It is my duty to keep as many Republican women gratefully attached to the party as possible and this is my chance." Upton also pointedly referred to the efforts of women who had worked for the election of state legislators and governors in 1922 as a reason to request the full appropriations authorized.[169]

---

[166]Harriet Taylor Upton to Warren G. Harding, June 16, 1921, ibid., Frame 385.

[167]Harriet Taylor Upton to Warren G. Harding, July 20, 1921, ibid., Frame 397.

[168]Harriet Taylor Upton to Warren G. Harding, November 21, 1921, ibid., Reel 194, Frames 1397–1398.

[169]Harriet Taylor Upton to Warren G. Harding, December 2, 1922, ibid., Reel

The same pattern occurred with respect to Upton's efforts on behalf of a proposed Department of Public Welfare. In 1921, Upton informed Harding that "a group of thirteen women's organizations" was objecting to an administration report concerning such a department, warning Harding that he should avoid "the appearance that there is a difference between the administration and any group or groups of women.[170] Similarly, Upton's lobbying efforts on behalf of a governmental commission to control the spread of sexually transmitted diseases were accompanied by references to independent women's organizations: "We have been working for months to have the work of the Interdepartmental Social Hygiene Board continued. My interest in it has been that five million women are asking for it";[171] "I am only trying to keep as many women friendly towards the party as possible";[172] "so many women are interested in this matter that I have found myself pushing it a little."[173]

Upton also referenced women's groups to Harding when lobbying for a commission on sex discrimination in the civil service ("This group of women have for some time, as have other groups, brought me facts concerning the discrimination against women in the different departments of the governmental service and now they say that it has been proposed that a commission be created which will look after this discrimination now existing. . . . women of the plain people seem to trust me when I tell them I will bring this matter to your attention and so, therefore, I must do it")[174] and for a federal prison for women ("I am not writing on the merits of the bill. I am only saying that there are large groups of women, influential key women, who believe in this bill and its passage now would mean more politically than I can make you or any one else realize").[175]

Another prominent issue that engaged Upton was to secure Harding's

---

211, Frames 383–384; Harriet Taylor Upton to Warren G. Harding, December 6, 1922, ibid., Reel 179, Frame 428; Harriet Taylor Upton to Warren G. Harding, December 7, 1922, ibid., Frame 429.

[170]Harriet Taylor Upton to George Christian, December 26, 1921, ibid., Reel 194, Frame 1417.

[171]Harriet Taylor Upton to George Christian, June 28, 1922, ibid., Reel 211, Frame 351.

[172]Harriet Taylor Upton to George Christian, July 11, 1922, ibid., Frame 354.

[173]Harriet Taylor Upton to Warren G. Harding, July 25, 1922, ibid., Frames 368–369; see also Harriet Taylor Upton to Warren G. Harding, December 1, 1922, ibid., Frame 382; Harriet Taylor Upton to Warren G. Harding, December 5, 1922, ibid., Frames 386–387.

[174]Harriet Taylor Upton to Warren G. Harding, January 14, 1922, ibid., Reel 192, Frame 929.

[175]Harriet Taylor Upton to Warren G. Harding, February 12, 1923, ibid., Reel 207, Frame 1448.

endorsement of the efforts of the Women's Bureau and most women's organizations to secure protective labor legislation for women, and to prevent his endorsing the efforts of the National Women's Party to secure an equal rights amendment to the Constitution, which would undermine protective legislation for women. When lobbying Harding on these matters, Upton made sure to reference the various women's organizations involved, oftentimes referring to the former group as the "industrial" group: "Since I saw you I have been able to help, because of my political condition, to straighten out an appropriation for the Woman's Bureau and thereby have made the industrial group feel grateful to us. I was awfully glad to be able to do this because they certainly have been 'touchy' over the Woman's Party amendment."[176]

In late 1922, Upton sought to have Harding speak at a conference on protective labor legislation for women sponsored by the Women's Bureau of the Department of Labor:

The leaders of all the women's organizations, such as the National Federation of Women's Clubs, the Parent-Teachers, the W.C.T.U. etc. are to be here [at the conference]. They have delegated me to ask you to open the conference with a few words of greeting. . . . they have suggested, because you have so often talked of the Eight-hour-a-day Law and the Welfare Department which you yourself proposed at Marion when a large number of these same women were present, that these topics could be referred to. I have gladly accepted the commission of asking you because I realize that the industrial people entered in to our defeat in November to a greater degree than any other one group.[177]

When Harding did not speak at the conference, Upton informed Harding's advisors of the consequences in terms of support for the administration by women's groups: "We had Woman's Day at Marion especially to get this group and the President's speech was great and took them and they came our way and we lost the leaders of seven or eight groups because I was not insistent."[178]

Upton also lobbied Coolidge on this issue after Harding's death in office, again referencing women's organizations: "the above organizations, powerfully strong, at their conventions in the past year, after due consideration, and discussion, passed resolutions against the Amendment proposed by the Woman's Party. I am . . . bringing the matter to

[176]Harriet Taylor Upton to Warren G. Harding, February 15, 1922, ibid., Reel 194, Frames 1463–1464.

[177]Harriet Taylor Upton to Warren G. Harding, December 21, 1922, ibid., Reel 192, Frames 952–953.

[178]Harriet Taylor Upton to George Christian, June 1923, ibid., Reel 195, Frames 215–216.

your attention again by sending you this duplicate list";[179] "[after again listing 'powerful' women's organizations as the League of Women Voters] it would not be wise to have [the ERA] mentioned in your message [to Congress], because such mention will not only further estrange the industrial women but will weaken the ardor of many groups toward the party, surely."[180]

Upton also sought to ensure the appointment of women to federal boards and commissions, particularly those advising Harding's conferences on disarmament and unemployment. Again Upton took pains to point out to Harding and his advisors that this was a concern of the League of Women Voters.[181] Upton arranged meetings between representatives of the league and Harding on the issue of appointments, and pushed Harding when she felt his support was flagging: "I have been able so far to steer clear of any kind of trouble with any women organizations but I find I must proceed cautiously on this employment commission or there will be trouble."[182]

Upton lobbied not only for women to be appointed to these boards and commissions, but for the "right" kind of women to be appointed, that is, women who would receive the approval of women's organizations. Harding's advisors were wont to appoint loyal Republican Party women to these positions, and Upton attempted to warn them off this strategy:

We must balance it up a little. If a woman like Miss West [Republican national committeewoman from Michigan] is put on [the advisory committee to Harding's Disarmament Conference] there must be a student and an internationalist for another. Two of the Unemployed Conference women were excellent. We ought to have had more still I am thankful for any. None of the names I submitted were lumber. Some of the men are.[183]

[179]Harriet Taylor Upton to Calvin Coolidge, n.d., Calvin Coolidge Papers, Reel 121, File 395.

[180]Harriet Taylor Upton to Calvin Coolidge, November 21, 1923, ibid., File 395–A.

[181]Harriet Taylor Upton to George Christian, August 15, 1921, Warren G. Harding Papers, Reel 194, Frame 1317.

[182]Harriet Taylor Upton to George Christian, September 6, 1921, ibid., Frame 1326; see also Harriet Flenner, Secretary to Harriet Taylor Upton, to George Christian, September 3, 1921, ibid., Frame 1323; Harriet Taylor Upton to George Christian, September 10, 1921, ibid., Frame 1331; Harriet Taylor Upton to George Christian, September 19, 1921, ibid., Frame 1328; George Christian to Harriet Taylor Upton, October 12, 1921, ibid., Frame 1372.

[183]Harriet Taylor Upton to George Christian, September 21, 1921, ibid., Frame 1332; see also Harriet Taylor Upton to George Christian, n.d., ibid., Frame 1310, concerning her recommendation of Mrs. Raymond Robins of the League of Women Voters for the Disarmament Advisory Committee; and Harriet Taylor Upton to Warren G. Harding, December 1, 1922, ibid., Reel 195, Frame 91, recommending against

Upton also warned Harding against appointing women associated with "the picketers," or the National Woman's Party, since these women were also opposed by the league and its allies:

Mrs. Reed of Connecticut . . . is one of the picketers and a militant. I know nothing of her ability but I know her appointment would not please women generally. . . . Mrs. Gardner [on the three-member Civil Service Commission] is trusted by women, knows the business, and should not be displaced by a woman.[184]

Upton went so far as to report to Harding in late 1922 that the Democratic National Committee was planning on making an appeal to women's organizations during the 1924 campaign on the issue of the number and kind of women appointed to office by Harding: "I am mentioning this because we all feel, you as much as the rest of us, that we must make a few more appointments of women but I continue to feel that we must be just as careful as we have been to get the right person in the right place."[185] The following month, in another cautionary memo about the possible appeal of the Democrats to women's organizations on this issue, Upton wrote Harding, "There has been no mistake made so far in woman's appointments – I figuratively knock on wood when ever I make this statement."[186]

Upton was not alone in the national party organization in referencing independent women's organizations when lobbying male party elites; national committeewomen would often pursue such a strategy in their lobbying efforts as well. A director of publicity for the Republican Party organization wrote Harding about his possible endorsement of Sheppard-Towner in July 1920: "I work in the field with the women and this is a measure that strikes home without any preliminaries. You know that this was one of the measures all the women's organizations of the country tried to get into our platform, and that they did not succeed. In fact they met with some unfortunate levity in response to their plea, and this we Republican women are trying to 'explain.' Your personal endorsement of this measure will more than undo all that has been done ill or left undone."[187] The Republican national committeewoman from

appointing a woman to the federal judiciary because of the opposition of women's organizations.

[184] Harriet Taylor Upton to Warren G. Harding, March 22, 1922, ibid., Reel 194, Frame 1466.

[185] Harriet Taylor Upton to Warren G. Harding, November 29, 1922, ibid., Reel 195, Frame 90.

[186] Harriet Taylor Upton to Warren G. Harding, December 27, 1922, ibid., Frames 99–101.

[187] Mary Stewart to Warren G. Harding, July 14, 1920, ibid., Reel 77, Frame 779.

California sought an endorsement from Harding on protective labor legislation with the following: "The National Y.W.C.A., the General Federation of Women's Clubs, the W.C.T.U., the National League of Women Voters and other women's organizations have in their annual and biennial conventions declared for these measures. There is therefore a widespread demand and interest on the part of the women of this country. . . . a statement that you were sympathetic with [a national minimum wage for women] if it can be done constitutionally would bring to our party thousands of women now 'on the fence.' "[188] And in 1924, the women on the Republican National Convention's platform committee publicly consulted with member organizations of the Women's Joint Congressional Committee in order to formulate a women's legislative agenda.[189]

Male Republican elites would have had incentives to respond to the efforts of women within the party as long as those women maintained ties with independent women's organizations that posed an electoral threat to the party's fortunes. The timing of male elites' response to the organizational demands of women's organizations certainly matches the timing of the NLWV's potential to pose an electoral threat. In addition, direct documentary evidence supports this conclusion.

First, Republican Party elites were clearly wary of the prospect of independently organized women's groups mobilizing in electoral contests. On numerous occasions the RNC chairman expressed, in the words of the *Times*, "deserved condemnation for the misguided sisters who are making the foolish and wicked mistake of standing apart from their brother voters and trying to perpetuate an aloofness and separation for which there is no longer either reason or excuse."[190] RNC Chairman Hays on occasion would go so far as to tell potential female voters that he would rather they become Democrats than follow the lead of independent women's organizations. Hays was not alone in these speeches to women; United States Senator and prospective Republican presidential nominee Warren G. Harding also spoke out denouncing the League of Women Voters and its campaign against New York Senator Wadsworth in early 1920.[191]

Harding's first speech to Republican women after the ratification of the federal suffrage amendment reiterated Republican male sentiment on the issue of independent women's organizations: "I want you to meet

---

[188]Katherine Philips Edson to Warren G. Harding, September 12, 1920, ibid., Reel 34, Frames 162–166.

[189]"Women to Be in Force at Party Conventions," *NYT*, June 1, 1924, VIII p. 4.

[190]"He Showed Sense and Wisdom," *NYT*, May 24, 1919, p. 12.

[191]Harriet Taylor Upton to Warren G. Harding, February 26, 1920, Warren G. Harding Papers, Reel 30, Frames 815–817.

this obligation [of citizenship] in the political parties. Nothing in the world would make me so much regret the coming of suffrage as to see the segregation of women because of sex."[192] Harding also referred here to the intention of former suffragists to campaign against antisuffragists, and pleaded with his audience not to engage in such "prejudice."

In two widely reported addresses to Republican women's clubs in New York during the campaign, Harding expressed approval of their choices in "allying themselves with a party" and asserted that, "certainly, there should be no division in the electorate along sex lines."[193] In Harding's final speech to Republican women in the campaign, he made a clear reference to the league and denounced its stated aims:

First to the women. . . . Our citizenship should recognize no selfish group allegiance. . . . it would be the supreme disappointment if the coming of women into our political life should mean the organization of any considerable part of them into a woman's party, built upon a spirit of demand, and thereby made repugnant to that consecration which must ever be the foundation of true American citizenship. . . . I beg you, the women and all the new voters of America, to keep this in your minds. I know how easy it is to find satisfaction, and at least a transitory hope, in that which some choose to call "political independence." But I urge you, as I would urge all Americans, so long as their conscience will allow them to do so, to put faith in the ultimate responsiveness of our political parties to the aspirations of our people.[194]

Once in office, President Harding continued to return to the theme that women should follow the electoral cues of one of the two major parties rather than those of an independent women's organization. In November 1921 Harding prepared a message for the convention of the National League of Women Voters, in which he denounced the idea of women uniting as a "class," and said that "Nothing could be more unfortunate than to give limited assent to the proposal of organizing our citizenship into groups according to sex."[195] In May 1922, in a speech to Republican women in New Jersey, Harding hit the same theme: "I believe with all my heart that women can only play their part fully and best when they play it in connection with recognized political organi-

[192]Text of Harding speech, August 27, 1920, ibid., Reel 239, Frames 123–132.

[193]Warren G. Harding to Mary Hatch Willard, President, Republican Committee of One Hundred, New York City, September 10, 1920, ibid., Reel 58, Frames 503–504; Text of Harding speech to the Women's Harding and Coolidge Club, New York City, September 15, 1920, ibid., Reel 78, Frames 1210–1213; "Harding Pleads for Women's Vote," *NYT*, September 16, 1920, p. 3.

[194]"New Voters Throng to Harding Porch," *NYT*, October 19, 1920, p. 2.

[195]"Harding Warns Women Voters against Uniting as a Class," *NYT*, November 23, 1921, p. 19.

zations. . . . No group of women could tell precisely what would be best for them without consulting some man or men, any more than a group of men may know what is best for them. . . . I believe it with all my heart, and I would look with very great sorrow upon the day when we had in America party divisions along lines of sex."[196]

Harding was not alone in these implicit or explicit denunciations of membership in the League of Women Voters during this period. Other elites in the national Republican organization joined Harding in pronouncing the league forbidden territory for women in the Republican organization. At the first anniversary celebration of the Women's National Republican Club in New York, the *New York Times* reported that several nationally prominent Republicans attacked the league:

Women were urged to affiliate themselves with the regular political parties and to avoid membership in non-partisan organizations such as the League of Women Voters and the Woman's Party by practically all the speakers at the birthday luncheon of the Women's National Republican Club at the Hotel Biltmore yesterday. . . . John T. Adams, Chairman of the Republican National Committee, said he would rather have a woman be a Democrat than belong to some nonpartisan or woman's organization.[197]

Later that spring Ohio Republican Senator Frank B. Willis reiterated the official Republican denunciation of the league, warning women to "not descend to the untenable position that with suffrage now extended to them political action hereafter should be based on sex alignment."[198] And upon his ascension to the presidency Calvin Coolidge made it clear that he supported the Republican line that membership in an independent women's organization rendered a Republican Party activist suspect. In speaking to a Republican women's group in the spring of 1924, he said, "I am glad to welcome you because you represent a desire for party organization. . . . It is necessary to have party organization if we are to have effective and efficient government. . . . I don't know of any one that has represented the real ideals of America any better than of those of party loyalty, either on the one side or the other."[199]

Could these public attacks on the electoral activities of women's organizations in general, and the NLWV in particular, have been motivated by a sincere belief in the absence of meaningful political differences

[196]"Harding Declares for Frelinghuysen," *NYT*, May 13, 1922, p. 1.
[197]"Partisan Loyalty Urged upon Women," *NYT*, January 15, 1922, II p. 2; "Attacks Surprise Women's League," *NYT*, January 16, 1922, p. 13.
[198]"Willis Advises Women," *NYT*, June 8, 1922, p. 3.
[199]"Coolidge Stresses Rule by Party," *NYT*, May 9, 1924, p. 7.

between men and women? This is unlikely. First, the Republican Party obviously maintained its own internal organization by sex. Second, in private correspondence male Republican elites expressed concern over the electoral threat posed by these organizations, and by the NLWV in particular. In early 1920 Harding's campaign manager warned the candidate to take the NLWV seriously because of its electoral potential.[200] Later in the campaign, a national Republican campaign official expressed concern over the guest list for Harding's front porch "Social Justice Day":

Apparently, according to confidential advice handed me today, a number of women have been invited to this function who are members of the League of Women Voters which is fighting Senator Wadsworth in New York, Senator Brandegee in Connecticut, Senator Moses in New Hampshire and whose affiliations with the Republican Party are of a dangerously tenuous sort. There has been a serious blunder somewhere which should be rectified before any of this outfit have an opportunity to get into the limelight. You of course know the party treason of Mary Garrett Hay and also you might as well know that it is only a question of days before Mrs. "Charlie Chaplin" Catt announces her adherence to the Cox-Roosevelt ticket. There are other women intimately connected with this coterie of mal-contents which have been invited to the Marion function. . . . Someone has been playing with fire.[201]

Because of their concerns over the electoral threat posed by women's organizations, Republican Party elites commissioned a study in 1920 to "find out what women want to know about politics, what they demand that their ballot shall effect, and to calculate therefrom what they will do with their ballot." The RNC's director of publicity studied the issue for two years and reported back to his party superiors that women favored a distinctive legislative agenda, and that male party elites would be well advised to respond to these legislative demands:

There will be a period when [women] will constitute the majority of the shifting vote; there will be a period during which the greater part of them will change readily from one of the established parties to the other. Therefore, I believe that it behooves both of the great parties carefully to preserve the enthusiasms that they have created; Democrats and Republicans must alike labor to keep the women members that they have acquired. Woman must have her full share in the party councils, and if she is to be won or retained the interparty contest must become, at least for a time, a fairer race toward the adoption of her some-

---

[200]Harry M. Daugherty to Warren G. Harding, May 13, 1920, Warren G. Harding Papers, Reel 28, Frame 1078.
[201]"Highly Confidential" to George Christian, n.d., ibid., Reel 53, Frame 1058.

times exacting, but generally well-inspired, demands as to platform and policies.[202]

As did their Republican counterparts, women in the national Democratic Party often warned male party leaders that the female vote would be distinct and significant. For example, in 1919 the head of the Democratic Party's national women's division told the Democratic National Committee that "the women" would determine the result of the 1920 presidential election.[203] At the 1920 Democratic National Convention, female party leaders declared that if a Democratic state were to ratify the federal suffrage amendment, women would remember that fact in the fall election.[204]

In addition, female Democratic leaders also maintained ties with women's organizations that were publicly committed to the mobilization of women's votes. Emily Newell Blair continued to be a member of the NLWV during her tenure in office, and also participated in the "Little Cabinet" of the leaders of women's organizations and the major parties. Her work on behalf of league measures was in fact recognized at the 1923 NLWV convention.[205]

In 1924, Eleanor Roosevelt appointed to her women's platform committee representatives from the major women's organizations (including the National League of Women Voters), apparently without much regard for their partisanship.[206] She also scheduled open hearings at which representatives of any women's organizations not represented on the women's platform committee itself could present their legislative requests for consideration.[207] The final women's legislative agenda was annotated by a list of the women's organizations which supported each plank.[208]

In short, throughout the 1920s, in all four party organizations, female party leaders maintained ties with independent women's organizations, including the NLWV. Many female leaders also warned, at times bluntly

[202]Reginald Wright Kauffman, "Her Whims as Voter," *NYT*, October 1, 1922, VIII p. 3.
[203]"Democrats Plan for Women's Vote," *NYT*, September 28, 1919, p. 7.
[204]"Democratic Women Count on Tennessee," *NYT*, June 24, 1920, p. 2.
[205]Papers of the National League of Women Voters, Pt. II, Reel 5, Frame 225. More information on the lobbying efforts of Democratic women within their organization was not readily available for this period.
[206]*NYT*, May 18, 1924, p. 2, reporting the membership of Eleanor Roosevelt's committee.
[207]"Women Democrats to Discuss Planks," *NYT*, June 8, 1924, II p. 1; "Women Democrats to Offer Planks," *NYT*, June 12, 1924, p. 6; "Women Democrats Propose Dry Plank," *NYT*, June 13, 1924, p. 21.
[208]"Women Plan Fight on Any Wet Plank," *NYT*, June 25, 1924, p. 15; "Anti-Klan Plank Pressed," *NYT*, June 25, 1924, p. 4.

and at other times more subtly, of the potential electoral threat posed by those organizations in alliance with partisan women. Male party elites displayed an awareness of this potential electoral threat, oftentimes expressed in denunciations of independent political organizations of women. While this documentary evidence is of course open to interpretation, it is certainly consistent with our hypothesized causal mechanism producing concessions for female party leaders in the early 1920s but not in the latter half of that decade.

CONCLUSION

In order to use changes in the internal structure of the party organizations as an additional dependent variable upon which to test our argument, we first required that certain conditions be satisfied. The first of these conditions was that women within the party organizations actually sought access to the men's party committees. This certainly appears to have been the case. Many female party leaders in all four party organizations did not quietly accept their subordinate status within the party organizations, protesting repeatedly during this period their exclusion from male party committees and their lack of control over their own organization.

Precisely because of this lack of female control over the parties' women's divisions, however, female party elites were unlikely to see a favorable response to their policy and organizational demands. Because the women's divisions were at first entirely appointed by male party elites, those elites originally had direct control over these divisions. Later, women were elected to some party positions by all-male party committees. Even after women were admitted to party posts that were elected by both male and female voters, male party committees retained the power to nominate the candidates for these positions, nominations that were only rarely contested. After women had been admitted to these latter committees, they were able to have a voice in the nomination of their successors. But male party elites were initially able to nominate enough female party loyalists to these posts, in addition to women from independent women's organizations, to undermine the possibility that these women would combine their votes to elect female party leaders other than those selected and/or supported by male party elites.[209]

Moreover, for all four parties examined here, several documented instances exist of male party elites using their control of the women's

[209]Melanie Gustafson also documents male control of the women's committees for the Progressive Party of 1912 and the concomitant lack of influence by female Progressive leaders. See "Partisan Women," chap. 7.

divisions to remove outspoken or otherwise troublesome women. In their stead were appointed women who were widely reputed to be much more receptive to the wishes of male party elites. These well-publicized incidents would certainly have given pause to any other female partisan leaders who sought to threaten party leaders with women's votes if their concessions were not granted.

Given the ease with which male party elites could remove trouble-makers from their positions in the women's party organizations, we should not have seen *any* movement by male elites to respond to the demands of women's party leaders. Organizational concessions could be costly, in terms of both votes and power, and there was no need to make such concessions as long as male party leaders could count on loyal female partisans to mobilize female votes using incentives other than policy promises.

Yet NLWV elites were both aware of and lobbied in support of the demands being made by women within the parties. Did male party elites respond to the potential electoral threat from the NLWV between 1920 and 1924? The answer to this question, for the four different party organizations, constitutes the test for our hypothesis concerning the sources of policy and party organizational change. Organizational concessions to women within the party organizations should have been made when the NLWV and its affiliates constituted a potential electoral threat, but not after that organization had renounced electoral mobilization.

There were in fact organizational concessions made by male party elites between 1920 and 1925 in all four party organizations. This matches the pattern we saw in Chapter 1, where independently organized women enjoyed a steady stream of policy victories in Congress through 1924, but after the 1924 elections saw those successes end rather dramatically. Similarly, after 1924, with the exception of the development of the law regulating access to the parties' state committees in New York State, organizational concessions by male party elites ceased as well.

Given the control that male party elites continued to exercise over the parties' women's divisions throughout this period, the only incentive that those elites could have had to respond to the demands from party women for greater representation would have been an *external* incentive, such as that from an electoral threat backed up by the potential of retaliation from the National League of Women Voters. If the league remained an electoral threat, the demands of women in the parties for greater access to male party committees could not be ignored as long as female party leaders maintained close ties with the league and its organizational allies. The timing of successes and failures experienced by

207

those seeking to secure representation on party committees corresponds quite neatly to the timing of the league's withdrawal from participation in electoral contests. Moreover, the documentary evidence discussed in this chapter further supports the argument that the links between the parties' women's divisions and independent women's organizations provide the causal mechanism producing a response to female demands up to 1925 but not thereafter.

The response of male elites to the organizational demands of women in the parties thus matches the response of electoral elites more generally to the lobbying efforts of independent women's organizations to secure policies designed to benefit women and children. The connection between the league's electoral power and its lobbying efficacy, hypothesized in Chapter 2, can thus be inferred with greater confidence than if the responses of electoral elites to the two different kinds of lobbying had not corresponded in their timing.

The next and final chapter suggests ways in which the story concerning the unequal competition between the NLWV and the parties evolved over time. As noted in Chapter 1, policy and party concessions for women were absent for many decades in the United States, but resumed rather suddenly in 1970. Why the change in 1970? That is, what could have occurred in the 1960s to undermine the competitive advantages held by the parties in the electoral mobilization of women?

6

The Reemergence of Policy and Party Benefits for Women, 1970–Present

If the arguments made in the preceding pages are correct, then by the mid-1920s the promise suffrage had held for women's organizations had already been eviscerated. Suffrage leaders had for decades publicized their quest for the vote not merely as a symbol or a right, but as a tool with which women's interests could more securely be protected. But the vote proved to be an unwieldy tool. Even if many women voted as a coordinated group, that in itself would not produce policy benefits for women. If those votes were coordinated by *party* female leaders rather than *independent* female leaders, then a vote might very well bring nothing but the benefit of approval from the members of one's partisan women's club. And independent women's organizations could not overcome their disadvantages in the competition with the parties to provide such solidary benefits.

How long did this unfortunate situation endure? With respect to the success rate of women's organizations lobbying for policy benefits, there appears to be a consensus in the historical literature that independent women's organizations had little to no influence during the period between 1925 and 1970. Organizations existed and lobbied, but won few policy concessions. And yet, in 1970 a new trend of policy benefits for women as a group suddenly developed. What accounts for the abrupt resumption of such benefits?

THE REEMERGENCE OF POLICY BENEFITS FOR WOMEN, 1970–PRESENT

As in the case of the 1920s, we have three different arguments for the reemergence of policy benefits for women in 1970. Jo Freeman has made both the policy network and the ideological climate arguments for the reemergence of these benefits; according to Freeman, some combination of a flowering of new women's organizations joining forces with more established women's organizations, plus the favorable change-oriented ideological climate of the 1960s, contributed to the reemergence of the willingness of office-seeking legislators to grant women policy concessions.[1] However, neither of these arguments is particularly satisfying. Women's lobbying organizations maintained close ties with administration officials throughout the 1960s without seeing any policy concessions. The woman who was made director of the Women's Bureau in the Department of Labor under the Kennedy administration was even given the brief to strengthen administration relationships with independent women's organizations. Esther Peterson did this by decentralizing Women's Bureau operations to render the bureau more accessible to those organizations as well as by hosting a series of regional conferences to bring together representatives from the Women's Bureau and women's organizations.[2] Similarly, Kennedy's 1961 President's Commission on the Status of Women was directed by Kennedy himself to work primarily through independent women's organizations.[3] Yet no congressional policy concessions were forthcoming from this policy network.

Likewise, the ideological climate argument does not fit the pattern of concessions to women's organizations particularly well. David Mayhew's comprehensive study of patterns of law making dates the ideological surge of the 1960s from approximately 1963 to 1975 or 1976.[4] But the pattern of benefits for women as a group is not neatly demarcated by those dates.

Helene Silverberg has made an electorally centered argument for the reemergence of this policy trend; she attributes the renewed interest of legislators in creating policy benefits for women to the coeval reemergence of women as an important electoral bloc.[5] Thus women apparently did not constitute such a bloc or group from 1925 to 1970. We have seen that this argument does not work particularly well for the 1920s; does it work any better for the later period?

[1]Jo Freeman, *The Politics of Women's Liberation: A Case Study of an Emerging Social Movement and Its Relation to the Policy Process* (New York: David McKay, 1975).

[2]Helene Norma Silverberg, "Political Organization and the Origin of Political Identity: The Emergence and Containment of Gender in American Politics, 1960–1984" (Ph.D. dissertation, Cornell University, 1988), pp. 53–58.

[3]Ibid., pp. 61–65; Esther Peterson oral history interview, pp. 23, 55, 59, 71, 93, John F. Kennedy Library, Boston, Massachusetts.

[4]David R. Mayhew, *Divided We Govern: Party Control, Lawmaking, and Investigations, 1946–1990* (New Haven: Yale University Press, 1991), pp. 81–91.

[5]Silverberg, "Political Organization."

The Reemergence of Benefits

The short answer is no. The somewhat longer answer is that women reemerged as a significant electoral group in the calculations of office-seeking elites as early as 1952, some twenty years before the renewal of policy benefits for women as a group.

Immediately following the 1952 presidential election, party elites as well as political commentators began remarking on the significance of an apparently materializing "women's vote," which was significantly more Republican than the men's vote. According to future Kennedy advisor Louis Harris, in 1952 women as a group "broke with the Democratic Party way of voting which they had taken to enthusiastically under Roosevelt": women turned out at a higher rate than men and voted for Eisenhower significantly more than did men.[6] The combination of the apparent emergence of this women's vote, primarily among middle-class women, and the defection of suburban Democrats were thought to have thrown the election to the Republicans.[7] Harris warned electoral elites of the significance of this development, arguing that the election demonstrated the emergence of women as "a potent, more independent force in politics . . . perhaps less predictable than some other groups, and . . . apt to have standards for voting different from men."[8] Democratic leaders did not necessarily need Harris's warning; even before the publication of Harris's book in 1954, Democratic Party leaders were well aware of "the reported trend of women voters toward the Republican ticket,"[9] and discussed this trend in party meetings held after their loss in 1952.[10]

The response of these leaders to the apparent emergence of a gender gap was not to develop policy initiatives designed to appeal to this emergent group, but rather to discuss new techniques of attracting women's votes through the organizational auspices of the women's Democratic organization. At one of the first Democratic National Executive Committee (DNEC) meetings held after their November loss, national Democratic elites discussed new methods of organizing women to vote on a

[6]Louis Harris, *Is There a Republican Majority? Political Trends, 1952–1956* (New York: Harper & Brothers, 1954), p. 104. The estimated increase in turnout for women between 1948 and 1952 was 22 percent; the comparable figure for men was 11 percent. Roper-NBC surveys in November of 1952 showed that women preferred Eisenhower to Stevenson by a margin of 17 percentage points; the comparable figure for men was 5 percentage points. Ibid., pp. 108, 116.

[7]Silverberg, "Political Organization," p. 42.

[8]Harris, *Is There a Republican Majority?*, p. 117.

[9]Stephen Mitchell, "Report to Members of the Democratic National Committee and State Chairmen," January 20, 1953, Democratic National Committee (DNC) Papers, Box 113, John F. Kennedy Library.

[10]Transcript of Democratic National Executive Committee (DNEC) meeting, April 1, 1953, ibid., Box 119, pp. 97, 103–108, 111.

neighborhood basis, such as through the social medium of women's neighborhood coffee hours.[11] Agreement was expressed among discussants that special organizational programs for women were the best way to get women involved with the Democratic Party, and that the DNC could serve as a source of guidance on creating and maintaining those programs in the various states.[12]

The congressional elections of 1954 saw the Office of Women's Activities of the DNC compiling a packet of nonpolicy oriented campaign materials specifically for women, and helping to organize women's campaign activities such as coffee hours and "Drop a Dollar in a Hat Box" drives.[13] In February 1955 the DNC began issuing a newsletter entitled *News and Comments for and about Women* as a means to appeal to this important electoral group. In the 1956 presidential campaign the Democrats sought to expand their organizational appeals to women through special campaign activities, as well as through a neighborhood program specifically directed at suburban women.[14]

Following the Democrats' defeat in the 1956 presidential election, Chairman Paul Butler told the DNEC that women as an electoral group were the source of the Democratic Party's woes: "the most important segment of the electorate, so far as the future plans of the Democratic party is [*sic*] concerned, is the women of America. I think that we have failed to keep pace with the Republican organization in our appeal to the women."[15] A lengthy discussion was held on how best to win more of this group for the party.[16] The following spring, the leader of the party's national women's organization reminded Butler of his arguments: "Emphasis is continually placed on the importance of the role of women. You have been a most determined spokesman for this thesis. You have pointed out on many occasions that women and young people are the segments of the population with which we need to do the most work."[17]

[11]Ibid., pp. 97, 103–105.
[12]Ibid., pp. 106–108, 111.
[13]Report of Mrs. Katie Louchheim, Director of the Office of Women's Activities, December 4, 1954, ibid., Box 116.
[14]Katie Louchheim to Paul Butler, "Democratic Women's Campaign Program," September 5, 1956, ibid., Box 442; Katie Louchheim to Paul Butler, "Budget: Office of Women's Activities," September 20, 1956, ibid.; Office of Women's Activities, "Operation Crossroads," October 2, 1956, ibid.; Office of Women's Activities, "Suburban Good Neighbor Policy," n.d., ibid.
[15]Paul Butler, in transcript of DNEC meeting, November 27, 1956, ibid., Box 119, p. 177.
[16]Ibid., pp. 169–179, 187; transcript of DNC meeting February 15, 1957, ibid., pp. 85–88.
[17]Katie Louchheim to Paul Butler, confidential memo, June 26, 1957, ibid., Box 442.

The Reemergence of Benefits

In preparation for the 1958 congressional elections, a national Democratic women's meeting was held for the first time in many years and candidates were urged not to overlook women in their campaigns.[18] Again in 1960, Democratic Party elites focused on trying to win back lapsed suburban and female Democrats and also any independent potential voters.[19] Democratic presidential candidate John F. Kennedy had even expressed the belief that women would hold the balance of power in the 1960 election as early as 1957.[20] Women were targeted with an appeal to their domestically oriented concerns with social welfare and peace.[21] The focus was on the last appeal, with a special program established to appeal to women's alleged pacifism, "Strategy for Peace."[22] "Kennedy Ladies" were also deployed throughout the campaign to attract potential female voters through tea parties featuring female members of the Kennedy family.[23]

According to a Gallup poll held in December 1960, Kennedy broke even with middle-aged women and bested Nixon by a 10 percent margin among young women.[24] Given the closeness of the election, Kennedy advisors continued to be concerned about this electoral group. A confidential strategy memorandum from presidential advisor Clayton Fritchey to Kennedy in 1963 noted that "Women now compose a majority of the electorate and this majority is constantly increasing," and that "Some now say that women are indifferent to political recognition of their sex, but I think this is also a miscalculation."[25] The President's Commission on the Status of Women, established in late 1961, was apparently urged by Vice-President Lyndon Johnson as a forum for at-

[18]Office of Women's Activities, "Report to the DNC on Women's Activities," February 21, 1958, ibid., Box 121; Office of Women's Activities, "Candidate Memo-Gram," 1958, ibid., Box 442.
[19]Silverberg, "Political Organization," p. 45.
[20]Ibid., p. 42.
[21]"Women's Committee for New Frontiers," Robert F. Kennedy (RFK) Pre-Administration Political Files, Box 52, John F. Kennedy Library; transcript of Henry Fonda interview of Senator and Mrs. John F. Kennedy, November 2, 1960, ibid., Box 38.
[22]Margaret Price to Robert Kennedy, "Strategy for Peace Program," September 27, 1960, RFK Papers, Box 24, John F. Kennedy Library; "Campaign Bulletin: Strategy for Peace," RFK Pre-Administration Political Files, Box 35; "Report to the Chairman and Vice Chairman of the Democratic National Committee on the Strategy for Peace Program, 1960 Campaign," RFK Pre-Administration Political Files, Box 38.
[23]"Final Report on the Activities of the Kennedy Ladies in the 1960 Presidential Campaign," RFK Pre-Administration Political Files, Box 36.
[24]Silverberg, "Political Organization," p. 50.
[25]Clayton Fritchey to John F. Kennedy, July 22, 1963, Presidential Subject Files, Box 374, John F. Kennedy Library.

tracting women to the party, and was picked up by the White House as such.[26] In 1964 Johnson himself embarked on a well-publicized campaign to end "stag government" as yet another electoral ploy to attract this group.[27]

By the mid-1950s, then, the Democrats' electoral strategies clearly included women as a distinct electoral group. According to the simple strategic account, electoral calculations should have resulted at least in part in attempts by congressional lawmakers to cater to the policy preferences of women in efforts to win the group's votes. And those efforts did in fact begin occurring in 1970. But there was a gap of approximately twenty years between the reemergence of women as a distinct and significant electoral group and the response of legislators and party elites to women's policy demands.

According to the arguments made in Chapter 2, if legislators began to respond favorably to the lobbying efforts of women's organizations in 1970, then those organizations must have wielded a credible electoral threat. We already know that party elites considered women to be a distinct electoral group from the mid-1950s onward. The question is, Were women's organizations seeking to coordinate women's votes independently of the party organizations?

The answer is no, for the period prior to 1968, and yes for the period after 1968. Before 1968, no women's organizations pursued a strategy of mobilizing women as an electoral group in order to win policy concessions from reluctant legislators. In 1966, however, the National Organization for Women (NOW) was formed to pursue the removal of legal barriers to women's economic, political, and social advancement.[28] In 1967 NOW President Betty Friedan recommended the organization of a feminist voting bloc in the 1968 elections, to punish and/or reward legislators from both parties as needed.[29] NOW's electoral activity was quickly joined by other women's organizations, which in 1970 united in a coalition pursuing congressional passage of the ERA. As articulated by Lucille Shrier, national director of the National Federation of Business and Professional Women's Clubs (NFBPWC), the coalition's electoral threat was unambiguous: "If this amendment is defeated, we would cooperate with other major women's groups in trying to get rid of those Congressmen who fought us. That's where we would direct our cam-

---

[26]Esther Peterson oral history interview, pp. 59, 71, 93; Silverberg, "Political Organization," p. 61.

[27]Esther Peterson oral history interview, p. 93; Silverberg, "Political Organization," pp. 79–80.

[28]Betty Friedan, *It Changed My Life: Writing on the Women's Movement* (New York: Random House, 1976), pp. 80–86.

[29]Ibid., p. 101.

paign this fall."[30] The NFBPWC and NOW orchestrated a letter-writing campaign to pressure indecisive Representatives to sign a discharge petition forcing the ERA to the floor of the House for a vote, and the House passed the amendment shortly thereafter.[31]

For every other piece of legislation during the 1970s that involved conferring benefits on women as a group, independent women's organizations testified at hearings and organized grass-roots activity to pressure vote-minded legislators.[32] Although the conventional wisdom is that women's organizations turned to electoral politics only in the 1980s, most famously with NOW's first official endorsement of a presidential ticket in 1984, in fact all the lobbying activity engaged in by those organizations throughout the 1970s was clearly electoral in nature. And after this wave of independent electoral pressure on political elites began in 1970, policy defeats for these organizations appear to have come not from the inattention of elites to their demands, but rather from the victories of a competing network of independent women's organizations that developed to stop ratification of the ERA and to oppose the liberalization of abortion policies.[33]

We can test this argument by looking at women in the party organizations. As in the preceding chapter, we would not expect women seeking greater status in those organizations to see any concessions to their demands unless they were backed by independent women's organizations wielding credible electoral threats.

First, we know that no credible electoral threats were being made by such organizations before approximately 1968. Therefore, women in the party organizations should not have seen any concessions to their demands prior to 1968.

This appears to have been the case for women in both national party organizations between 1925 and 1968. In the Democratic Party, no major changes occurred in women's status within the party organization throughout the New Deal years. We know from existing studies that women in the national party organization protested their status, but to no avail. For instance, the leader of the party's women's organization during the New Deal years would later write that "Women believed that it was a 'New Deal' for our sex but since then nothing has happened more than a few routine appointments."[34] Questionnaires administered by political scientist Marguerite J. Fisher in 1944 and 1946 to the Dem-

[30]*NYT*, September 20, 1970, p. 98.
[31]Friedan, *It Changed My Life*, p. 101.
[32]Silverberg, "Political Organization," pp. 153–206.
[33]Ibid., pp. 223–269.
[34]Susan Ware, *Partner and I: Molly Dewson, Feminism and New Deal Politics* (New Haven: Yale University Press, 1987), p. 184.

ocrats' national committeewomen and state vice-chairwomen indicated widespread dissatisfaction with their lack of influence in the party organization.[35]

In 1953 the Democratic Party officially "integrated" its women's division with its men's organization.[36] This move had not been a demand of the leaders of the women's division; in fact, organization women had not been consulted nor even informed of their changed status before the public announcement of such.[37] Although this announcement was couched in the rhetoric of equal rights, as admitted by the DNC chairman the integration was no more than a budget-cutting measure.[38] "Integration" did not mean that women were no longer to be considered a distinct electoral group; as former (now deposed) women's division leader India Edwards said shortly after "integration," "we know there always will have to be some special progams for women."[39]

But those special programs were to be managed by a greatly reduced staff after "integration." Of the only six women remaining on the permanent staff of the women's division in 1952, three were moved to other divisions and one secretary was fired, leaving an assistant and a secretary for the director of the renamed Office of Women's Activities (OWA).[40] This was to remain the staff of the OWA throughout the 1950s and 1960s, with only a few additional workers hired during election years.[41] The women's magazine, the *Democratic Digest*, was taken away from the women's division and made the publicity organ of the entire party.[42]

The announcement itself occasioned a series of discussions held in DNC and DNEC meetings on the position of women in the Democratic organizational hierarchy. In these meetings it was openly stated by both India Edwards and the national party chairman that women had always been relegated to a subordinate status within the party organization; these statements were not disputed.[43] India Edwards in fact derided the

---

[35]Marguerite J. Fisher and Betty Whitehead, "Women and National Party Organization," *American Political Science Review* 38 (October 1944): 901–902; Marguerite J. Fisher, "Women in the Political Parties," *Annals of the American Academy* 151 (May 1947): 87–93.

[36]Press Release, Democratic National Committee, January 26, 1953, DNC Press Releases, Box 4, John F. Kennedy Library.

[37]Transcript of DNC meeting, September 15, 1953, p. 25, DNC Papers, Box 119.

[38]Transcript of DNEC meeting, April 1, 1953, p. 114, ibid.

[39]Ibid., pp. 93–94, also see pp. 97, 103–104, 106–108, 111.

[40]Ibid., p. 118.

[41]See India Edwards, *Pulling No Punches: Memoirs of a Woman in Politics* (New York: Putnam, 1977), p. 252.

[42]Ibid.

[43]See, e.g., transcript of DNEC meeting, February 14, 1953, pp. 58–61, 64–65, DNC Papers, Box 119; transcript of DNEC meeting, April 1, 1953, pp. 91–93, 100–102, 105–6, ibid.; transcript of DNC meeting, September 15, 1953, pp. 25–26, ibid.

"integration" language used by male party elites in a mock press release which she read to the DNEC:

"The Executive Committee of the Democratic National Committee unanimously passed a resolution this morning endorsing the new policy of integration of women into full Party operations at all levels and recommending to the National Committee that henceforth National Committee men and women have equal authority and that there be two co-chairmen, a woman and a man, of every committee, instead of a man chairman and a woman vice chairman, as the custom now. The National Committee man and woman and the co-chairmen of the committees will share policy-making, fund-raising and all other activities in which they engage as they perform their work of leading the Democratic Party to victory. The Executive Committee also recommended that the Democratic Manual be amended or rewritten to conform to this new policy of integration." April Fool![44]

Needless to say, Edwards's suggestions were not taken seriously. One other suggestion made by Edwards was that, in the spirit of integration, more women who were not members of Congress be appointed to the Democratic National Congressional Committee, as was evidently allowed by party rules.[45] This suggestion was also not followed.

After "integration" male party elites continued to control the fortunes of female party elites, as had always been the case. Edwards herself was soon asked to leave her position as director of the Office of Women's Activities by then Democratic National Chairman Stephen Mitchell, which she did in late 1953.[46] In November 1955 the DNC added three more male vice-chairmen to its executive committee, increasing the number of male vice-chairmen from two to five, while only one female vice-chairman of the committee remained.[47] This move was made over the protest of that female vice-chairman, who had requested that at least one of the new vice-chairmen (chosen to represent the House, the Senate, and the state governors) be a woman so as not to alter the male–female balance of this decision-making body. In 1957 the DNC created a new advisory committee on political techniques to consist of six male regional advisors; this move again occasioned complaints from female national committeewomen about the increasing burden of male supervision of their activities.[48] At the same time the DNC chairman created a new position of deputy chairman of the DNC, which OWA director Katie

[44]Transcript of DNEC meeting, April 1, 1953, pp. 91–92, ibid.
[45]Ibid., p. 284.
[46]Edwards, *Pulling No Punches*, p. 260.
[47]Transcript of DNC meeting, May 3, 1957, pp. 122–124, DNC Papers, Box 121.
[48]Katie Louchheim to DNC Chairman, June 26, 1957, ibid., Box 442.

Louchheim personally opposed because it implied yet another layer of male hierarchy between herself and the leadership of the party.[49]

In addition to these specific instances, which were protested by the leaders of the women's division, there were other complaints after "integration" as well. Democratic national committeewomen complained that they were not consulted on matters within their jurisdictions,[50] and that they should be recognized as "Co-Chairmen" with the men rather than always vice-chairmen to male chairmen.[51] In 1957 the director of the OWA protested to the DNC chairman that the female partisan workers would like to work more but that the men would not give them the opportunity.[52] And in late 1958 the former women's vice-chairman of the DNC and head of the women's division, India Edwards, wrote an angry letter to Chairman Paul Butler complaining of treatment as a "second class person" and arguing that women had a higher status at Democratic national headquarters in the 1940s than they now had ten years later.[53] Edwards was later to write that the "integration" of the party's women's division was "in theory a step up for women but actually a step way down."[54] No further significant changes were made to the status of women in the party organization during the 1960s.

A similar story may be told for the Republican Party. While during the New Deal years Republican national conventions passed rules that appeared favorable to women, in actuality those rules were infrequently implemented. In 1940 the Republican National Convention passed a rule that stated that, "when possible," RNC subcommittees would be composed of equal numbers of men and women. According to later reports by women in the national Republican organization, such action was rarely "possible."[55] In 1944 a similar rule was passed with respect to the national convention's resolution committee; in subsequent convention years some state delegations would select a man and a woman to sit on this committee but many would not.[56] Also in 1944 the director of the party's women's division, who had once held the title of vice-chairman of the Republican National Committee, was further demoted from assistant chairman to "assistant to the chairman."[57] And as

[49]Ibid.
[50]Minutes of DNEC meeting, May 6, 1954, ibid., Box 119.
[51]Transcript of DNC meeting, February 15, 1957, pp. 87–88, ibid.
[52]Katie Louchheim to DNC Chairman, June 26, 1957, ibid., Box 442.
[53]India Edwards to Paul Butler, December 8, 1958, ibid., Box 439.
[54]Edwards, *Pulling No Punches*, p. 261.
[55]Josephine L. Good, *Republican Womanpower: The History of Women in Republican National Conventions and Women in the Republican National Committee* (Washington, D.C.: Republican National Committee, 1963), pp. 22, 24, 35.
[56]Ibid., p. 26.
[57]Ibid., pp. 24, 27, 33, 37.

with the Democrats, questionnaires administered by political scientist Marguerite J. Fisher in 1944 and 1946 to the Republicans' national committeewomen and state vice-chairwomen indicated widespread dissatisfaction with their status in the party organization.[58]

At the 1952 Republican National Convention the Women's Division of the Republican Party was officially abolished, and the position of director of the women's division was thus eliminated as well. From that point on the coordinator of women's mobilization activities for the national Republican Party held the title of assistant to the RNC chairman and director of women's activities, and managed a much reduced staff.[59] As with the women in the Democratic Party, women in the Republican Party were not consulted prior to the decision to eliminate many of the organizational resources of the former women's division.[60] Also in 1952 the RNC was expanded to allow seats for state chairmen under certain conditions, thereby undermining the male–female balance on that committee established in 1924, and giving party leaders a justification for similarly imbalanced RNC subcommittee appointments.[61] In 1960, the Republican National Convention extended the 1944 rule on the male–female balance of the resolutions committee to all convention committees ("when possible"), but the resolutions committee itself was still imbalanced.[62] No significant changes in women's status within the party organization occurred during the 1960s.

We know that women's organizations renewed a policy of electoral mobilization in 1968. Did those organizations pursue, in addition to policy benefits, an improvement of the status of women within the party organizations? The answer is a resounding yes. The National Women's Political Caucus (NWPC) was formed in July 1971 out of a conference called by NOW to discuss the place of women in politics. At that conference, participants passed a resolution calling for both parties to select women to 50 percent of their national convention delegate positions in 1972. The caucus's first meeting was held in September 1971; its first strategy session, held the following month, developed as the caucus's first priority the lobbying of both parties to ensure a healthy representation of women at both national party conventions.[63]

[58]Fisher and Whitehead, "Women and National Party Organization"; Fisher, "Women in the Political Parties," pp. 87–93.

[59]Clare B. Williams, *The History of the Founding and Development of the National Federation of Republican Women* (Washington, D.C.: Women's Division, Republican National Committee, 1963), pp. 32–33.

[60]Eugenia Kaledin, *Mothers and More: American Women in the 1950s* (Boston: Twayne Publishers, 1984), pp. 84–85.

[61]Good, *Republican Womanpower*, p. 36.

[62]Ibid., p. 41.

[63]Byron E. Shafer, *Quiet Revolution: The Struggle for the Democratic Party and*

As noted in Chapter 1, the Democratic Party's Commission on Party Structure and Delegate Selection, otherwise known as the McGovern-Fraser Commission, had by this point already generated from among its own ranks a statement prohibiting sex discrimination in the delegate selection process for national conventions. However, the commission had left unclear the means by which that prohibition was to be implemented: a "reasonable relationship" was to exist between a state's demographic makeup and a state's delegation to the party's national convention, but the criteria for establishing "reasonableness" were left unspecified. A footnote to these guidelines placed the commission as being on record against quotas.[64] In the fall of 1971 the NWPC lobbied the commission to amend its guidelines to ensure proportional demographic representation of women on the 1972 state delegations to the Democratic National Convention.

The caucus, with close links to women's organizations threatening to engage in electoral mobilization, was successful. The commission issued guidelines, ratified by the DNC, that required state parties to select women as national convention delegates roughly in proportion to their presence in the state's general population. If a state delegation were composed of fewer women than this proportion, then the burden of proof would be on state party officials to prove that they had not discriminated in the delegate selection process.[65] The rule had immediate effects; in 1972, the percentage of Democratic national convention delegates who were women rose to 40 percent from 13 percent in 1968. Explicit quota provisions for women in the Democratic Party were then further expanded in subsequent years. Republican Party elites acted similarly: a national committee on party reform authorized by the 1968 Republican National Convention recommended the expansion of affirmative action language in the selection of national convention delegates. The 1972 national convention, at which female delegates composed 30 percent of the delegates compared with 17 percent in 1968, approved this recommendation and created a committee to work with state parties to implement this reform.[66]

In short, the changes in the status of women in the party organizations

---

the *Shaping of Post-Reform Politics* (New York: Russell Sage Foundation, 1983), pp. 465–466.

[64]Ibid., pp. 138–142, 169–172.

[65]Ibid., pp. 466–486.

[66]Winifred Wandersee, *On the Move: American Women in the 1970s* (Boston: Twayne Publishers, 1988), pp. 20, 25; Denise Baer, "The National Federation of Republican Women: Women's Auxiliary or Feminist Force?," paper delivered at the Annual Meeting of the American Political Science Association, Chicago, August 31–September 3, 1995, p. 3.

mirrored the changes in the willingness of congressional legislators to grant policy concessions to women's organizations. In both cases, the best explanation for those changes appears not to be a women's policy network, a favorable ideological climate, or the emergence of women as an electoral group. Rather, the best explanation appears to be the willingness of *independent* women's organizations, rather than *partisan* women's organizations, to coordinate the electoral mobilization of women.

As with the 1920s, the apparent importance of the willingness of women's organizations to seek the electoral mobilization of women raises the issue of why it was that those organizations came to see such a strategy as both feasible and desirable in the late 1960s. Why did these organizations resume an electoral strategy that was dropped by the NLWV in the mid-1920s?

THE REEMERGENCE OF AN ELECTORAL STRATEGY FOR WOMEN'S ORGANIZATIONS, 1968–PRESENT

Surprisingly little attention has been devoted to explaining the reemergence of an electoral strategy on the part of independent women's organizations in the late 1960s. Students of these organizations have perhaps concluded that women did not pursue an electoral policy until 1984, with the first endorsement of a presidential ticket by the National Organization of Women (NOW).[67] But as we have seen, this is simply incorrect.

In the absence of competing explanations for the endorsement of an electoral strategy by these organizations, we can at least ask whether the arguments made in Chapter 2 help to explain this strategic choice. According to the arguments made there, the primary reason women's organizations were not able to compete effectively with the major parties in the mobilization of women's votes after enfranchisement was institutional: women's organizations were disadvantaged by their prior institutional position in the race with the parties to initiate women's electoral mobilization. Therefore, if women's organizations were able to contest the parties' women's divisions for the mobilization of female voters in the late 1960s, then some feature of the institutional context of electoral politics, affecting either the party organizations, women's organizations, or both, must have changed first. That is, some change exogenous to our model must have occurred in the context of electoral politics, which either weakened the parties organizationally or strength-

---

[67]See, e.g., Silverberg, "Political Organization," pp. 205, 309.

ened the ability of women's organizations to compete with the parties. Fortunately for our argument, just such a change did occur.

Studies of several different measures of the parties' capacities to turn out voters have all demonstrated a severe decline in that capacity during the 1960s.[68] The dating is relatively precise for the initiation of this decline, which appears to have begun between 1964 and 1967. At that time the proportion of the white electorate who identified as independents, both "pure" independents and "leaners," began to increase significantly after a long period of stability. At the same time, the proportion of the electorate that identified as strong partisans began to decrease significantly, after a similar period of stability. These changes in the electorate have continued, albeit with a slowing-down period in the 1980s, into the 1990s.[69] Importantly, the rise of political independents at this time was not due simply to generational change such as the entrance of "baby boomers" into the electorate and/or period change such as the civil rights movement, the Vietnam War, political scandals, and increases in both inflation and unemployment in the early 1970s. Rather, there was a dramatic change in the way in which voters of all ages *responded* to such shocks: before 1965–1967, economic conditions, political scandals, and election campaigns did not produce switching between partisans and independents, but after this period they did. In other words, changing economic and political conditions began to produce in voters the response of abandoning their partisan identifications. The parties simply had a weaker hold on the electorate after the mid-1960s.[70]

Moreover, the weakening hold of the parties on the electorate appears to have been due not to increasing negative evaluations of the parties by voters, but rather to voters' increasing sense that the parties were simply irrelevant. The percentage of the electorate that offers a net negative evaluation of either party in national surveys has remained relatively small and stable (under 10 percent) between 1952 and 1992, while the percentage of the electorate that offers a net neutral evaluation of the parties or offers no opinion whatsoever began to increase dramatically between 1968 and 1972.[71] Similarly, the percentage of the electorate that

[68]See John H. Aldrich, *Why Parties? The Origin and Transformation of Party Politics in America* (Chicago: University of Chicago Press, 1995), chaps. 6 and 8, for an overview of this literature.

[69]Philip E. Converse, *The Dynamics of Party Support: Cohort-Analyzing Party Identification* (Beverly Hills, Calif.: Sage, 1976); Aldrich, *Why Parties?*, pp. 245–248.

[70]Harold D. Clarke and Motoshi Suzuki, "Partisan Dealignment and the Dynamics of Independence in the American Electorate, 1953–1988," *British Journal of Political Science* 24 (January 1994): 57–77.

[71]Martin P. Wattenberg, *The Decline of American Political Parties: 1952–1988* (Cambridge, Mass.: Harvard University Press, 1990); Aldrich, *Why Parties?*, pp. 248–250.

believes that it does not matter which party holds office for solving what it takes to be the most important problem facing the country began to increase dramatically between 1964 and 1968, and the percentage of the electorate that thinks that political parties do not make elected officials pay more attention to voters likewise began to increase significantly between 1968 and 1972.[72]

Evidence of the decreasing capacity of the parties to mobilize voters is given more directly by looking at aggregate election results in addition to survey data. Shively demonstrated that a change in the nature of presidential election results appears to have occurred between 1956 and 1960. Prior to 1960, presidential elections were primarily won or lost by the efforts of parties to mobilize their supporters and demobilize their opponents. But beginning with the election of 1960, presidential elections appear to have been won or lost primarily by voters switching from one party's candidate in one election to the other party's candidate in the next election.[73] Likewise, Rabinowitz, Gurian, and Macdonald found that presidential elections were structured primarily by party prior to 1960, but that after that date they began to be structured more by ideology.[74]

Similar findings apply to congressional elections. Alford and Brady found in their examination of personal incumbency effects in Congress that the advent of those effects can be precisely dated to 1966.[75] Before that time, any incumbency advantage was due to party rather than personal characteristics. This pattern holds true for Senate as well as for House elections, although personal incumbency advantage in the Senate appeared in approximately 1960 and is of a smaller magnitude than in the House.

According to scholars who have studied these trends, the best reason for these changes is organizational: in the 1960s, parties were simply much less able than previously to influence the outcome of elections by using their organizational resources to turn out supporters. Why was this the case? The most often cited cause for the organizational decline of the parties during this period is the advent of new campaign tech-

[72]Aldrich, *Why Parties?*, pp. 250–251.

[73]W. Phillips Shively, "From Differential Abstention to Conversion: A Change in Electoral Change, 1864–1988," *American Journal of Political Science* 36 (May 1992): 309–330.

[74]George Rabinowitz, Paul-Henri Gurian, and Stuart Elaine Macdonald, "The Structure of Presidential Elections and the Process of Realignment, 1944 to 1980," *American Journal of Political Science* 28 (November 1984): 611–635.

[75]John R. Alford and David W. Brady, "Personal and Partisan Advantage in U.S. Congressional Elections, 1846–1986," in Lawrence C. Dodd and Bruce I. Oppenheimer, eds., *Congress Reconsidered*, 4th ed. (Washington D.C.: CQ Press, 1989), pp. 153–169.

nologies, particularly television, which allowed candidates more immediate access to voters through their own campaign organizations. Prior to the development and spread of these new technologies, campaigns were very labor-intensive affairs, which required the local provision of electoral information to voters. Because the parties were organizationally much stronger than any individual candidate's organization, candidates relied on the organizational resources of the parties to win elections.

But the appearance of television, computerized direct mail, and other nationalizing campaign technologies allowed candidates to bypass the party organizations. After all, in 1960 88 percent of American families owned a television set, compared with only 11 percent in 1950.[76] Candidates found that they could do without the parties' mobilization operations if they had enough capital to acquire the technical expertise necessary for a media-heavy campaign. In presidential campaigns, John F. Kennedy was perhaps the first to do this effectively. Despite his background in electoral politics, Kennedy was still an outsider to the regular Democratic Party organization in 1960. In order to demonstrate to the latter that he could in fact win in elections outside his native state of Massachusetts, despite his religion and background of privilege, Kennedy built his own campaign organization and entered enough primaries to demonstrate his electoral appeal to party regulars. The success of this strategy was a novel occurrence in the history of presidential nominations. And it set a precedent both for Kennedy's general campaign, largely run by Kennedy confidants rather than party regulars, and for later developments in both parties' presidential nomination processes.[77]

Kennedy's successful efforts to bypass the regular party organization were subsequently adopted by both parties' presidential candidates. In congressional campaigns as well, beginning in the 1960s incumbents were able to take advantage of the atrophying of party organizations to build their own campaign organizations during their tenure in Congress, fed with congressional resources.[78] In both cases, these independent campaign organizations were enabled by parties no longer able to monopolize the flow of information to voters.[79]

In short, until the 1960s campaigns were run by party elites rather

---

[76]Theodore H. White, *The Making of the President, 1960* (New York: Atheneum, 1969).

[77]John H. Aldrich, "Presidential Campaigns in Party- and Candidate-Centered Eras," in Mathew D. McCubbins, ed., *Under the Watchful Eye: Managing Presidential Campaigns in the Television Era* (Washington, D.C.: CQ Press, 1992), pp. 59–82.

[78]Alford and Brady, "Personal and Partisan Advantage."

[79]See also Gary C. Jacobson, *The Politics of Congressional Elections*, 3d ed. (New York: Harper-Collins, 1992).

than candidates. It is true that the dominance of the party organizations in campaigning was gradually eroded over the course of the twentieth century. Even before the advent of television and other nationalized media, high-speed travel, and new campaign technologies, the parties were being slowly weakened by reforms wrought in the Populist and Progressive eras, by New Deal legislation which took from party leaders the job of distributing material benefits to voters, and by the increasing educational levels of the electorate.[80] The final blow to the parties as mobilization organizations came in the 1960s, however, as candidates became able to run campaigns without the assistance of the parties.

Gradually, the parties evolved to provide technical services to candidates rather than votes themselves.[81] But even in this capacity parties as organizations were simply much less present during electoral campaigns than previously. Voters thus quite rationally responded to this diminished organizational presence by following partisan cues to a much lesser extent. First in particular vote choices, and subsequently in their reported identification with parties, voters demonstrated increasing independence from the parties.[82]

Relatedly, the weakening of the parties as mobilization organizations implied a greater ease for interest groups in mobilizing particular blocs of voters to win concessions from office-seeking elites.[83] The weaker the parties in appealing to voters, the more susceptible would voters be to following electoral cues based on some identity other than a purely partisan identity.

What impact would these more general changes in the environment of electoral politics have had on the competition between the women's divisions of the major party organizations and benefit-seeking women's organizations? First of all, we would predict that the more general decline of the parties as mobilization organizations would have extended to the parties' women's divisions as well. And in fact, documentary ev-

---

[80]Walter Dean Burnham, *Critical Elections and the Mainsprings of American Politics* (New York: Norton, 1970); Sidney M. Milkis, *The President and the Parties: The Transformation of the American Party System since the New Deal* (New York: Oxford University Press, 1993).

[81]Aldrich, "Presidential Campaigns in Party- and Candidate-Centered Eras," pp. 59–82.

[82]Wattenberg, *The Decline of American Political Parties*; Martin P. Wattenberg, *The Rise of Candidate-Centered Politics: Presidential Elections of the 1980s* (Cambridge, Mass.: Harvard University Press, 1991).

[83]Aldrich, *Why Parties?*, chaps. 6 and 8; Aldrich, "Presidential Campaigns in Party- and Candidate-Centered Eras"; Mathew D. McCubbins, "Party Decline and Presidential Campaigns in the Television Age," in Mathew D. McCubbins, ed., *Under the Watchful Eye: Managing Presidential Campaigns in the Television Era* (Washington, D.C.: CQ Press, 1992), p. 17.

idence from the Democratic Party's women's division is quite consistent with this inference.

As mentioned previously, the 1953 "integration" of the DNC's women's division into the committee's other operations was admitted to be a budget-cutting measure by the DNC chairman. The staff of the former women's division was reduced by 66 percent and the women's magazine was made the general party magazine.[84] While additional staff was hired by the OWA as needed during campaigns, the number of temporary staff used by the OWA declined after "integration." Whereas in 1952 the women's division had an augmented election year staff of twenty, for the 1956 campaign the OWA had less than half that number to coordinate state-level efforts to mobilize potential female voters.[85] In 1957 the OWA's budget was cut even further.[86] Throughout 1956 and 1957 the OWA's director, Katie Louchheim, complained to the DNC chairman that she had neither the staff nor the money to coordinate the mobilization efforts among women that seemed to be a priority with party strategists.[87] In particular, Louchheim predicted that her inability to hire female campaign field workers would have an adverse impact on the party's efforts to mobilize women because female voters in the states would not respond as readily to male party workers.[88]

By January 1959 the financial problems of the OWA had progressed to the point where the organization had to cease publication of its newsletter, *News and Comments for and about Women*, which had been its only separate publication since it had lost control of the Democratic women's magazine.[89] Published for only four years, the women's newsletter became a small section in the general party magazine after 1959.

There thus appears to be suggestive evidence that the Democratic Party's women's division was growing organizationally weaker throughout the 1950s and 1960s. Logically, this increasing organizational weakness would have affected party leaders' ability to mobilize female voters as partisans. The story of the party's women's division is thus in accord with the broader story told by party scholars about the changes undergone by the party organizations during the 1960s: institutional and technological changes (during the 1950s in particular) were undermining the advantages held by the party organizations in coordinating the labor-

[84]Transcript of DNEC meeting, April 1, 1953, pp. 114, 118, DNC Papers, Box 119; Edwards, *Pulling No Punches*, p. 252.
[85]Katie Louchheim memo, 1956, DNC Papers, Box 442.
[86]Katie Louchheim to DNC Chairman, June 26, 1957, ibid.
[87]Ibid., transcript of DNEC meeting, November 27, 1956, p. 176, ibid., Box 119.
[88]Katie Louchheim to DNC Chairman, June 26, 1957, ibid., Box 442.
[89]Katie Louchheim to Thomas, January 29, 1959, ibid., Box 462.

intensive mobilization of voters. The women's divisions of the parties would not have been exempt from these trends.

We would also predict that these same exogenous changes were making it easier for both candidates and independent benefit-seeking organizations to mobilize female voters independently of the party organizations. And this also appears to have been the case. The Kennedy campaign of 1960 used its own cadre of female workers outside the regular party organization, including Kennedy family women, to direct the mobilization of women.[90] Once elected, Kennedy and his advisors sought to build ties with independent benefit-seeking women's organizations. The woman that Kennedy chose to direct his administration's efforts to reach out to women as an electoral group was herself not of the party hierarchy but rather had worked for national labor unions.[91] This woman, Esther Peterson, was made director of the Women's Bureau in the Department of Labor and was instructed, as already noted, to strengthen administration relationships with independent women's organizations.[92] During congressional consideration of the Equal Pay Act in 1963, Peterson organized a women's grass-roots lobbying campaign independently of the Democratic Party organization.[93] The head of the party's OWA, Margaret Price, apparently never met with either Kennedy or Johnson throughout the 1960s.[94]

The most publicized effort on the part of the Kennedy administration to reach out to independent women's organizations came through the President's Commission on the Status of Women. Originally suggested by Johnson as a means to appeal to middle-class female voters, the idea was picked up by Kennedy and given to Peterson to administer. No Democratic Party women were asked to be on the commission, which had as a Kennedy directive to work primarily through independent women's organizations.[95] Encouraged by the Kennedy administration and its political allies in the states, the National Federation of Business and Professional Women's Clubs in fact undertook a project to encour-

---

[90]"Final Report on the Activities of the Kennedy Ladies in the 1960 Campaign," RFK Pre-Administration Political Files, Box 36; memo from Mrs. Moynihan, Director of Women's Activities for Citizens for Kennedy, Syracuse, N.Y., John F. Kennedy Pre-Presidential Papers, Box 976, John F. Kennedy Library; Lawrence F. O'Brien, *No Final Victories: A Life in Politics from John F. Kennedy to Watergate* (Garden City, N.Y.: Doubleday, 1974), p. 32.

[91]Esther Peterson oral history interview, pp. 18, 36.

[92]Silverberg, "Political Organization," pp. 53–58.

[93]Esther Peterson oral history interview, p. 55.

[94]Edwards, *Pulling No Punches*, p. 252.

[95]Silverberg, "Political Organization," pp. 61–65; Esther Peterson oral history interview, pp. 23, 55, 59, 71, 93.

age the formation of state commissions on the status of women to carry forward this project.[96] It was at a conference of these state commissions in 1966 that the National Organization of Women was formed.

Secondary sources reveal a similar pattern in the Republican Party, as one would expect given that the institutional and technological changes of the 1950s affected both parties alike. As already noted, the women's division of the RNC was eliminated in 1952, leaving behind only an assistant to the RNC chairman responsible for coordinating women's electoral mobilization.[97]

At the same time, and relatedly, the Republican organization began to grant more autonomy to the National Federation of Republican Women (NFRW), an auxiliary organization of women's clubs formed by the regular Republican organization in 1938. Until 1952 the director of the RNC's women's division had also served as the executive director of the NFRW, and clubs requesting affiliation with the NFRW were required to obtain the approval of their state's national committee-woman and vice-chairman of the state committee. But when the women's division was abolished, the NFRW was thereby given more organizational independence and was permitted to abolish the position of executive director formerly held by the director of the regular organization's women's division. The organizationally elected president of the NFRW was also given an ex-officio seat on the RNC's executive committee.[98]

The NFRW continued to win more independence from the regular Republican organization.[99] And just as the creation of NOW was essentially subsidized by the Democratic Party's efforts to nurture a network of sympathetic yet independent women's organizations in the state commissions on the status of women, it was from within the ranks of the NFRW that Phyllis Schlafly rose and eventually left in 1967 in order to start her own benefit-seeking women's organization. Initially coordinated through *The Phyllis Schlafly Report*, this organization received a more distinct form in 1972 as STOP-ERA. Schlafly went on to coordinate STOP-ERA with the developing antiabortion movement, and appears to have enjoyed considerable success along with other conservative

[96]Silverberg, "Political Organization," pp. 68, 72.
[97]Williams, *The History of the Founding and Development of the National Federation of Republican Women*, pp. 32–33.
[98]Ibid.
[99]The NFRW became financially self-sustaining by 1977 and was given a voting membership on the RNC's twenty-eight-member Executive Council in 1988. Denise Baer, "The National Federation of Republican Women: Women's Auxiliary or Feminist Force?," p. 3.

entrepreneurs in winning policy concessions from Republican Party elites.[100]

The inference is clear: because of the decline of the parties' women's divisions as organizations for mobilizing women, there was now the possibility for independent women's organizations to begin making effective electoral appeals to women. Indeed, candidates appear to have come to rely on such organizations for their electoral needs. And the fact that these women's benefit-seeking organizations were independent of the parties meant that, in contrast to the parties' own women's divisions, their leaders would have been able to use women's votes to leverage policy concessions from vote-minded legislators.

CONCLUSION: INSTITUTIONS, HISTORY, AND DEMOCRATIC THEORY

Modern democratic theory, in a conceptual break with its classical heritage, argues that the competition of self-interested electoral elites is the best method of ensuring the representation of voters' preferences. It is not necessary for our representatives to embody civic virtue and to have the public good at heart; rather, in a democracy, it is better for us, the citizenry, if those elites are single-mindedly seeking election for their own personal ends of power and ambition. This is so because the discipline of periodic elections will force those elites to seek out our policy preferences, make promises to satisfy those preferences, and act on those promises if they are elected. Just as firms have incentives to seek out consumers' preferences in an economic market, the pressures of the electoral market will ensure that strategic electoral elites will leave unrepresented the policy preferences of no sizable electoral group.[101]

The recognition of the collective action problem in voting threw a wrench into this theory, leading theorists to predict that because voters had insufficient incentives to vote on the basis of their policy preferences, office-seeking electoral elites would have insufficient incentives to cater to those preferences once in office. But recent solutions to the collective

---

[100]Silverberg, "Political Organization," pp. 223–241.

[101]Some of the best works in modern democratic theory are E. E. Schattschneider, *Party Government* (New York: Rinehart, 1942); Joseph A. Schumpeter, *Capitalism, Socialism, and Democracy* (New York: Harper & Brothers, 1942); Robert A. Dahl, *A Preface to Democratic Theory* (Chicago: University of Chicago Press, 1956); Anthony Downs, *An Economic Theory of Democracy* (New York: Harper & Row, 1957); and William H. Riker, *Liberalism against Populism: A Confrontation between the Theory of Democracy and the Theory of Social Choice* (San Francisco: W. H. Freeman, 1982).

action problem in voting have reconnected the policy preferences of voters and the policy decisions of electoral elites, albeit through the medium of benefit-seeking group elites. These benefit-seeking elites, so the story goes, will be motivated by the expectation of policy payoffs to mobilize groups to vote by offering them selective incentives such as the opportunity to act with others whose opinions matter to voters. By making such selective incentives available, group entrepreneurs can capitalize on the tendency for groups sharing a strong norm of group identification to jump on the bandwagon of group action. And by then bargaining with office-seeking elites over the votes of this reference group, group elites can win policy concessions for a voting group *even though* the group did not vote on the basis of its policy preferences.

The argument of this book has been, however, that this model will work only under certain conditions. The model must assume that group entrepreneurs will be able to initiate the electoral mobilization of a group, as coordination of a group by appeal to solidary benefits gives advantages to the first organization to begin group electoral mobilization. If office-seeking party elites are able to initiate the electoral mobilization of a group, then those party elites may very well be able to accrue enough of an advantage over benefit-seeking group elites to prevent the latter from effectively coordinating the group's electoral mobilization. This requirement of the model implies that benefit-seeking group elites must have either informational or organizational advantages over office-seeking party elites which allow them to initiate a group's electoral mobilization.

If we assume an institutional context of suffrage, it is at least plausible that either or both of these informational and organizational advantages could exist for benefit-seeking group elites. For instance, those group elites are likely to have "inside" information on the development of a group's norm of solidarity. Group elites' privileged access to group-specific information could immediately be acted upon through electoral mobilization. Similarly, group-specific organizations may more efficiently reach group members than the geographically organized parties.

In the absence of suffrage, however, neither of these advantages for benefit-seeking group elites is plausible. In the case of informational advantages, that information cannot be acted upon through electoral mobilization. The information can be used to coordinate group collective action, but that collective action must take place outside of the context of electoral politics. Such public collective action will undermine the informational advantage that the model must assume is possessed by benefit-seeking group elites.

Benefit-seeking female elites were indeed the first to recognize and to

230

capitalize on a norm of gender identification that was evidently strong enough in the early years of this century to facilitate collective action by women as a group. But this collective group action could not take the form of electoral mobilization, as in most states women could not vote. Rather, the coordination of women as a group was put in the service of a task peculiar to a disfranchised group, namely the task of educating and converting the voting friends and family members of the disfranchised group to support suffrage. At the same time, the exclusively female parades and rallies of the suffrage movement would have provided office-seeking party elites with illustrations of the extent to which women could be mobilized by appeal to gender solidarity. Party elites would have been enticed by the postsuffrage opportunity to mobilize women themselves by creating "women's organizations" within the political parties.

Similarly, an organizational advantage for benefit-seeking elites is also dependent upon the availability of suffrage to the group. Only where a group can vote will group entrepreneurs have incentives to invest in the kind of organizations that can coordinate the group's electoral behavior in support of a legislative agenda. Where a group cannot vote, astute group entrepreneurs will invest in a different kind of organization, one that can coordinate the group to persuade voters to support suffrage for the disfranchised group. Mobilizing public opinion in support of suffrage is not the same thing as mobilizing votes in support of a broader legislative agenda, and the organizations that best perform those tasks will be significantly different.

During the years before constitutional female suffrage, many leaders of women's organizations turned to the suffrage drive as the logical first step to achieving their legislative agendas. And the major suffrage organization itself deferred the pursuit of a broader legislative agenda until suffrage had been won. As a result, procedures to formulate such an agenda were never developed within the NAWSA.

These two consequences of disfranchisement imply a third. Where a group can vote before it develops a norm of group identity, then group elites will likely have both the incentives and the opportunity to initiate the group's electoral mobilization, thereby deterring party elites from competing with group elites. But where a group develops the potential for mobilization before it can vote, then group entrepreneurs will have neither the incentives nor the opportunity to foreclose competition in that mobilization from party entrepreneurs. Moreover, because group entrepreneurs will have invested in organizations that are not appropriate to the task of electoral mobilization in support of a legislative agenda, they will need to adapt these organizations to their new institutional context once suffrage has been attained. That adaptation will take time, and the party organizations will be able to use that temporal window to initiate the group's electoral mobilization.

Both the major party organizations and the NAWSA began planning for women's electoral mobilization in early 1918. The NAWSA's elites no longer had an informational advantage over party elites in their knowledge of women's shared norm of group identification; all these elites were aware of women's potential to be mobilized as a group and all relevant elites thus began to plan for that mobilization simultaneously. But not only did the NAWSA no longer have an informational advantage over party elites in initiating women's electoral mobilization, but it also was at a disadvantage organizationally with respect to the parties. The suffrage organization could not adapt immediately to the organizational requirements for mobilizing women in support of a legislative agenda. Most significantly, the various state and local NAWSA affiliates had to be coordinated to agree upon a more diverse legislative agenda, and procedures for inducing that agreement had to be developed. These and other tasks delayed the NAWSA almost three years before it was ready to begin mobilizing women for electoral politics, in a 1920 New York senatorial campaign.

But in the meantime, the parties in New York State, and indeed nationally, had quickly assembled organizations of women and had been assiduously cultivating followings of women who responded to the voting cues of female party leaders. These women's organizations had been easy to create, as they had required merely the appointment of women as party auxiliaries at every level of party organization. No time-consuming organizational revisions were necessary to create the parties' women's divisions, the parties being already functioning electoral organizations with time-worn procedures for linking their electoral operations with candidate selection and policy choice. And to the potential female voter, these organizations would have looked remarkably like "authentic" women's organizations. Male party elites were quite astute in inducing many prominent women with histories in independent women's organizations to take positions in the parties' women's divisions, which were not only organizationally distinct from the men's party committees but which also had no other function but to build partisan networks of women using gender-specific appeals.

The model of group electoral mobilization discussed in Chapter 2 does not predict how much of a temporal advantage an organization will have to accumulate in order to generate enough of a bandwagon to deter others from contesting that particular group's mobilization. The model simply tells us that the bigger an organization's temporal lead, the more likely it will be that later entrepreneurs will not be able to generate bandwagons and will therefore not be able to mobilize a group solely by appeal to group solidarity. Conversely, of course, the smaller the temporal gap between organizations' mobilization campaigns, the less likely it is that the first entrepreneur will be able to deter a later entrepreneur from contesting that group's mobilization.

In New York State between 1917 and 1920, neither party would have had much of a competitive advantage over the other in the electoral mobilization of women. Because the parties essentially began competing at the same time to mobilize women, neither party had much of a temporal advantage over the other. Both parties, however, had a sizable temporal advantage over the League of Women Voters. By 1920, the league would have been at a serious disadvantage in its efforts to convince women that they would be acting with the bulk of other women by following the electoral cues of league elites. And shortly after the disappointing 1920 election results, NLWV elites made a provisional (and private) decision not to make statements endorsing or opposing candidates for office.

Barring some external disruption, it is the nature of a bandwagon to grow stronger rather than weaker. There would thus have been little reason for NLWV elites to find it a promising course of action once again to mobilize women for electoral contests. NLWV elites did still consider electoral mobilization to be at least an option worth considering in the first years after suffrage, leaving their suspension of candidate endorsements provisional until 1923. In that year, however, NLWV elites made that suspension permanent. In the second half of the 1920s, the league's prohibition of electoral involvement was never seriously reconsidered.

That league elites would not find taking sides in electoral contests a promising course of action throughout the 1920s is not surprising, given the apparently increasing success of the major party organizations, particularly the Republican Party, in mobilizing women by appeal to gender solidarity during this period. Buoyed by what they considered to be demonstrations of the responsiveness of women to gender-specific mobilization efforts in 1922 and 1924, Republican elites believed that these mobilization efforts could have a significant impact on a national scale if the proper organizational means could be found to reach the large pool of still unmobilized women in the second half of the 1920s. Those elites mounted a women's club operation on an unprecedented scale in the presidential campaign of 1928, and after the election the seemingly unanimous conviction of those elites was that women, voting as a group, had been the single most important factor in Herbert Hoover's massive victory. Given the reported scale of and returns to the party's mobilization efforts among women, and given the Democratic Party's attempts to match those efforts, the NLWV had no realistic chance of success in competing with either party for the electoral loyalties of most women.

We can have more confidence in these inferences by looking at partisan registration data from the limited number of areas that kept data separately for men and women. Men and women registering to vote during the 1920s exhibited interesting differences in their registration patterns. While both newly registering men and women displayed a bias toward their locally dominant party (with the exception of wealthy "Yankees" in Democratic Boston), newly registering women were even *more* biased toward the dominant party than newly registering men. This is what we would expect to be the case if women's organizations were *uniquely* disadvantaged in competition with the party organizations for the loyalties of potential female registrants. Group-specific men's organizations, such as unions or immigrants' associations, could compete with the parties for the loyalties of potential male registrants. Group-specific women's organizations, however, plausibly could not compete with the women's divisions of the parties for the loyalties of potential female registrants due to the parties' temporal advantage in mobilizing those potential registrants. We would therefore *expect* women to have been more biased toward their locally dominant party than were men.

What were the consequences of this sequence of events for the electoral leverage of women's organizations? Recall that from basic assumptions about self-interested electoral elites one can conclude that those elites have as their primary goal the winning of office, whether for themselves or for their candidates. All other goals, including policy making, are secondary to this goal. Not only are policies merely a means to win elections, but they are costly to electoral elites, who seek both to maintain consistency with earlier policy positions and to maximize their flexibility to make future policy concessions.

In the absence of self-interested group elites, the collective action problem in voting would allow electoral elites to mobilize voters without either making or keeping policy promises. Because instrumentally rational individuals do not have any incentives to vote on the basis of their policy preferences, given the infinitesimal impact their votes will have on the outcome of an election, party elites would be free to mobilize voters purely on the basis of selective incentives such as group, occupational, or regional identities. In the absence of independent group organization, that is, even intense two-party competition for votes would not necessarily (or even plausibly) result in competition to satisfy voters' policy preferences.

The timing of the congressional legislation that was passed at the urging of the NLWV and its female allies in the Women's Joint Congressional Committee corresponds quite neatly to the period during which party elites would still have considered the league to be a potential competitor for women's votes during electoral campaigns. League elites made no public announcement of their provisional repeal of the organization's candidate endorsement policy at the close of 1920, as they again did not in 1923. On the other hand, the 1922 NLWV convention debate on that policy was reported, as was the league's lack of a clear resolution one way or the other. Party elites would have had to infer the league's policy from its actions during electoral campaigns. After two national elections in which no league action was taken on either side of the partisan contest, those elites would have been safe in concluding that the league was by now hopelessly outclassed by the parties' women's divisions, and had no intention of contesting those divisions' mobilization efforts among potential female voters.

After 1924, the policy concessions to the league's lobbying efforts simply stopped coming, and the league's first big national policy victory was repealed by the end of the decade. This occurred despite the fact that the parties were still assiduously competing for the votes of women as a group, and despite the fact that the nationally dominant Republican Party was proclaiming increasing success in securing those votes. As the foregoing argument demonstrates, it would seem to be a sound inference to conclude that the reason why those policy concessions ceased is that the parties no longer had any reason to fear the league would threaten women's votes if those concessions were not forthcoming.

This inference is strengthened by the way in which party elites, in New York State and nationally, responded to the demands of the leaders of the parties' women's divisions for greater representation on male party committees, demands that were backed up by the NLWV. These divisions were always under the control of male party elites who, as per the preceding argument, would have been reluctant to make any concessions to the demands of female party leaders. Yet because through 1924 male party elites did make concessions to the demands of women within the parties, albeit unwillingly, we must conclude that they had some incentive to do so. The potential for electoral retaliation from the NLWV if those concessions were not made would have given those elites such an incentive. After 1924, those concessions ceased to be granted, and earlier concessions were at least partially rescinded. Again, the inference must be that there was no longer an independent electoral threat to party elites if they did not continue to make such concessions.

In short, there appears to have been a critical difference between male and female voting between 1920 and 1970. Male votes arguably had more leverage than did female votes, because of the incentives of the elites who coordinated those votes. And this differential leverage appears to have resulted from the sequence of office-seeking and benefit-seeking organizations' efforts to mobilize women in electoral politics. The consequences of the timing of the entrance of these competing organizations into the market for women's mobilization were significant. And the counterfactual is clear: if women had already possessed suffrage at the time that they began developing a shared identity around a norm of public motherhood, then the same leaders who in the nineteenth century began mobilizing women for suffrage by appealing to that identity could instead have been mobilizing female voters in support of candidates. Possessing suffrage during that period would not have guaranteed women's organizations success in either women's electoral mobilization or in winning policy concessions, of course, but it would at least have given those organizations the same chance as various male organizations had (and would continue to have) to compete with the party organizations in the mobilization of voters. Instead, even after having won the vote, women's organizations ultimately ended up with no more leverage over policy than they had had as a disfranchised group.

Finally, as this chapter has argued, the conclusion to this story was also predictable. If bandwagons are to a large extent self-reinforcing, then we would expect the partisan bandwagons initiated among new female voters to have endured until some exogenous change undermined their stability. As a corollary, we would expect those bandwagons to have continued to deter benefit-seeking women's organizations from contesting the market in women's electoral mobilization until such an exogenous change. And what we know about the 1960s is that such a change exogenous to the (implicit) competition between the parties and women's organizations for women's electoral loyalties did occur, with the expected effects.

What, then, does this story tell us about the predictions of modern democratic theory? Most obviously, it tells us that those predictions are quite sensitive to the institutional context of electoral competition. But more subtly, the story tells us that those predictions, because they imply a causally linked chronological sequence of events, are sensitive to institutionally determined *initial conditions*. In other words, history matters for the ability of electoral systems based on modern democratic theory to generate predicted results. Perhaps most significantly, this line of reasoning implies that political inequalities from previous historical periods may continue to exert influence even after their formal eradication.

This is a rather general statement, but in the case of women we can be much more specific. The history of the relationship between women and democracies has been one of formal exclusion succeeded more or less recently by formal inclusion. We have constructed our theories of

236

how democracies work on the assumption that once formal inclusion has been obtained, the previous condition of women's formal exclusion from electoral politics ceases to have relevance. As long as women have the vote, then they have equal opportunities to affect outcomes. Any differences between male and female organizations' successes in influencing the course of public policy must be the result of something like a lack of will by the mass of female voters or a lack of assertiveness by female leaders.

But these are not the only explanations for the difficulties faced by women's lobbying organizations in the United States, nor are they the best explanations. Women began the process of electoral mobilization under initial institutional conditions different from those of men. That unique starting point had downstream effects also unique to women as a group. In short, female disfranchisement proved to have a lasting legacy.

Bibliography

ARCHIVES AND COLLECTED PAPERS

Annual Report of the Board of Election Commissioners, 1922–1928. Boston Public Library, Boston, Massachusetts.

Calvin Coolidge Papers, microfilm edition, U.S. Library of Congress, Washington, D.C.

Democratic National Committee Papers, John F. Kennedy Library, Boston, Massachusetts.

Warren G. Harding Papers, microfilm edition, Ohio Historical Society, Columbus, Ohio.

Herbert Hoover Papers, Herbert Hoover Presidential Library, West Branch, Iowa.

Lou Henry Hoover Papers, Herbert Hoover Presidential Library, West Branch, Iowa.

John F. Kennedy Papers, John F. Kennedy Library, Boston, Massachusetts.

Robert F. Kennedy Papers, John F. Kennedy Library, Boston, Massachusetts.

Nathan William MacChesney Papers, Herbert Hoover Presidential Library, West Branch, Iowa.

Papers of the National League of Women Voters, 1918–1974, microfilm edition, University Publications of America, Frederick, Maryland.

Esther Peterson oral history interview, John F. Kennedy Library, Boston, Massachusetts.

PERIODICALS

New York Times, 1917–1932.
Pennsylvania State Manual, 1925–1936.
The Woman Citizen, 1917–1920.
The Woman Voter, 1910–1920.

Bibliography

ARTICLES, BOOKS, AND DISSERTATIONS

Aldrich, John H. "Presidential Campaigns in Party- and Candidate-Centered Eras." In Mathew D. McCubbins, ed., *Under the Watchful Eye: Managing Presidential Campaigns in the Television Era*, pp. 59–82. Washington, D.C.: CQ Press, 1992.

Why Parties? The Origin and Transformation of Party Politics in America. Chicago: University of Chicago Press, 1995.

Alford, John R., and David W. Brady. "Personal and Partisan Advantage in U.S. Congressional Elections, 1846–1986." In Lawrence C. Dodd and Bruce I. Oppenheimer, eds., *Congress Reconsidered*, pp. 153–169. 4th ed., Washington, D.C.: CQ Press, 1989.

Allswang, John M. *A House for All Peoples: Ethnic Politics in Chicago, 1890–1936.* Lexington: University Press of Kentucky, 1971.

Alpern, Sara, and Dale Baum. "Female Ballots: The Impact of the Nineteenth Amendment." *Journal of Interdisciplinary History* 16, no. 1 (Summer 1985): 43–67.

Andersen, Kristi. *No Longer Petitioners: Women in Partisan and Electoral Politics after Suffrage.* Chicago: University of Chicago Press, 1996.

Artle, Roland, and Christian Averous. "The Telephone System as a Public Good: Static and Dynamic Aspects." *Bell Journal of Economics and Management Science* 4, no. 1 (Spring 1973): 89–100.

Baer, Denise. "The National Federation of Republican Women: Women's Auxiliary or Feminist Force?" Paper delivered at the Annual Meeting of the American Political Science Association, Chicago, August 31–September 3, 1995.

Baker, Jean. *Affairs of Party: The Political Culture of Northern Democrats in the Mid-Nineteenth Century.* Ithaca, N.Y.: Cornell University Press, 1983.

Baker, Paula C. "The Domestication of Politics: Women and American Political Society, 1780–1920." In Linda Gordon, ed., *Women, the State, and Welfare*, pp. 55–91. Madison: University of Wisconsin Press, 1990.

The Moral Frameworks of Public Life, 1870–1930. New York: Oxford University Press, 1991.

Barry, Brian. *Sociologists, Economists, and Democracy.* Chicago: University of Chicago Press, 1970.

Bell, Winifred. *Aid to Dependent Children.* New York: Columbia University Press, 1965.

Berry, Jeffrey. *The Interest Group Society.* New York: Harper Collins, 1989.

Black, Naomi. *Social Feminism.* Ithaca, N.Y.: Cornell University Press, 1989.

Bourque, Susan C., and Jean Grossholtz. "Politics an Unnatural Practice: Political Science Looks at Female Participation." *Politics and Society* 4, no. 2 (Winter 1974): 225–266.

Breckenridge, Sophonisba. *Women in the Twentieth Century.* New York: McGraw-Hill, 1933.

Brennan, Geoffrey, and James Buchanan. "Voter Choice: Evaluating Political Alternatives." *American Behavioral Scientist* 28, no. 2 (December 1984): 185–201.

Bibliography

Burnham, Walter Dean. *Critical Elections and the Mainsprings of American Politics.* New York: Norton, 1970.

Catt, Carrie Chapman. *Woman Suffrage and Politics: The Inner Story of the Suffrage Movement.* New York: C. Scribner's Sons, 1923.

Chafe, William Henry. *The American Woman: Her Changing Social, Economic, and Political Roles, 1920–1970.* London: Oxford University Press, 1972.

Chambers, Clarke A. *Seedtime of Reform: American Social Service and Social Action, 1918–1933.* Minneapolis: University of Minnesota Press, 1963.

Chepaitis, Joseph Benedict. "The First Federal Social Welfare Measure: The Sheppard-Towner Maternity and Infancy Act, 1918–1932." Ph.D. dissertation, Georgetown University, 1968.

Chong, Dennis. *Collective Action and the Civil Rights Movement.* Chicago: University of Chicago Press, 1991.

Clarke, Harold D., and Motoshi Suzuki. "Partisan Dealignment and the Dynamics of Independence in the American Electorate, 1953–1988." *British Journal of Political Science* 24 (January 1994): 57–77.

Clemens, Elisabeth S. "Organizational Repertoires and Institutional Change: Women's Groups and the Transformation of U.S. Politics, 1890–1920." *American Journal of Sociology* 98, no. 4 (January 1993): 755–798.

Cohen, Lizabeth. *Making a New Deal: Industrial Workers in Chicago, 1919–1939.* Cambridge: Cambridge University Press, 1990.

Converse, Philip E. *The Dynamics of Party Support: Cohort-Analyzing Party Identification.* Beverly Hills, Calif.: Sage, 1976.

Costain, Anne N. *Inviting Women's Rebellion.* Baltimore: Johns Hopkins University Press, 1992.

"Women's Claims as a Special Interest." In Carol Mueller, ed., *The Politics of the Gender Gap,* pp. 150–172. Newbury Park, Calif.: Sage, 1988.

Costain, W. Douglas, and Anne N. Costain. "The Political Strategies of Social Movements: A Comparison of the Women's and Environmental Movements." *Congress & the Presidency* 19 (Spring 1992): 1–27.

Cott, Nancy F. "Across the Great Divide: Women in Politics before and after 1920." In Louise Tilly and Patricia Gurin, eds., *Women, Politics and Change,* pp. 153–176. New York: Russell Sage Foundation, 1990.

The Grounding of Modern Feminism. New Haven: Yale University Press, 1987.

Dahl, Robert A. *A Preface to Democratic Theory.* Chicago: University of Chicago Press, 1956.

Downs, Anthony. *An Economic Theory of Democracy.* New York: Harper & Row, 1957.

DuBois, Ellen Carol, ed. *Elizabeth Cady Stanton; Susan B. Anthony: Correspondence, Writings, Speeches.* New York: Schocken Books, 1981.

"Working Women, Class Relations, and Suffrage Militance: Harriot Stanton Blatch and the New York Woman Suffrage Movement, 1894–1909." *Journal of American History* 74, no. 1 (June 1987): 34–58.

Edwards, India. *Pulling No Punches: Memoirs of a Woman in Politics.* New York: Putnam, 1977.

240

Bibliography

Erie, Steven P. *Rainbow's End: Irish-Americans and the Dilemmas of Urban Machine Politics, 1840–1985.* Princeton: Princeton University Press, 1988.

Ethington, Philip J. "Women Voters and Politicians in American Cities during the Progressive Era: A Report on Mass and Elite Participation." Paper presented at the Annual Meeting of the Social Science History Association, Baltimore, November 5, 1993.

Fenno, Richard. *Congressmen in Committees.* Boston: Little, Brown, 1973.

Ferejohn, John A., and Morris P. Fiorina. "The Paradox of Not Voting: A Decision Theoretic Analysis." *American Political Science Review* 68 (1974): 525–535.

Ferguson, Thomas. *Golden Rule: The Investment Theory of Party Competition and the Logic of Money-Driven Political Systems.* Chicago: University of Chicago Press, 1995.

Fisher, Marguerite J. "Women in the Political Parties." *Annals of the American Academy* 251 (May 1947): 87–93.

Fisher, Marguerite J., and Betty Whitehead. "Women and National Party Organization." *American Political Science Review* 38 (October 1944): 901–902.

Flanagan, Maureen A. "The Predicament of New Rights: Suffrage and Women's Political Power from a Local Perspective." *Social Politics* 2, no. 3 (Fall 1995): 305–330.

Flexner, Eleanor. *Century of Struggle: The Woman's Rights Movement in the United States.* Cambridge, Mass.: Harvard University Press, 1975.

Fraser, Steven. *Labor Will Rule: Sidney Hillman and the Rise of American Labor.* New York: Free Press, 1991.

Freeman, Jo. *The Politics of Women's Liberation: A Case Study of an Emerging Social Movement and Its Relation to the Policy Process.* New York: David McKay, 1975.

Friedan, Betty. *It Changed My Life: Writings on the Women's Movement.* New York: Random House, 1976.

Frohlich, Norman, and Joe A. Oppenheimer. "I Get By with a Little Help from My Friends." *World Politics* 23, no. 1 (October 1970): 104–120.

Modern Political Economy. Englewood Cliffs, N.J.: Prentice-Hall, 1978.

Frohlich, Norman, Joe A. Oppenheimer, and Oran Young. *Political Leadership and Collective Goods.* Princeton: Princeton University Press, 1971.

Gamm, Gerald H. *The Making of New Deal Democrats: Voting Behavior and Realignment in Boston, 1920–1940.* Chicago: University of Chicago Press, 1989.

George, Alexander L., and Timothy J. McKeown. "Case Studies and Theories of Organizational Decision Making." *Advances in Information Processing in Organizations* 2 (1986): 21–58.

Ginzberg, Lori. *Women and the Work of Benevolence: Morality, Politics, and Class in the Nineteenth-Century United States.* New Haven: Yale University Press, 1990.

Glazer, Amihai. "A New Theory of Voting: Why Vote When Millions of Others Do." *Theory and Decision* 22 (1987): 257–270.

Bibliography

Glazer, Nathan, and Daniel Patrick Moynihan. *Beyond the Melting Pot.* Cambridge, Mass.: MIT Press and Harvard University Press, 1963.

Good, Josephine L. *Republican Womanpower: The History of Women in Republican National Conventions and Women in the Republican National Committee.* Washington, D.C.: Republican National Committee, 1963.

Gordon, Felice D. *After Winning: The Legacy of the New Jersey Suffragists, 1920–1947.* New Brunswick, N.J.: Rutgers University Press, 1986.

Gosnell, Harold F. *Getting Out the Vote: An Experiment in the Stimulation of Voting.* Chicago: University of Chicago Press, 1927.

Greenstone, J. David. *Labor in American Politics.* New York: Alfred A. Knopf, 1969.

Gustafson, Melanie S. "Partisan Women: Gender, Politics, and the Progressive Party of 1912." Ph.D. dissertation, New York University, 1993.

Hansen, John Mark. *Gaining Access: Congress and the Farm Lobby, 1919–1981.* Chicago: University of Chicago Press, 1991.

Hanson, Russell L. "Federal Statebuilding during the New Deal: The Transition from Mothers' Aid to Aid to Dependent Children." In Edward S. Greenberg and Thomas F. Mayer, eds., *Changes in the State*, pp. 93–114. Newbury Park, Calif.: Sage, 1990.

Hardin, Russell. *Collective Action.* Baltimore: Johns Hopkins University Press, 1982.

———. *One for All: The Logic of Group Conflict.* Princeton: Princeton University Press, 1995.

Harper, Ida H., ed. *History of Woman Suffrage.* Vol. 5. New York: J. J. Little and Ives, 1922.

Harris, Louis. *Is There a Republican Majority? Political Trends, 1952–1956.* New York: Harper & Brothers, 1954.

Harrison, Cynthia. *On Account of Sex: The Politics of Women's Issues, 1945–1968.* Berkeley: University of California Press, 1988.

Hart, Oliver. "An Economist's Perspective on the Theory of the Firm." *Columbia Law Review* 89 (1989): 1757–1774.

Harvey, Anna L. "The Legacy of Disfranchisement: Women in Electoral Politics, 1917–1932." Ph.D. dissertation, Princeton University, 1995.

———. "The Political Consequences of Suffrage Exclusion: Organizations, Institutions, and the Electoral Mobilization of Women." *Social Science History* 20, no. 1 (Spring 1996): 97–132.

———. "Votes without Leverage: The Political Consequences of Black and Female Disfranchisement." Paper presented at the Annual Meeting of the American Political Science Association, Washington, D.C., September 2–5, 1993.

———. "Women, Party, and Policy, 1920–1970: A Rational Choice Approach." *Studies in American Political Development* 11, no. 2 (Fall 1997): 292–324.

Heclo, Hugh. "Issue Networks and the Executive Establishment." In Anthony King, ed., *The New American Political System*, pp. 87–124. Washington, D.C.: American Enterprise Institute, 1978.

Hewitt, Nancy. *Women's Activism and Social Change: Rochester, New York, 1822–1872.* Ithaca, N.Y.: Cornell University Press, 1984.

Bibliography

Howard, Christopher. "Sowing the Seeds of 'Welfare': The Transformation of Mothers' Pensions, 1900–1940." *Journal of Policy History* 4, no. 2 (1992): 188–227.

Huckfeldt, R. Robert. "Political Participation and the Neighborhood Social Context." *American Journal of Political Science* 23, no. 3 (August 1979): 579–592.

Huckfeldt, R. Robert, and John Sprague. "Political Parties and Electoral Mobilization: Political Structure, Social Structure, and the Party Canvass." *American Political Science Review* 86, no. 1 (March 1992): 70–86.

Huntington, Samuel P. *American Politics: The Promise of Disharmony.* Cambridge, Mass.: Harvard University Press, 1981.

Jacobson, Gary C. *The Politics of Congressional Elections,* 3d ed. New York: Harper-Collins, 1992.

Kaledin, Eugenia. *Mothers and More: American Women in the 1950s.* Boston: Twayne Publishers, 1984.

Kenny, Christopher B. "Political Participation and Effects from the Social Environment." *American Journal of Political Science* 36, no. 1 (February 1992): 259–267.

King, Gary, Robert O. Keohane, and Sidney Verba. *Designing Social Inquiry: Scientific Inference in Qualitative Research.* Princeton: Princeton University Press, 1994.

Kingdon, John W. *Agendas, Alternatives, and Public Policies.* Boston: Little, Brown, 1984.

Knack, Stephen. "Civic Norms, Social Sanctions, and Voter Turnout." *Rationality and Society* 4, no. 2 (April 1992): 133–156.

Koch, Jeffrey W. *Social Reference Groups and Political Life.* Lanham, Md.: UPI, 1995.

Kramer, Gerald H. "The Effects of Precinct-Level Canvassing on Voter Behavior." *Public Opinion Quarterly* 34 (1970): 560–572.

Ledyard, John O. "The Paradox of Voting and Candidate Competition: A General Equilibrium Analysis." In George Horwich and James P. Quirk, eds., *Essays in Contemporary Fields of Economics,* pp. 54–80. West Lafayette, Ind.: Purdue University Press, 1981.

"The Pure Theory of Large Two Candidate Elections." *Public Choice* 44 (1984): 7–41.

Lemons, J. Stanley. *The Woman Citizen: Social Feminism in the 1920s.* Chicago: University of Chicago Press, 1975.

Mayhew, David R. *Congress: The Electoral Connection.* New Haven: Yale University Press, 1974.

Divided We Govern: Party Control, Lawmaking, and Investigations, 1946–1990. New Haven: Yale University Press, 1991.

McCubbins, Mathew D. "Party Decline and Presidential Campaigns in the Television Age." In Mathew D. McCubbins, ed., *Under the Watchful Eye: Managing Presidential Campaigns in the Television Era,* pp. 9–58. Washington, D.C.: CQ Press, 1992.

McGerr, Michael. *The Decline of Popular Politics: The American North, 1865–1928.* New York: Oxford University Press, 1986.

Bibliography

"Political Style and Women's Power, 1830–1930." *Journal of American History* 77, no. 3 (December 1990): 864–885.

Mettler, Suzanne Bridget. "Divided Citizens: State Building, Federalism, and Gender in the New Deal." Ph.D. dissertation, Cornell University, 1994.

Milkis, Sidney M. *The President and the Parties: The Transformation of the American Party System since the New Deal.* New York: Oxford University Press, 1993.

Miller, Arthur H., Patricia Gurin, Gerald Gurin, and Oksana Malanchuk. "Group Consciousness and Political Participation." *American Journal of Political Science* 25 (August 1981): 494–511.

Miller, Arthur H., Christopher Wlezien, and Anne Hildreth. "A Reference Group Theory of Partisan Coalitions." *Journal of Politics* 53, no. 4 (November 1991): 1134–1149.

Mink, Gwendolyn. *The Wages of Motherhood: Inequality in the Welfare State, 1917–1942.* Ithaca, N.Y.: Cornell University Press, 1995.

Mohr, Lawrence B. *Impact Analysis for Program Evaluation.* Chicago: Dorsey Press, 1988.

Monoson, S. Sara. "The Lady and the Tiger: Women's Electoral Activism in New York City before Suffrage." *Journal of Women's History* 2, no. 2 (Fall 1990): 100–135.

Muncy, Robyn. *Creating a Female Dominion in American Reform, 1890–1935.* New York: Oxford University Press, 1991.

Nelson, Barbara J. "The Origins of the Two-Channel Welfare State: Workmen's Compensation and Mothers' Aid." In Linda Gordon, ed., *Women, the State, and Welfare,* pp. 123–151. Madison: University of Wisconsin Press, 1990.

Nichols, Carole. *Votes and More for Women: Suffrage and After in Connecticut.* New York: Haworth Press, 1983.

North, Douglass C. *Institutions, Institutional Change, and Economic Performance.* Cambridge: Cambridge University Press, 1990.

O'Brien, Lawrence F. *No Final Victories: A Life in Politics from John F. Kennedy to Watergate.* Garden City, N.Y.: Doubleday, 1974.

Oestreicher, Richard. "Urban Working-Class Political Behavior and Theories of American Electoral Politics, 1870–1940." *Journal of American History* 74, no. 4 (March 1988): 1257–1286.

Olson, Mancur. *The Logic of Collective Action: Public Goods and the Theory of Groups.* Cambridge, Mass.: Harvard University Press, 1965.

Orloff, Ann Shola. "Gender in Early U.S. Social Policy." *Journal of Policy History* 3, no. 1 (1991): 249–281.

Palfrey, Thomas R., and Howard Rosenthal. "Private Incentives in Social Dilemmas: The Effects of Incomplete Information and Altruism." *Journal of Public Economics* 35 (1988): 309–332.

"Voter Participation and Strategic Uncertainty." *American Political Science Review* 79 (1985): 62–78.

Patterson, Samuel C., and Gregory A. Caldeira. "Getting Out the Vote: Participation in Gubernatorial Elections." *American Political Science Review* 73 (December 1979): 1071–1089.

Bibliography

Perry, Elizabeth I. *Belle Moskowitz: Feminine Politics and the Exercise of Power in the Age of Alfred E. Smith.* New York: Oxford University Press, 1987.

Price, David E., and Michael Lupfer. "Volunteers for Gore: The Impact of a Precinct-Level Canvass in Three Tennessee Cities." *Journal of Politics* 35 (1973): 410–438.

Rabinowitz, George, Paul-Henri Gurian, and Stuart Elaine Macdonald. "The Structure of Presidential Elections and the Process of Realignment, 1944 to 1980." *American Journal of Political Science* 28 (November 1984): 611–635.

Riker, William H. *Liberalism against Populism: A Confrontation between the Theory of Democracy and the Theory of Social Choice.* San Francisco: W. H. Freeman, 1982.

Riker, William H., and Ordeshook, Peter C. *An Introduction to Positive Political Theory.* Englewood Cliffs, N.J.: Prentice Hall, 1973.

"A Theory of the Calculus of Voting." *American Political Science Review* 62 (1968): 25–42.

Rohlfs, Jeffrey. "A Theory of Interdependent Demand for a Communications Service." *Bell Journal of Economics and Management Science* 5, no. 1 (Spring 1974): 16–37.

Rosenstone, Steven J., and John Mark Hansen. *Mobilization, Participation, and Democracy in America.* New York: Macmillan, 1993.

Rosenthal, Naomi, Meryl Fingrutd, Michele Ethier, Roberta Karant, and David McDonald. "Social Movements and Network Analysis: A Case Study of Nineteenth-Century Women's Reform in New York State." *American Journal of Sociology* 90, no. 5 (1985): 1022–1054.

Salisbury, Robert H. "An Exchange Theory of Interest Groups." *Midwest Journal of Political Science* 13, no. 1 (February 1969): 1–32.

Sapiro, Virginia. "The Gender Basis of American Social Policy." In Linda Gordon, ed., *Women, the State, and Welfare*, pp. 36–54. Madison: University of Wisconsin Press, 1990.

Schattschneider, E. E. *Party Government.* New York: Rinehart, 1942.

Schelling, Thomas. *Micromotives and Macrobehavior.* New York: Norton, 1978.

The Strategy of Conflict. Cambridge, Mass.: Harvard University Press, 1960.

Schlesinger, Arthur M., Jr. *The Cycles of American History.* Boston: Houghton Mifflin, 1986.

Schlesinger, Joseph A. *Political Parties and the Winning of Office.* Chicago: University of Chicago Press, 1991.

"The Primary Goals of Political Parties: A Clarification of Positive Theory." *American Political Science Review* 69 (September 1975): 840–849.

Schuessler, Alexander. "Expressive Motivation and Mass Participation." Unpublished manuscript, Department of Politics, New York University.

Schumpeter, Joseph. *Capitalism, Socialism and Democracy.* New York: Harper & Brothers, 1942.

Scott, Anne Firor. *Natural Allies: Women's Associations in American History.* Urbana: University of Illinois Press, 1991.

245

Bibliography

Scriven, Michael. "Maximizing the Power of Causal Investigations: The Modus Operandi Method." *Evaluation Studies Review Annual* 1 (1976): 101–118.

Sealander, Judith. "Moving Painfully and Uncertainly: Policy Formation and 'Women's Issues,' 1940–1980." In Donald T. Critchlow and Ellis Hawley, eds., *Federal Social Policy: The Historical Dimension*, pp. 79–96. University Park: Pennsylvania State University Press, 1988.

Shafer, Byron E. *Quiet Revolution: The Struggle for the Democratic Party and the Shaping of Post-Reform Politics.* New York: Russell Sage Foundation, 1983.

Sharkey, William W. *The Theory of Natural Monopoly.* Cambridge: Cambridge University Press, 1982.

Shingles, Richard D. "Black Consciousness and Political Participation: The Missing Link." *American Political Science Review* 75 (March 1981): 76–91.

Shively, W. Phillips. "From Differential Abstention to Conversion: A Change in Electoral Change, 1864–1988." *American Journal of Political Science* 36 (May 1992): 309–330.

Silverberg, Helene Norma. "Political Organization and the Origin of Political Identity: The Emergence and Containment of Gender in American Politics, 1960–1984." Ph.D. dissertation, Cornell University, 1988.

Skocpol, Theda. "The Enactment of Mothers' Pensions: Civic Mobilization and Agenda Setting or Benefits of the Ballot?: Response." *American Political Science Review* 89, no. 3 (September 1995): 720–730.

Protecting Soldiers and Mothers: The Political Origins of Social Policy in the United States. Cambridge, Mass.: Belknap Press of Harvard University Press, 1992.

Skocpol, Theda, and Gretchen Ritter. "Gender and the Origins of Modern Social Policies in Britain and the United States." In Theda Skocpol, ed., *Social Policy in the United States: Future Possibilities in Historical Perspective*, pp. 72–135. Princeton: Princeton University Press.

Stanton, Elizabeth Cady, Susan B. Anthony, and Matilda J. Gage. *History of Woman Suffrage.* Vol. 1. New York: Fowler & Wells, 1881.

History of Woman Suffrage. Vol. 2. Rochester, N.Y.: Charles Mann Printing Co., 1881.

Straits, Bruce C. "The Social Context of Voter Turnout." *Public Opinion Quarterly* 54, no. 1 (Spring 1990): 64–73.

Sugden, Robert. "Reciprocity: The Supply of Public Goods through Voluntary Contributions." *Economic Journal* 94 (December 1984): 772–787.

Uhlaner, Carole J. "Rational Turnout: The Neglected Role of Groups." *American Journal of Political Science* 33, no. 2 (May 1989): 390–422.

"'Relational Goods' and Participation: Incorporating Sociability into a Theory of Rational Action." *Public Choice* 62 (1989): 253–285.

Verba, Sidney and Norman H. Nie. *Participation in America: Political Democracy and Social Equality.* New York: Harper & Row, 1972.

Wagner, Richard. "Pressure Groups and Political Entrepreneurs: A Review Article." *Papers on Non-Market Decision Making* 1 (1966): 161–170.

Bibliography

Wandersee, Winifred. *On the Move: American Women in the 1970s.* Boston: Twayne Publishers, 1988.

Ware, Susan. *Beyond Suffrage: Women in the New Deal.* Cambridge, Mass.: Harvard University Press, 1981.

Holding Their Own: American Women in the 1930s. Boston: Twayne, 1982.

Partner and I: Molly Dewson, Feminism and New Deal Politics. New Haven: Yale University Press, 1987.

Wattenberg, Martin P. *The Decline of American Political Parties: 1952–1988.* Cambridge, Mass.: Harvard University Press, 1990.

The Rise of Candidate-Centered Politics: Presidential Elections of the 1980s. Cambridge, Mass.: Harvard University Press, 1991.

White, Theodore H. *The Making of the President, 1960.* New York: Atheneum, 1969.

Williams, Clare B. *The History of the Founding and Development of the National Federation of Republican Women.* Washington, D.C.: Women's Division, Republican National Committee, 1963.

Wilson, James Q. *Political Organizations.* New York: Basic Books, 1973.

Wolfinger, Raymond. "The Development and Persistence of Ethnic Voting." *American Political Science Review* 59, no. 4 (December 1965): 896–908.

"The Influence of Precinct Work on Voting Behavior." *Public Opinion Quarterly* 27 (1963): 387–398.

Young, Louise M. *In the Public Interest: The League of Women Voters, 1920–1970.* New York: Greenwood Press, 1989.

Zelman, Patricia. *Women, Work, and National Policy: The Kennedy-Johnson Years.* Ann Arbor, Mich.: UMI Research Press, 1982.

Index

Index

Index

251

Index

Index